Regulatory Frameworks for Water Resources Management

A Comparative Study

Law, Justice, and Development

The Law, Justice, and Development series is offered by the Legal Vice Presidency of the World Bank to provide insights into aspects of law and justice that are relevant to the development process. Works in the series present new legal and judicial reform activities related to the World Bank's work, as well as analyses of domestic and international law. The series is intended to be accessible to a broad audience as well as to legal practitioners.

Series Editor: Salman M. A. Salman
Editorial Board: Dominique Bichara, Hassane Cisse, Alberto Ninio, Kishor Uprety

Regulatory Frameworks for Water Resources Management

A Comparative Study

Salman M. A. Salman
Daniel D. Bradlow

THE WORLD BANK
Washington, D.C.

ISBN-10: 0-8213-6519-3   eISBN: 0-8213-6520-7
ISBN-13: 978-0-8213-6519-9   DOI: 10.1596/978-0-8213-6519-9

Library of Congress Cataloging-in-Publication Data
Salman, Salman M. A., 1948–.
    Regulatory frameworks for water resources management : a comparative
study / Salman M.A. Salman, Daniel D. Bradlow.
        p. cm — (Law, justice, and development)
    Includes bibliographical references and index.
    ISBN-13: 978-0-8213-6519-9
    ISBN-10: 0-8213-6519-3
        1. Water resources development—Law and Legislation.   I. Bradlow, Daniel D.
II. Title.   III. Series.

K3498.S25 2006
346.04'69115—dc22

                                                                    2005058019

Water is not a commercial product like any other but, rather, a heritage which must be protected, defended and treated as such.

Preamble to the European Union Water Framework Directive, 2000

Contents

Foreword

Water is a scarce and finite resource with no substitute, and upon which the very existence of life on earth depends. The challenges facing water resources are daunting. During the last century, the population of the world has more than tripled, from 1.6 billion to over 6 billion, while water resources have remained constant. Urbanization, industrialization, and environmental degradation are compounding the challenges. The United Nations World Water Development Report, 2003, presented a gloomy picture: About 2 billion people in over 40 countries are affected by water shortages, more than 1 billion people lack sufficient and safe drinking water, and 2.4 billion have no provisions for sanitation.

The Millennium Development Goals aim, *inter alia,* at reducing by half, by 2015, the proportion of people without sustainable access to safe drinking water and sanitation. Although progress thus far is not encouraging, it is hoped that necessary actions will be taken to achieve this goal during the remaining period. Such actions include financial, institutional, and legal measures. Indeed, without the appropriate legal framework, the ability of the state to regulate, control, and allocate its water resources is hampered; its role in ensuring their efficient and proper use is hindered; and its right to protect those resources is challenged.

The declarations and resolutions of the many different forums and conferences that have addressed the challenges of the water sector urged the states, *inter alia,* to adopt water legislation. They call for water legislation that lays down clear and comprehensive rules but that is sufficiently flexible to accommodate future challenges and changes in priorities and perspectives. Similarly, the World Bank Operational Policy on Water Resources Management underscores the importance of water legislation and confirms the Bank's readiness to assist its borrowers in establishing a strong legal and regulatory framework for water resources management.

This study of the regulatory frameworks for water resources management examines water legislation in sixteen jurisdictions and highlights, in a comparative manner, the key elements needed for an effective regulatory framework. The Legal Vice Presidency of the World Bank is pleased to offer this publication and hopes it will serve as a useful guide for policy makers and technical experts, international and civil society organizations, and all those concerned with water resources management, development, and protection.

Scott B. White
Acting Vice President and General Counsel
The World Bank

February 2006

Abstract

This study deals with the regulatory frameworks for water resources management. Chapter 1 traces the relevance and importance assigned to water legislation by the different international conferences and forums, including the Mar del Plata, Dublin, and Rio, and the guidance provided by those conferences for preparing such legislation. Chapter 2 surveys the regulatory frameworks for water resources management in sixteen jurisdictions, based on certain key elements. Those jurisdictions were selected based on the availability and accessibility of a water law, as well as on the need to represent different regions and legal systems of the world. Chapter 3 presents a comparative analysis of these regulatory frameworks based on the same elements. The analysis examines the main similarities and differences in the approaches adopted by the jurisdictions selected. Chapter 4 highlights essential elements that need to be addressed in any regulatory framework for water resources management and identifies emerging trends in water legislation. Finally, Chapter 5 underscores the relevance and importance of the regulatory framework and specifies conditions supporting its utility and efficacy.

Acknowledgements

The work on this study has been quite extensive and demanding, and it is not possible to mention all the colleagues who have assisted with it in different ways. However, we would like to extend our thanks and appreciation to Gabriel Eckstein, Aboubacar Fall, Karin Krchnak, and Robyn Stein, as well as Fuad Bateh, Alberto Ninio, Tjaarda Storm Van Leeuwen, and Kishor Uprety for reviewing the manuscript and providing detailed and valuable comments. Our thanks are also extended to Awadh Bahamish, Miguel Barrios Lozano, Mohammed Bekhechi, Sidi M. Boubacar, Hassane Cisse, Charles Di Leva, Ousmane Dione, Junko Funahashi, Le Thanh Long, Jackson Morrill, Kenneth Mwenda, Hoi-Chan Nguyen, Götz Reichert, Brian Steven Smith, Ashok Subramanian, Patrice Talla Takoukam, and Wang Xi for assistance, helpful comments, and advice on the country study sections of this manuscript.

Our sincere thanks are also due to Scott B. White, Acting Vice President and General Counsel of the World Bank, and David Freestone, Deputy General Counsel, Advisory Services, for their support and continuous advice on this study. We also thank Laura Lalime-Mowry, Wendy Melis, Martha Weiss, Christian Jimenez Tomas, Linda Thompson, Mary May Agcaoili, Lakshmi Mathew, Melissa Frisck, Nicole Rothe and Salimatou Diallo for assistance in various ways with this study, and Shéhan de Sayrah for his advice and editorial assistance.

We acknowledge with appreciation the funding from the Bank-Netherlands Water Partnership Program (BNWPP) for this study, and thank the colleagues who facilitated such funding.

Acronyms and Abbreviations

ANA	National Water Agency (*Brazil*)
CBA	Catchment Basin Authority (*Morocco*)
CMA	Catchment Management Agency (*South Africa*)
CNA	National Water Commission (*Mexico*)
DMC	Developing Member Countries (*Asian Development Bank*)
EC	European Community
EU	European Union
GWP	Global Water Partnership
HTS	Hydro Technical Structures (*Armenia*)
IWRM	Integrated Water Resources Management
LWR	Law on Water Resources (*Vietnam*)
MARD	Ministry of Agriculture and Rural Development (*Vietnam*)
NCA	National Water Commission (*Mexico*)
NIS	National Information System
NWA	National Water Act (*South Africa*)
NWRA	National Water Resources Authority (*Yemen*)
NWRP	National Water Resources Policy (*Brazil*)
OP	Operational Policy of the World Bank
PROFEPA	Procuraduría Federal de Protección al Ambiente (*Mexico*)
SAGE	Schémas d'aménagement et de gestion des eaux (*France*)
SDAGE	Schéma directeurs d'aménagement et de gestion des eaux (*France*)
TAC	Technical Advisory Committee of the GWP
UNCED	United Nations Conference on Environment and Development
WRA	Water Resources Act (*Nepal*)
WSA	Water Services Act (*South Africa*)
WUA	Water Users' Associations

CHAPTER 1

Introduction

The authority and ability of any state to regulate, allocate, and control its water resources depend primarily on whether the state has in place a legal framework for dealing with water resources and, if it does, what approach the framework prescribes for ownership and allocation of water. This framework could be a separate water law, as in most states; provisions in different laws; administrative or executive decrees or regulations; customary or traditional law; or court decisions. Increasingly, states are making explicit references in their constitutions to their water resources and the need to manage them properly and efficiently; they may even lay down basic principles of management and allocation.[1] In a number of constitutions and laws of federal states, provisions are included that clarify the responsibilities of each of the federal and provincial or state governments over water resources management and lay down procedures for resolution of inter-states water disputes.[2]

---

[1] The constitutions of Brazil and South Africa can be cited as examples for inclusion of references to innovative aspects of water resources issues. The Constitution of Brazil requires, in art. 21 (XIX), the establishment of "a national system for management of water resources" and defines criteria for granting rights of water use. This is the only constitution that explicitly requires establishing a national water resources management system. The Constitution of South Africa establishes a right, *inter alia,* to water in art. 27, which reads "Everyone has the right to have access to health care services, including reproductive health care, sufficient food and water, and social security." This is the first constitution to make explicit reference to the right to water.

[2] The Indian constitution, for example, lays down the division of authority between the Union government and the state governments. Entry 17 of List III of the Seventh Schedule to the Constitution endows the State governments with authority over "water, that is to say, water supplies, irrigation and canals, drainage and embankments, water storage and water power, subject to the provisions of Entry 56 of List I." Entry 56 gives the Union Parliament legislative authority "over regulation and development of inter-state rivers and river valleys to the extent to which such regulation and development under the control of the Union is declared by Parliament by law to be expedient in the public interest." For discussion of inter-states water disputes in India, *see* B. R. Chauhan, *Settlement of International and Inter-State Water Disputes in India,* Part II, 107 (Indian Law Institute 1992). *See also* Salman M. A. Salman, *Inter-States Water Disputes in India: An Analysis of the Settlement Process,* 4 Water Policy 223 (2002); and R. Maria Saleth, *Water Institutions in India—Economics, Law, and Policy* (Institute of Economic Growth 1996). It should also be noted that in the United States of America, water *quality* issues are under the authority of the federal government, while *quantity and ownership* issues are under the authority of individual states. Water quality issues are dealt with in a comprehensive manner in the

As water becomes an increasingly scarce resource, threatened both quantitatively and qualitatively, and as competing demands between different uses and users become steadily sharper, many states are moving faster in the direction of adopting water resources legislation to address in detail the vast array of issues facing or emerging in the water sector. Some countries that already have water legislation in place are realizing that there are major shortcomings with such legislation. The United Nations Water Conference that was held in Mar del Plata, Argentina, in 1977 noted such deficiencies. The Conference observed that existing legislation in many countries is often complex, lags behind modern water management practices and techniques, and perpetuates an undesirable fragmentation of responsibilities between different entities within a government.[3] In a number of countries, provisions that regulate water resources are scattered through different laws and regulations, and in some instances they may even be incompatible with each other or with existing practices and traditional rights. Overlapping jurisdiction of different entities working on water resources management is also common.

Although the above statement was made in 1977, its content is still valid and has been repeatedly confirmed by recent similar statements. The World Bank Water Resources Management Policy Paper, 1993 (the Policy Paper), pointed out that in most legislation, allocations and priorities are often vaguely stated or are absent, and many uses, such as in-stream or environmental uses, may be overlooked. The Policy Paper further noted that the procedures to be followed for reallocation of water to higher-priority or higher-valued purposes are not explicitly stated; thus reallocation may not take place at all or may follow *ad hoc* decisions that carry a high cost.[4] Similarly, the African Development Bank Policy for Integrated Water Resources Management 2000 noted that in the African Continent

---

Clean Water Act, 1972. For an analysis of this act, *see* Water Environment Federation, *The Clean Water Act, A Desk Reference: 25th Anniversary Edition* (WEF 1997). For the division of authority over water between the Federal and State governments in the United States, and the process for resolving inter-states water disputes, *see* George William Sherk, *Dividing the Waters—The Resolution of Interstate Water Conflicts in the United States* (Kluwer Law International 2000).

[3] *See* Report of the United Nations Water Conference (hereinafter the Report), Mar del Plata, March 14–25, 1977, U.N. Publications, Sales No. E 77.II.A.12 (1977), at 33. For a critical analysis of existing legislation in some selected countries *see* Dante A. Caponera, *National and International Water Law and Administration,* 137 (Kluwer Law International 2003). *See also* Antonio Embid Irujo, *Water Law in Spain After 1985,* 28 Water Intl. 290 (2003); and Aynur Aydin Coskun, *Water Law—The Current State of Regulation in Turkey,* 28 Water Intl. 70 (2003).

[4] *See* World Bank, *Water Resources Management—A World Bank Policy Paper* 44 (World Bank 1993).

"water legislation is at a very early stage of development. This is not surprising, since, in the majority of countries . . . national water polices, which provide the basis for legislation, have not been formulated."[5] Furthermore, the Asian Development Bank Water Policy observed that most of the governments of the Bank Developing Member Countries (DMCs) "have yet to adopt effective policies to regulate water allocation and conservation. Legislation to grant users rights to water, and to empower users to protect and advance their rights, is commonly absent in DMCs. Responsibilities for managing water are frequently fragmented and overlapping."[6]

It is noteworthy that most, if not all, of the international conferences and forums held since 1970 urged governments to adopt legislation that not only lays down a clear set of rules for dealing with water resources issues but is sufficiently flexible to accommodate future changes in priorities and perspectives. The Mar del Plata Water Conference is the first international water conference to lay out, among many other features, a detailed road map for both water legislation and a national water policy.[7] The Action Plan issued by the Conference included resolutions and recommendations covering a broad spectrum of water resources issues. With regard to water legislation, the Action Plan recommendations are still highly relevant and valid. Those recommendations can be summarized as follows:[8]

> First, a review of existing rules and regulations on water resources should be prepared in order to improve and streamline their scope to cover aspects pertaining to water resources management, protection of quality, prevention of pollution, penalties for undesirable effluent discharges, licensing, abstraction, and ownership.

> Second, the legislation should be comprehensive; yet it should be framed in the simplest way possible and be consistent with the need to spell out the

---

[5] *See* African Development Bank & African Development Fund, *Policy for Integrated Water Resources Management* 22 (April 2000).

[6] *See* Asian Development Bank, *Water for All: The Water Policy of the Asian Development Bank* 10 (2001). For a list of the DMCs, visit http://www.adb.org/Countries/default.asp.

[7] It should, however, be noted that the Stockholm Declaration, which was issued by the United Nations Conference on the Human Environment in 1972, stated in principle 2 that "The natural resources of the earth, including the air, water, land, flora and fauna . . . must be safeguarded for the benefit of present and future generations through careful planning or management, as appropriate." Although the Declaration did not address the issue of the legal framework for natural resources, it is understood that "careful planning and management" would require, of necessity, a legal and regulatory framework.

[8] *See* the Report, *supra* n. 3, at 33.

respective responsibilities and powers of governmental agencies and the means for conferring rights to use water on individuals.

Third, the legislation should allow for the easy implementation of policy decisions, which should be made in the public interest while protecting the reasonable interests of individuals.

Fourth, the legislation should define the rules of public ownership of water projects, as well as the rights, obligations, and responsibilities, and should emphasize the role of public bodies at the proper administrative level in controlling both the quantity and quality of water. It should also spell out, either in the primary or subordinate legislation, administrative procedures necessary for the coordinated, equitable, and efficient control and administration of all aspects of water resources and land use problems,[9] as well as the conflicts that may arise from them.

Fifth, the legislation should take into account the administrative capacity to implement it.

Sixth, priority should be accorded to the effective enforcement of the provisions of the legislation and, where necessary, administrative and other arrangements should be strengthened and rendered more effective to achieve this objective.

Seventh, countries should make necessary efforts to adopt measures for obtaining effective participation in the planning and decision-making process involving users and public authorities. Every effort should be made to convince the public that participation is an integral component in the decision-making process, and there should be a continuous two-way flow of information.

Eighth, in the field of community water supply and sanitation, special emphasis should be given to the situation and role of women.

Ninth, water tariff policies should be evaluated in accordance with the general development policies and restructured and readjusted as necessary so that they may be effectively used as policy instruments to promote better management of demand, while encouraging better use of available resources without causing undue hardship to poorer sections and regions of

---

[9] As will be discussed later, protecting the ecosystems of a watercourse requires paying close attention to the use of the lands contiguous to it. *See infra,* nn. 41 and 257. It is quite interesting that the Mar del Plata Water Conference noted and underscored this fact as early as 1977, at a time when the concept of environmental impact assessment was still at the infant stage.

the community.[10] Water charges should as far as possible cover the costs incurred unless governments as a policy choose to subsidize them.

The Mar del Plata Conference recommended that national water policy should be conceived and carried out within the framework of an interdisciplinary national economic, social, and environmental development policy and should recognize water development as an essential infrastructural facility in the country's development plans, with land and water managed in an integrated manner. The policy should also call for defining the goals for different sectors of water use, including provision of safe water supply and waste disposal facilities; provision for agriculture, stock-raising, and industrial needs; transport by water; and development of hydropower in such a way as to be compatible with the resources and characteristics of the area concerned.[11] In estimating available water resources, account should be taken of water reuse and water transfer across basins. The policy also needs to develop and apply techniques for identifying, measuring, and presenting the economic, environmental, and social benefits and costs of development projects and proposals and for the systematic evaluation of such projects, with a view to learning lessons for the future, particularly in relation to social benefits and ecological changes. Furthermore, the policy should also formulate master plans for sectors and river basins to provide a long-term perspective for planning, including resource conservation,

---

[10] The Mar del Plata Conference adopted the famous, and often-quoted, recommendation that "All peoples, whatever their stage of development, and their social and economic conditions, have the right to have access to drinking water in quantities and of a quality equal to their basic needs." *See* the Report, *supra* n. 3, Resolution II (a), at 66. A number of authors consider this recommendation to have laid the foundation for the concept of the human right to water. *See* Salman M. A. Salman & Siobhán McInerney Lankford, *The Human Right to Water—Legal and Policy Dimensions* 8 (World Bank 2004). *See also* Peter Gleick & Jon Lane, *Large International Water Meetings: A Time for a Reappraisal,* 30 Water Intl. 410 (2005); Stephen McCaffrey, *A Human Right to Water: Domestic and International Implications,* 5 Geo. Intl. Envtl. L. Rev. 13 (1992); and Peter Gleick, *The Human Right to Water,* 1 Water Policy 492 (1998).

[11] *See* the Report, *supra* n. 3, at 30. Most national water policies more or less follow this outline. *See, for example,* the National Water Policy of Tanzania (issued by the Ministry of Water and Livestock Development in July 2002). This is a fairly comprehensive and elaborate policy. Similarly, the India National Water Policy, issued by the Ministry of Water Resources in September 1987, addresses in a shorter but focused manner the issues highlighted in the Mar del Plata Recommendations. *See also* the National Water Plan in Botswana, discussed and analyzed in C. T. Ganesan, *Water Resources Development and Management—A Challenging Task for Botswana,* 26 Water Intl. 80 (2001); and *Water Demand Management: Towards Developing Effective Strategies for Southern Africa* 100 (M. Goldblatt, J. Ndamba, B. van der Merwe, F. Gomes, B. Haasbroek & J. Arntzen, eds., IUCN 2000).

using such techniques as systems analysis and mathematical modeling as planning tools and reviewing and adjusting targets to keep pace with changing conditions.[12]

The Action Plan and Recommendations of the Mar del Plata Conference are without a doubt comprehensive and of significant importance, and their subsequent endorsement by the United Nations General Assembly provided further strengthening and weight for them.[13] They continue to provide the basis for declarations and resolutions on water resources management that have been issued since that time. Indeed, the Dublin Statement on Water and Sustainable Development that was issued in 1992 is based largely on the recommendations of the Mar del Plata Water Conference.

The Dublin Statement was issued by the International Conference on Water and the Environment—Development Issues for the 21st Century that was held in Dublin, Ireland, on January 26–31, 1992. The Conference participants, totaling more than 500, called for fundamentally new approaches to the assessment, development, and management of freshwater resources that can only be brought about through political commitment and involvement from the highest levels of government to the smallest communities. Such commitment will need to be backed by substantial and immediate investments, public awareness campaigns, technology development, capacity-building programs, and legislative and institutional changes.

The four guiding principles adopted by the Conference came to be known as the Dublin Principles.[14] They are:

1. Fresh water is a finite and vulnerable resource, essential to sustain life, development, and the environment.
2. Water development and management should be based on a participatory approach, involving users, planners, and policymakers at all levels.
3. Women play a central part in the provision, management, and safeguarding of water.

---

[12] For guidance on the preparation of a national water policy, plan, or strategy, *see National Water Master Plans for Developing Countries* (Asit K. Biswas, Cesar Herrera Toledo, Héctor Garduño Velasco & Cecilia Trotajada Quiroz, eds., Oxford University Press 1997). *See also* Guy Le Moigne, Ashok Subramanian, Mei Xie & Sandra Giltner, *A Guide to the Formulation of Water Resources Strategy,* World Bank Technical Paper No. 263 (World Bank 1994).

[13] *See* United Nations General Assembly Resolution 32/158, 107th Plenary meeting, 19 December 1977. Paragraph I of the Resolution adopted the Report of the Conference and approved the Action Plan and other agreements reached at the Conference.

[14] For the Dublin Statement on Water and Sustainable Development, *see* 41 J. Water SRT Aqua (1992), at 129. The Dublin Statement is reproduced as appendix I to this study.

4. Water has an economic value in all its competing uses and should be recognized as an economic good.[15]

Since their issuance in 1992, the Dublin Principles have retained a central role in the ongoing debate on water resources management and development and have had a major influence on water legislation world-wide.[16] The Dublin Statement can indeed be considered the *magna carta* for water resources management.

The recommendations of the Mar del Plata Water Conference and the Dublin Statement have, *inter alia*, laid the foundation for the concept of integrated water resources management (IWRM). The concept of IWRM aims to ensure the coordinated development and management of water, land, and related resources by maximizing economic and social welfare without compromising the sustainability of vital environmental systems.[17]

The Dublin Conference was planned as a preparatory meeting for the United Nations Conference on Environment and Development (UNCED) that was held in Rio de Janeiro, Brazil, in June 1992 (the Rio or the Earth Summit). Agenda 21 of the Summit "Programme of Action for Sustainable Development" included a separate chapter (Chapter 18) on freshwater resources.[18] The Programme of Action noted that the widespread scarcity, gradual destruction, and aggravated pollution of freshwater resources in many parts of the world, combined with the progressive encroachment of incompatible activities, demanded integrated water resources management and development. Such integration should cover all types of freshwater bodies, including both surface and groundwater, and should deal with both the quantity and quality of water. The Programme called, *inter alia*, for the establishment of appropriate policy frameworks and national priorities, as

---

[15] For an analysis of the last principle *see* Peter Rogers, Ramesh Bhatia & Annette Huber, *Water as a Social and Economic Good: How to Put the Principle into Practice,* Global Water Partnership (GWP), Technical Advisory Committee (TAC) Background Papers, No. 2 (GWP/Swedish Intl. Dev. Coop. Agency 1998).

[16] *See* Miguel Solanes & Fernando Gonzalez-Villarreal, *The Dublin Principles for Water as Reflected in a Comparative Assessment of Institutional and Legal Arrangements for Integrated Water Resources Management,* Global Water Partnership (GWP), TAC Background Papers, No. 3 (GWP/Swedish Intl. Dev. Coop. Agency 1999).

[17] *See* Global Water Partnership, Technical Advisory Committee, *Integrated Water Resources Management,* TAC Background Papers, No. 4 (GWP 2000).

[18] *See* Earth Summit, Agenda 21, United Nations Programme of Action from Rio, U.N. ISBN 92-1100509-4; Sales No. E.93.1.11.166 (United Nations Publications 1993). The title of chapter 18 is "Protection of the Quality and Supply of Freshwater Resources: Application of Integrated Approaches to the Development, Management and Use of Water Resources." *See also Agenda 21, The Earth Summit Strategy to Save Our Planet* (Daniel Sitarz, ed., Earthpress 1994).

well as the establishment of the institutional capacities of countries, including legislative and regulatory arrangements.[19] It also urged that appropriate institutional, legal, and financial mechanisms be identified and strengthened or created to ensure that water policy and its implementation are a catalyst for sustainable social progress and economic growth.[20]

Similarly, the World Bank Policy Paper on Water Resources Management underscores the importance of regulatory frameworks. It states that legislation provides the basis for action by governmental and nongovernmental entities, such as water users' associations, and individuals when dealing with issues like water rights.[21] World Bank Operational Policy 4.07 (OP 4.07), which governs Bank operations in the water sector, states that the Bank assists its borrowers in "establishing strong legal and regulatory frameworks to ensure that social concerns are met, environmental resources are protected, and monopoly pricing is prevented. The Bank requires legislation or other appropriate arrangements to establish effective coordination and allocation procedures for inter-states water resources."[22] In line with the Dublin Principles and the Bank Policy Paper, the Operational Policy calls for decentralization in water services, involving users in planning water projects, and encouraging stakeholders to contribute to policy formulation. It also calls for pricing and incentives policies that achieve cost recovery, water conservation, and better allocation of water resources.[23] Along those lines, the African Development Bank Water Policy states that "Effective implementation of IWRM requires that stakeholders have a consensus on the legitimacy of decisions and actions of the institutions regulating different aspects of water resources management."[24]

---

[19] *See* United Nations Programme of Action from Rio, *id.* at 170.

[20] *See id.* at 167.

[21] *See* World Bank, *supra n.* 4, at 44. It is worth noting that the World Bank issued its Policy Paper in 1993, shortly after the Dublin and Rio Conferences. The Policy Paper reflected the consensus forged at those two meetings and incorporated the principles enunciated in the Dublin Statement. *See id.* at 23–25. For an assessment of how the World Bank implemented this policy, *see* World Bank Operations Evaluation Department, *Bridging Troubled Waters—Assessing the World Bank Water Resources Strategy* (World Bank 2002). The assessment underscored the relevance and validity of the Policy Paper but suggested the need for an implementation strategy. Consequently, in 2004 the World Bank issued *Water Resources Sector Strategy—Strategic Directions for World Bank Engagement.*

[22] *See* OP 4.07, Water Resources Management 1993, para. (f). This OP was reissued in April 2000 and is reproduced as appendix II to this study.

[23] *See id.* paras. (c) and (d).

[24] *See supra* n. 5, at 22. Similarly, the Asian Development Bank noted the need for empowering water users to protect and advance their rights. *See supra* n. 6, at 10.

A specific reference to the relevance and importance of legal and institutional issues related to water resources is also included in the Marrakech Declaration, which was issued by the First World Water Forum, held in Marrakech, Morocco, in 1997. The Declaration states that the participants in the Forum "recognize and note the urgent need for a better understanding of all the complex issues— quantitative and qualitative, political and economic, legal and institutional, social and financial, educational and environmental—that must go into shaping a water policy for the next millennium."[25] Although the Ministerial Declaration of the Second World Water Forum, held at The Hague in 2000, missed the legal and regulatory issues, the Third World Water Forum, held in Kyoto, Japan, in 2003, made specific and clear reference to them. Paragraph 25 of the Kyoto Ministerial Declaration urged countries to review, and when necessary establish, appropriate legislative frameworks for the protection and sustainable use of water resources.[26]

Along the same lines, the United Nations Millennium Declaration, issued on September 8, 2000, stressed, under a separate part of the Declaration, the need to protect the common environment.[27] The Declaration stated the resolve of the parties to "stop the unsustainable exploitation of water resources by developing water management strategies at the regional, national and local levels which promote both equitable access and adequate supplies."[28] The eight Millennium Development Goals proclaimed by the Millennium Declaration include reducing by half, by the year 2015, the proportion of people who are unable to reach or to afford safe drinking water.[29]

---

[25] *See* Third Paragraph of the Marrakech Declaration. For a detailed discussion of the Marrakech Water Forum and its Declaration, *see Water, the World's Common Heritage,* Proceedings of the First World Water Forum, Marrakech, Morocco (Mohamed Aït-Kadi, Aly Shady & Andras Szöllösi-Nagy, eds., Elsevier 1997).

[26] For an analysis of the first three World Water Forums, *see* Salman M. A. Salman, *From Marrakech Through The Hague to Kyoto—Has the Global Debate on Water Reached a Dead End?* Part One, 28 Water Intl. 491 (2003), and Part Two, 29 Water Intl. 11 (2004).

[27] The United Nations Millennium Declaration was issued as General Assembly Resolution 55/2. Part IV of the Declaration (paras. 21 to 23) deals with "Protecting our Common Environment."

[28] *See id.* para. 23. This paragraph reaffirmed "support for the principles of sustainable development, including those set out in Agenda 21, agreed upon at the United Nations Conference on Environment and Development."

[29] *See id.* para. 19. It should be clarified in this regard that the Millennium Declaration dealt only with the issue of reducing by half the proportion of people without access to safe drinking water; it did not address the issue of sanitation. This unfortunate oversight was corrected two years later at the World Summit on Sustainable Development held in September 2002 in Johannesburg, South Africa. Paragraph 7 of the Plan of Implementation issued by the Summit added the sanitation component. Since the Johannesburg Summit, reference to the water component of the Millennium Development Goals has been read to include sanitation. This reading was further emphasized by the United Nations

Furthermore, the Declaration of the Ministerial Session of the International Conference on Freshwater that was held in Bonn, Germany, in December 2001 (the Bonn Declaration) addressed the issue of water governance.[30] It confirmed that the primary responsibility for ensuring the sustainable and equitable management of water resources rests with governments. It called on each country to have in place arrangements for the governance of water affairs at all levels and, where appropriate, to accelerate water sector reforms.[31]

The relevance and importance of the policies, legislation, strategies, and plans for water resources management continue to be debated and emphasized in international conferences. In September 2005, the Heads of States and Governments, gathered at the World Summit at the United Nations Headquarters in New York and issued a Resolution entitled the "2005 World Summit Outcome."[32] Paragraph 56(h) of the Resolution proclaimed the resolve of the participants to assist developing countries with their efforts to prepare integrated water resources management and water efficiency plans as part of their national development strategies. The same paragraph went on to stress the importance of achieving the Millennium Development Goal of reducing by half, by the year 2015, the proportion of people without sustainable access to safe drinking water and sanitation. Accordingly, the World Summit established a clear link between those water resources management plans and efforts to achieve the Millennium Development Goal with regard to water.[33]

The issue of regulatory frameworks for water resources management has thus occupied a considerable place in international conferences and forums. Its relevance and importance to water resources management and protection have been

---

General Assembly Resolution 58/217, "International Decade for Action, Water for Life 2005–2015," issued on December 23, 2003. The Resolution includes a reference to both water and sanitation goals. For an analysis of this Resolution, *see* Salman M. A. Salman, *United Nations General Assembly Resolution: International Decade for Action, Water for Life, 2005–2015,* 30 Water Intl. 415 (2005).

[30] The Bonn Conference was held to assess progress in implementing Agenda 21 and to prepare for the World Summit on Sustainable Development, which was held in August/September 2002 in Johannesburg, South Africa. Thus, this Conference was the equivalent of the Dublin meeting in relation to the Rio Summit. However, it should be clarified that the Bonn Conference was not a United Nations–sponsored conference but was organized on the initiative of the German government.

[31] For discussion and analysis of the concept of water governance, *see* Peter Rogers & Alan W. Hall, *Effective Water Governance,* Global Water Partnership, Technical Committee, TEC Background Papers, No. 7 (GWP 2003). *See also* Karin M. Krchnak, *Improving Water Governance Through Increased Public Access to Information and Participation,* 5 Sust. Dev. L. & Pol. 34 (2004).

[32] *See* United Nations General Assembly Resolution A/RES/60/1, 16 September 2005.

[33] *See id.,* para. 56(h).

underscored by the different declarations, resolutions, and action plans issued at those meetings. This reflects a clear and unequivocal conviction by all the actors involved in water resources of the significant place of water legislation in integrated water resources management. However, it should be emphasized that water resources management is a dynamic and evolving concept; regulatory frameworks need to take into account the socioeconomic and cultural setting of each state, rather than follow a specified model form or blueprint. Nonetheless, and despite the differences in settings, there are still some common, basic principles that water legislation needs to address, though the details will depend upon the socioeconomic and cultural milieu.

The purpose of this study is to examine how the regulatory frameworks in sixteen jurisdictions have addressed the various basic issues related to water resources management, and to provide a comparative analysis of those issues. The study furthermore discusses what it considers the essential elements for a regulatory framework for water resources management and identifies some emerging trends. Water, as a subject matter requiring a multidisciplinary approach,[34] will often have provisions pertinent to its use, management, development, and protection included in a variety of laws and regulations. This study is not intended as a comprehensive review of all provisions in every law and regulation dealing with water resources management in each jurisdiction; nor does it attempt to analyze how water legislation is being implemented in any jurisdiction. Rather, the intention of the study is to identify the main laws and regulations on water and to examine how they have addressed the use, development, management, allocation, and

---

[34] The issue of whether water is an interdisciplinary or a multidisciplinary subject was aptly addressed by Ben Dziegielewski when he stated:

> It is now widely recognized that water resources management decisions must go beyond the confines of technical disciplines of hydrology and civil engineering. Multidisciplinary, interdisciplinary, or even transdisciplinary approaches are often recommended for dealing with the multifaceted water resources problems. While these "buzzwords" are often used interchangeably, some writers make distinctions between these terms as they apply to research. The term "multidisciplinary" usually refers to research that draws on knowledge from different disciplines but stays within the boundaries of the researcher's own discipline. In contrast, an interdisciplinary approach implies that researchers have to move out to the fringe of their disciplinary boundary and attempt integration of concepts, methodologies, procedures, theories, terminology, and data from other disciplines to create a new interdisciplinary field (OECD, 1998, *Interdisciplinary in Science and Technology*. Directorate for Science, Technology and Industry. Paris: OECD). By continuing in this context, a transdisciplinary approach would be an extension of the interdisciplinary method that is far-reaching and holistic. Possibly, the integrated water resources management (IWRM) approach would be a good example of a transdisciplinary approach.

See Ben Dziegielewski, *Message from the Executive Editor,* 30 Water Intl. 269 (2005).

protection of the water resource. The primary objective of the study is to provide countries that are preparing water legislation, or revising existing legislation, with a toolkit where they can find out how some basic issues related to such legislation have been addressed by the water regulatory frameworks of other countries.

The research for this study was completed in June 2004. Since that time some amendments or new provisions may have been introduced in one or more laws or regulations in some of the jurisdictions included in this study. Except for a few cases, this study does not take into account those changes.

CHAPTER 2

Country Study of Regulatory Frameworks for Water Resources Management

This chapter describes and analyzes the regulatory frameworks for water resources management in sixteen jurisdictions. Those jurisdictions were selected based on a number of factors, among them the existence and availability of a water law.[35] Attention was also given to representation of the different regions and legal systems of the world. The chapter discusses constitutional provisions; the main laws, decrees, or regulations that deal with water resources management in those countries; and the underlying principles and priorities set forth in each of those instruments. Furthermore, it discusses issues related to water resources, including regulation of water uses, protection of water, regulation of water infrastructure, institutional and financial arrangements, and the enforcement of regulations and dispute settlement in each country represented.

---

[35] A number of countries with a federal system of government do not have a national water law because the constitutions of those countries place the main responsibilities for water resources, as a general rule, on the Provinces or the states of the country, giving limited authority to the central government. Therefore, water resources would be regulated by laws issued by each of those states or Provinces. In some of these countries, however, there may be other laws or policies granting the Federal government specific authority over water. India and Pakistan are examples. India issued its National Water Policy in 1997. Although this policy has no legally binding effect, its main purpose is to provide guidance for the Indian states on the issues to be addressed in their water laws and on how to deal with them. However, as discussed earlier, there is a role for the central government in inter-states water disputes (*see supra* n. 2). Pakistan has drafted a national water policy that would establish a national water council, to be headed by the Prime Minister, to take decisions on water-related issues and inter-provincial disputes. However, at the time this study was completed, the draft policy was still under discussion and had not been adopted. Thus, the major responsibility over water in Pakistan is still vested with the Provinces. On the other hand, in Brazil and Canada, which both have a Federal system of government, there is a division of authority over water between the Federal and state governments, and both countries have a national water law. *See* the country study for Brazil in section 2.2 in this chapter.

2.1 Armenia

2.1.1 Statutory Framework

There are two statutes dealing with water issues in Armenia, one of which was still in draft form when this study was completed. Those statutes are:

- Water Code of the Republic of Armenia, adopted by the National Assembly of the Republic of Armenia on June 4, 2002 (Water Code); and
- Law of the Republic of Armenia on Water Users' Associations and Unions of Water Users' Associations (WUA Law). This law was still in draft form when the research for this study was completed. The WUA Law states that the activities of Water Users' Associations (WUA) and Unions of WUA are regulated by the WUA Law, the Water Code, the Civil Code of Armenia, and the charters of WUA and their associations.

2.1.2 Underlying Principles and Priorities

The main purpose of the Water Code is to provide the legal basis for conserving the national water reserve and satisfying the water needs of Armenian citizens and the economy through effectively managing usable water resources and securing the ecological sustainability of water resources (Water Code, art. 6). More specifically, the objectives of the Water Code include the establishment of appropriate water resource management mechanisms, the conservation and protection of water resources, ensuring an adequate quantity and quality of water supply to the population and economy, and the organization of the management, protection, and development of water systems (Water Code, art. 7).[36]

Article 5 of the Water Code states that the basic principles applicable to the management, use, and protection of water resources and water systems in Armenia include satisfaction of the basic needs of present and future generations, maintenance and increase of the volume of the "national water reserve,"[37] protection of aquatic and related ecosystems and their biological diversity, encouragement of fair and efficient use of water resources, and consideration of

---

[36] For a thorough discussion of Armenian policies and strategies in the water sector, *see* World Bank, *Armenia: Towards Integrated Water Resources Management,* ECSSD Working Paper No. 35 (World Bank 2002).

[37] The "national water reserve" is defined in art. 1 of the Water Code as the "quality and quantity of water that is required to satisfy present and future basic human needs, as well as protect aquatic ecosystems, and to secure sustainable development and use of that water resource."

the "economic value"[38] of water in the procedures applicable to the use, allocation, and protection of water resources. This article also mandates that the authorities must charge fees for water use that are based on the abated price of water scarcity in order to make available the minimum sufficient quantity and quality of water, and must charge fees for water use generally. Finally, the article recognizes the importance of public participation and awareness in the management and protection of water resources and prohibits the satisfaction of water users' needs at the expense of "ecological water releases" (Water Code, art. 5(24)).

Pursuant to these principles, the Water Code requires the formulation of a national water policy that sets out the objectives and challenges involved in the strategic development of water resource use and protection; the implementation of the objectives and principles of the Water Code relating to the development of water basin strategies and plans for the next ten to fifteen years; and a preliminary assessment of the quantity and quality of water available for allocation among the various demands for water from the population and the economy (Water Code, art. 15).

The objective of the WUA Law is to regulate the establishment and operation of WUA and unions of WUA and their activities (WUA Law, art. 1).

2.1.3   Regulation of Water Uses

2.1.3.1   *Ownership of Water and Establishment of Water Rights*

Water resources in Armenia are considered, pursuant to article 4 of the Water Code, to be the property of the state. However, state-owned water systems can be under either state or private management (Water Code, art. 48).

The right to use water is established by obtaining a water use permit unless the Water Code specifically provides that a permit is not required (Water Code, art. 21). The Water Code establishes six uses for which a permit is not required; these are known as "free water uses." These free uses are listed in article 22; they are: uses that do not have a profit-making purpose, recreation, swimming and water sports, nonentrepreneurial fishing and hunting, use of precipitation on privately held lands, fire prevention, and water flows to maintain the ecological balance for sanitary purposes. The Water Code provides that the Water Resources Management and Protection Body can make exceptions to the free use of water for these purposes (Water Code, art. 22).

---

[38] Art. 5(11) of the Water Code stipulates that the "economic value" of water consists of the sum of the "drinking, environmental, energetic potential and agricultural values of water."

A landowner has the first right to acquire a groundwater use permit relating to groundwater on his or her property. A groundwater use permit relating to groundwater use on another's property may only be issued with that landowner's written permission (Water Code, art. 25).

2.1.3.2   Allocation of Right to Use Water

The Water Code defines "water use" in article 1 as the removal of water from or otherwise reducing water in a water resource, storing water, impeding or diverting its flow, polluting a water resource, discharging wastewater into a water resource, disposing or storing hazardous substances in a manner that is detrimental to the water resource, and altering the beds, banks, course, or characteristics of a water resource.

In general, water resources cannot be allocated, extracted, or used in a way that envisages a decrease in the national economy (Water Code, art. 18). Moreover, in order to establish a right to use water, it is necessary to obtain a water use permit. These permits are issued by either the Water Resources Management and Protection Body or a Water Basin Management Authority (Water Code, art. 30), pursuant to the procedures (Water Code, arts. 27–30) and criteria (Water Code, art. 31) established in the Water Code. One requirement of the procedures is that there be public notice of the permit application (Water Code, art. 20). The permit should describe, *inter alia,* the types of water uses allowed, the quantity of water that can be used, the time periods when water can be used, the water standards with which the permit holder must comply, water use permit fees, and the payment schedule (Water Code, art. 32). The period of permit validity varies from three to forty years, depending on the location of the water resource and the investment costs involved in the water use (Water Code, art. 33). Permits are renewable pursuant to article 33.

The Water Code also provides for the issuance of water system use permits. "Water systems" are defined as "hydrotechnical structures" that cause alteration of the water flow, such as dams, dikes, canals, pumping plants, water storage facilities, and the machinery and equipment used in the construction of such structures.[39] A "noncompetitive water supply system" is a system of structures that has as its primary purpose the storage of water to supply the public with drinking water, wastewater treatment, and irrigation services and that is the only available source of such services (Water Code, art. 1).

Noncompetitive water suppliers are required, pursuant to article 38, to hold valid water system use permits. These permits describe the rights of the permit

---

[39] Water Code, art. 1. A "water system" includes, according to this article, both an integrated system of such structures and the separate parts of such a system.

holder to use the water supply system, the tariffs to be charged, and the requirements relating to the quality of services to be provided by the permit holder
(Water Code, art. 38). The Water Code stipulates the form of the water system use
permit (Water Code, art. 39) and the process (Water Code, arts. 40–43) for applying for and obtaining a water use permit, which requires, *inter alia,* that there be
public notice of the permit application (Water Code, art. 20). One prerequisite for
obtaining a water system use permit is that the applicant must first hold a water
use permit that is commensurate with the requirements of the proposed noncompetitive water system's use and management (Water Code, art. 42). Water systems
use permits are valid for no more than twenty-five years unless initial investment
costs warrant a longer period, in which case the licenses will be valid for forty
years (Water Code, art. 45).

Water system managers have the right to use the water system in compliance
with the requirements of the Water Code and of their permit and to enforce their
rights under the Water Code and their permits (Water Code, art. 59). They are
responsible for providing water users with water of the quality and quantity specified in their permits, to perform the other duties required by the water system use
contracts, and to comply with applicable environmental rules and regulations
(Water Code, arts. 60–61).

2.1.3.3   Transfer of Water Rights

Water use permit holders can sell or otherwise transfer a portion of their permitted water right to a third party, provided they comply with the procedures established by the government and their permits do not specifically prohibit them from
doing so (Water Code, art. 35).

Water system use permits can be sold or otherwise transferred only if this is
stipulated in the permit (Water Code, art. 47). If so, the right to use a water system can be transferred through the use of a trust management contract, a concession agreement, the creation of a commercial organization, or a lease (Water
Code, art. 49).[40] Trust management arrangements are established through a
tender process (Water Code, arts. 50–52). Concession agreements are concluded

---

[40] Art. 49 of the Water Code, "Types of Water System Use Rights Transfer," states:

The right of use of a water system can be transferred in the following forms:

1) Trust Management Contract;

2) Concession Agreement;

3) Creation of a commercial organization;

4) Lease.

The procedures for transfer types shall be established by the legislation.

between the entity accepting the responsibility to manage the water system through the concession and the Water Systems Management Body (Water Code, art. 53). The commercial organizations to which water systems use permits can be transferred can have private persons owning up to 49 percent of the total equity in the organizations, with the remaining equity owned by the state (Water Code, art. 54). In lease arrangements the lessor is the Water Systems Management Body (Water Code, art. 55).

2.1.3.4   Loss of Right to Use Water

Water use permits can be suspended, amended, or revoked (Water Code, art. 34). Permit holders can also be deemed to have abandoned their permits if they fail to use a permit for three consecutive years and there is no legal reason that precludes them from making use of the water right. An abandoned permit is null and void (Water Code, art. 36).

Water system use permits can be suspended, amended, or revoked (Water Code, art. 46). They can also be terminated (Water Code, art. 57).

2.1.4   Protection of Water

Article 99 of the Water Code stipulates that the "water resources in the Republic of Armenia shall be protected." In furtherance of this objective, the Article formulates a series of primary requirements for their protection. These requirements include that water use is only permitted in conditions that allow for water resource protection and restoration; water is a constituent part of the ecosystem[41]

---

[41] The Water Code does not define the term "ecosystem." Malin Falkenmark gave a comprehensive definition of the term when she stated

Basically, the term ecosystem refers to a set of interacting organisms and the solar-driven system that they compose, comprising both primary producers and consumers and decomposers. In combination they mediate the flow of energy, the cycling of elements (including water) and spatial and temporal patterns of vegetation. An ecosystem may be of any scale from global all the way down to local. At the upper end of the scale the life support system of our planet is an ecosystem energized by solar energy and kept together by the circulating water that functions as the bloodstream. At the lower end of the scale the local biotic systems are spoken of as ecosystems: a grass land, a forest, a lake, a stream, and so on.

See Malin Falkenmark, *Water Management and Ecosystems: Living with Change,* Global Water Partnership, Technical Committee, TEC Background Papers, No. 9, at 9 (GWP 2003). The Convention on Biological Diversity defines the term "ecosystem" to mean "a dynamic complex of plant, animal and micro-organism communities and their non-living environment interacting as a functional unit." *See* Convention on Biological Diversity, art. 2, 1760 U.N.T.S. 79. This definition was adopted by the Millennium Ecosystem Assessment, which defined the term "ecosystem" to mean "a dynamic complex of plants,

and its protection demands the maintenance of balance within a given ecosystem (Water Code, art. 66)[42]; water resources are to be protected from pollution, littering, infection, and depletion; and specific activities, such as irrigation with wastewater (Water Code, arts. 66, 101), can be restricted or prohibited in certain water resources. Article 20 requires any person who becomes aware of water pollution or a situation that is adversely affecting the quality of water to notify the Water Resources Management and Protection Body.

Pursuant to the objective of protecting the nation's water resources, the Water Code stipulates that the National Water Program, which covers all water resources within the Republic of Armenia, must establish a "national water reserve."[43]

The Water Resources Management and Protection Body and interested state management bodies are jointly responsible for developing water quality standards, which may vary according to the specific situation in each water basin management area (Water Code, art. 66). The standards should address such issues as degradation, depletion and contamination of water, as well as establishing minimum environmental flows (Water Code, art. 66). The Water Resources Management and Protection Body is responsible for ensuring that these standards comply with water quality criteria (Water Code, art. 59).

The state body authorized to monitor water resources shall follow all procedures established in law for monitoring water resources. It shall also provide the data required to create the Water Cadastre (Water Code, art. 19). Moreover, it is worth noting that the development of the National Water Policy and Program, and of standards for water, is subject to public notice (Water Code, art. 20).

2.1.5 Regulation of Water Infrastructure

The government is responsible for use, protection, capital investment in, and safety of all state-owned water reservoirs (Water Code, art. 82). The owners and operators of hydrotechnical structures (HTS) are required to provide for the safety of these structures at all times (Water Code, art. 83).[44] The Water Systems

---

animals, microbes, and physical environmental features that interact with one another." *See* Millennium Ecosystem Assessment, *Ecosystems and Human Well-Being: Opportunities and Challenges for Business and Industry* 3 (World Resources Institute 2005). Along those lines, the World Bank Water Resources Management Policy Paper defines "ecosystem" to mean "A complex system formed by the interaction of a community of organisms with its environment." *See* World Bank, *supra* n. 4, at 6. Thus, the concept of the ecosystem is broad, and includes flora, fauna, and land contiguous to the water source.

[42] *See also* Water Code, art. 98.

[43] *See supra* n. 37.

[44] *See also* arts. 84 and 85.

Management Body, in consultation with relevant state management bodies, is required to establish a Technical Commission to monitor the performance of all HTS (Water Code, art. 86).

2.1.6 Institutional Arrangements

The ultimate responsibility for the management and protection of water rests with the Government of the Republic of Armenia, acting through various state bodies (Water Code, art. 3). The highest advisory body is the National Water Council, which makes recommendations to the Government on the National Water Policy, the National Water Program, and related matters (Water Code, art. 8). The Council is chaired by the Prime Minister; its members include the heads of the Water Resources Management and Protection Body, the Water Systems Management Body, and the Regulatory Commission. The Prime Minister can decide which other state bodies should be represented on the Council (Water Code, art. 9).

The Water Resources Management and Protection Body is responsible for coordinating preparation of the National Water Policy and National Water Program, implementing water resource management and protection within the framework of this Policy and Program, and issuing water use permits (Water Code, art. 9). The Water Resources Management and Protection Body is also responsible for appointing representatives to the Water Basin Management Authority, which falls under the jurisdiction of the Water Resources Management and Protection Body (Water Code, arts. 10–11).

The Water Systems Management Body is responsible for the management and safe use of state-owned HTS (Water Code, art. 12). It also participates in preparation and implementation of the National Water Program and submits to the Regulatory Commission proposals on water systems use permits and their terms and conditions and on regulated tariffs (Water Code, art. 12). The Water Code does not contain any information on the composition of the Water Systems Management Body or its relationship to the Water Resources Management and Protection Body.

The procedures for establishing the Regulatory Commission, which is an independent body fulfilling the functions of a state management body, are established by law but are not contained in the Water Code (Water Code, art. 14). Its function is to define tariff policy with regard to water affairs and to issue water systems use permits for noncompetitive water suppliers.[45]

---

[45] Art. 14 of the Water Code, states as follows:

  The Regulatory Commission shall define tariff policy in water relations and shall issue water systems use permits to non-competitive water suppliers.

2.1.6.1　River Basin Authorities

The Water Basin Management bodies are responsible for developing water management plans for the applicable water basin that are consistent with the National Water Program (Water Code, art. 11). These bodies also link the Water Resources Management and Protection Body with the communities that use the applicable water basin. The bodies are responsible for ensuring that the use of the applicable water basin complies with legal and regulatory requirements and with the terms of water use permits. In addition to the representatives of the Head of the Water Resource Management and Protection Body, the membership of Water Basin Management bodies will include citizens' representatives and representatives of water users' associations and other organizations. These latter categories of representatives have the right to an "advisory vote" (Water Code, art. 11).

2.1.6.2　Water Users' Associations

Water users' associations play an important role in the management and use of water resources in Armenia.[46] They are nonprofit organizations that have a separate legal status and that implement plans for the exploitation and maintenance of the irrigation system for the public benefit (WUA Law, art. 4). They are responsible for managing the irrigation system within their service area, for providing water to the water users within their service area, and for collecting the applicable fees from both members and non-members within their service area (WUA Law, art. 4). The rules applicable to their establishment, operation, and termination are all spelled out in the WUA Law.

The Water Code and the WUA Law also provide for the establishment of unions of water users' associations that are voluntary associations of water users' associations or water users' companies (Water Code, art. 71).[47] The latter are nonprofit entities that operate in the public interest to carry out the operation and

---

The Regulatory Commission is an independent body fulfilling functions of a state management body. The procedure for its establishment and activity shall be established by law.

The Regulatory Commission shall develop and run the tariff policy, as well as issue water system use permits to non-competitive water suppliers in a procedure established by law according to the provisions of this Code.

[46] For further discussion of WUAs in Armenia, *see* Volker Branscheid, *Irrigation Development in Eastern Europe and the Former Soviet Union,* ECSRE Rural Development and Environment Sector Working Paper No. 3 (World Bank 1998).

[47] *See also* WUA Law, ch. 3, arts. 23–31. For a discussion of the role and responsibilities of such a union of water users' associations in Colombia, *see* Gilberto Garcia-Betancourt, *The Emergence of FEDERRIEGO: The Colombian Federation of Irrigation Districts,* International Irrigation Management Institute, Short Report No. 8 (1994).

maintenance of irrigations systems (Water Code, art. 72). The WUA Law provides, in article 32, that the Government of Armenia will establish a Regulatory Board that will be responsible for overseeing the affairs and activities of water users' associations and unions of water users' associations.

2.1.6.3 Advisory Committees

The National Water Council is the highest advisory body. As described above, the Council makes recommendations to the Government on the National Water Policy, the National Water Program, and related matters.

2.1.7 Financial Arrangements

The basic principle applicable to the economic regulation of the use, restoration, and protection of water resources, water supply, and wastewater systems is "chargeable water use" (Water Code, art. 76). The charges must be set at a level that is adequate to cover the costs associated with the operation of the water resource, its restoration and maintenance, and the effective management of water and to create economic incentives to promote efficient operation, restoration, and maintenance of water supply and wastewater systems (Water Code, art. 76). In furtherance of these objectives, fees are charged for permits for water use (Water Code, art. 77) and water system use permits (Water Code, art. 78). In addition, regulated tariffs are charged on noncompetitive water uses (Water Code, art. 79). The Water Code also provides that the state may provide financial assistance in the form of subsidies or tax benefits to water suppliers and water users to ensure equal conditions and to avoid discrimination in the supply and use of water. This assistance is to be set out in the Government's annual budget and must be approved by the National Assembly (Water Code, art. 81).[48]

In May 2001 Armenia established, as part of its reform of the financial sustainability of the water sector, the State Committee of Water Economy.[49] The Committee is responsible for regulatory tasks related to the provision of commercially oriented water services.[50] Subsequently, the Water Code addressed the role of the private sector in water service delivery. The Water Code provides in article 48 that state-owned water systems can be under state or private

---

[48] This article basically calls for the right to have access to water. For discussion of the article in the context of the human right to water, *see* Salman & McInerney Lankford, *supra* n. 10, at 72.

[49] Government of Armenia Decree No. 440, issued on May 17, 2001.

[50] *See* World Bank, *supra* n. 36, at v.

management, or both. The transfer of management rights must in all instances be conducted in a manner that provides for adequate public notice and conditions for competition. Prior to transferring management rights over state-owned water systems, the Water Systems Management Body responsible shall make certain that all necessary water use permits and water system use permits are in order. Article 48 further provides that preference is given to entities with more extensive professional experience and knowledge, and that the transfer of rights for the use of a water system shall not exceed the term specified in the water system use permit.

2.1.8 Enforcement of Regulations and Dispute Settlement

2.1.8.1 Enforcement of Regulations

The regulatory bodies are responsible for monitoring water resources according to the procedures established in article 19 of the Water Code. Most of the information collected through the monitoring of water resources is included in the State Water Cadastre, which is freely accessible to the public (Water Code, art. 19). Each year the state monitoring bodies submit to the Water Resources Management and Protection Body a comprehensive report on the water resources they are monitoring. These reports are incorporated into the annual report of the Water Resources Management and Protection Body on the implementation of the National Water Program (Water Code, art. 19).

Transactions that are inconsistent with applicable water law are invalid (Water Code, art. 113). Furthermore, people who enter into such invalid transactions or who otherwise fail to act in conformity with the applicable law can be held criminally and administratively liable for their actions (Water Code, art. 114). They may also be required to compensate those who suffer losses as a result of their invalid or unlawful actions (Water Code, art. 116).

2.1.8.2 Dispute Settlement

The Water Code establishes a Dispute Resolution Commission, pursuant to article 9, that is responsible for resolving disputes relating to water use permits. This Commission can use mediation and binding arbitration to resolve disputes. If its decisions are not complied with, the matter shall be resolved by the courts (Water Code, art. 9). The members of the Dispute Resolution Commission are appointed by the Prime Minister (Water Code, art. 9). The Commission is not authorized to adjudicate disputes to which the Republic of Armenia is a party (Water Code, art. 110). Disputes involving members of water users' associations and unions of water users' associations are resolved using their own procedures and boards (Water Code, art. 111).

2.2 Brazil

2.2.1 Statutory Framework

Water in Brazil is regulated by:

- A number of articles in the Constitution, including articles 20 (III) and 26 on ownership of water and article 21 (XIX) on the establishment of a national system for management of water resources;[51]
- The National Water Resources Policy (Law No. 9,433 of January 8, 1997) (the NWRP); and
- The National Water Agency Law (Law No. 9,984 of July 17, 2000) (the ANA Law).

2.2.2 Underlying Principles and Priorities

Under its Constitution of 1988 (as amended in 2004), Brazil is a federal state and authority over water is divided between the Union and the States. Article 20 of the Brazilian Constitution enumerates the property of the Union, which includes lakes, rivers, and any watercourses on lands that it owns; interstate waters; waters that serve as borders with other countries; and waters that extend into or come from a foreign territory. Article 26 stipulates that the property of the States includes surface water and groundwater, whether flowing, emerging or in reservoirs, except reservoirs, as permitted by law, resulting from works carried out by the Union. Article 21 (XIX) of the Constitution requires the Union to "establish a national system for management of water resources and define criteria for granting rights of their use."

The NWRP elaborates on these principles and establishes other principles regarding water resources, which include, *inter alia,* the following:

- Water is public property.
- It is a limited resource, which has economic value.
- In cases of shortage the highest priority should be given to using water resources for human consumption and for the watering of animals.
- The management of water resources should allow for multiple uses of water (NWRP, art. 1).

Article 1 of the NWRP also stipulates that the territorial unit to be used in implementing the law is the river basin, and that the management of water resources

---

[51] In addition, art. 255 of the Constitution of Brazil states that "Everyone has the right to an ecologically balanced environment, which is a public good for the people's use and is essential for a healthy life. The Government and the Community have a duty to defend and to preserve the environment for present and future generations."

should be decentralized and should involve users and communities as well as the Government.[52]

Article 2 states that the objectives of the NWRP are to ensure that both present and future generations have access to water of a quality that is adequate for their various uses; to ensure the rational and integrated use of water resources to achieve sustainable development; and to prevent water crises due to either natural disasters or the inappropriate use of natural resources. Implementation of the NWRP is guided by the following six general criteria:

1. The systematic management of water resources with equal regard to its quantity and quality;
2. The adjustment of water resources management to the specific physical, demographic, and social, economic, and cultural differences between the regions of Brazil;
3. The integration of water resources management with environmental concerns;
4. The coordination of water resources planning with users of water and with planning at the regional, state, and national level;
5. The coordination of water resources management with management of land use; and
6. The integration of river basin management with that of estuary systems and coastal zones.[53]

In implementing the NWRP, the responsible authorities can use a number of specific instruments, including water resources plans; classification of bodies of water according to the principal use made of the water; granting of rights to use water; charging of fees for the use of water; and the Water Resource Information System (NWRP, art. 5). It should be noted that the Union is required to coordinate with the States on the management of water of common interest to the State and the Union (NWRP, art. 4).[54]

---

[52] *See* Rubem La Laina Porto & Monica F. A. Porto, *Planning as a Tool to Deal with Extreme Events: The New Brazilian Water Resources Management System,* 27 Water Intl. 14 (2002).

[53] NWRP, art. 3.

[54] Art. 20 (III) of the Constitution of Brazil declares as the property of the Union, *inter alia,* "Lakes, rivers, and any watercourses on lands that it owns; interstate waters; waters that serve as borders with other countries; waters that extend into or come from a foreign country, as well as bordering lands and river beaches." On the other hand, art. 26 (I) indicates that the property of the States includes, *inter alia,* "surface or underground waters, whether flowing, emerging or in reservoirs, with the exception, in the latter case, as provided by law, of those resulting from works carried out by the Union."

2.2.3 Regulation of Water Uses

2.2.3.1 Ownership of Water and Establishment of Water Rights

Water is public property and the award of the right to use water in no way implies partial alienation of the water itself (NWRP, arts. 1 & 18). The NWRP states that the right to use water for the following purposes is subject to a Government award:

- Diversion or impoundment of water for final consumption or use in a productive process.
- Extraction of water from subterranean aquifers for final consumption or use in a productive process.
- Discharge of sewerage and waste into a body of water.
- Utilization of water for hydroelectric potential.
- Other uses that affect the flow, quantity, and quality of water existing in a body of water (NWRP, art. 12).

A Government award is not required for the following uses: meeting the needs of small population groups in rural areas; and diversions, catchments, and discharges that are "considered insignificant" (NWRP, art. 4).

Article 12 goes on to state that the award of water resource utilization for the generation of electric power must be provided for in the National Water Resources Plan. All awards to use water are subject to the priorities for land use established in the applicable Water Resources Plan and must maintain the principle of multiple uses of water (NWRP, art. 13). No award to use water can be made for longer than thirty-five years, but the awards are renewable (NWRP, art. 16).

Water Resources Plans are master plans that provide the bases for, and for implementation of, the National Water Resources Policy and water resources management (NWRP, art. 6). Article 7 states that Water Resources Plans are long-term plans that should have a time horizon that is compatible with the period over which the proposed programs and projects are to be implemented. They should contain the following information:

- A diagnosis of the current status of water resources;
- An analysis of population growth, the evolution of productive activity, and land-use patterns;
- A statement of the future supply of and demand for water resources in terms of quantity and quality, including identification of potential areas of conflict;
- Targets for rationalizing the use of water as well as improving its quantity and quality, and measures to be taken to reach these goals;

- Priorities for the awarding of water-use rights;
- Guidelines and criteria for water-use fees; and
- Proposals for the creation of areas with restrictions on water use that are designed to protect water resources (NWRP, art. 6).[55]

2.2.3.2 Allocation and Transfer of Right to Use Water

There are no provisions in the NWRP that give specific guidance on how rights to use water should be allocated. However, the statute requires that Water Use Plans should be developed for each river basin and State as well as for the entire country (NWRP, art. 8). Article 9 requires the authorities to classify bodies of water according to the principal uses made of the water body, the objective being (a) to ensure that the quality of the water is compatible with the most demanding use being made of each particular water body, and (b) to reduce the cost of combating water pollution through preventive action. There are no provisions in the NWRP that specifically address transfer of water rights.

2.2.3.3 Loss of Right to Use Water

An award of the right to use water can be partially or entirely suspended, either indefinitely or for a specified period of time, if, *inter alia*, the awardee fails to comply with the terms of the award or fails to use the resources for three consecutive years; there is an urgent need for the water because of a disaster; it is necessary to avoid or reverse major environmental degradation; or there is a need to provide for priority uses in the interests of the community (NWRP, art. 15).[56]

2.2.4 Protection of Water

The NWRP stipulates that one of the objectives of the water law is to protect the quality, quantity, and flow of water (NWRP, art. 12). The statute contains provisions that specifically address the issue of pollution and the protection of water. For example, article 9(ii) of the NWRP requires that the classification of bodies of water according to their principal uses shall have the objective of reducing the cost of combating water pollution through constant preventive actions.[57]

---

[55] *See* José Simas, *Issues Affecting the Irrigation and Drainage Sectors in Latin America: Lessons from Mexico, Argentina, and Brazil,* in *Institutional Reform for Irrigation and Drainage,* World Bank Technical Paper No. 524, 149 (Fernando J. Gonzalez & Salman M. A. Salman, eds., World Bank 2002).

[56] For an analysis of water rights in Brazil, *see* Alexander M. Baltar, Luiz Gabriel T. de Azevedo, Manuel Rego & Rubem La Laina Porto, *Decision Support Systems for Water Rights in Brazil,* Brazil, Water Series No. 3 (World Bank 2003).

[57] *See* Sergio Margulis, Gordon Hughes, Martin Gambrill & Luiz Gabriel T. de Azevedo, *Brazil: Managing Water Quality—Mainstreaming the Environment in the Water Sector,* World Bank Technical Paper No. 532 (World Bank 2002).

The NWRP, in article 5(VI), refers to the Water Resources Information System. This is a system for collecting, processing, storing, and retrieving information on water resources and the factors involved in their management (NWRP, art. 25). The objectives of this system are to collect, standardize, and disseminate data on the quality and quantity of water resources in Brazil; to update information on the availability and demand for water throughout the country; and to provide subsidies for the preparation of Water Resource Plans (NWRP, art. 27). There is guaranteed access to the data and information in this system for the "whole society" (NWRP, art. 26).

2.2.5 Regulation of Water Infrastructure

No provisions in the NWRP specifically address the issue of regulating water infrastructure. Article 25 of the NWRP states that the instruments for the National Water Resources Policy include, *inter alia*, Water Resources Plans that would deal, among other things, with water infrastructure. Moreover, article 25 of the ANA Law stipulates that the Executive Branch will implement decentralization of the activities of operating and maintaining reservoirs, canals, and pipelines controlled by the Federal Government and undertake infrastructure projects forming part of the Brazilian Interconnected System, operated by the National System Operator. As will be discussed below, article 4 of the ANA Law also grants the National Water Agency (ANA) authority over the National Water Resources Policy.

Moreover, Brazil recently adopted Federal Law 11,097 of 2004 on Public-Private Partnerships. The law regulates the planning, approval, and bidding process for infrastructure projects, including water infrastructure projects.

2.2.6 Institutional Arrangements

The role of the Federal executive branch in the implementation of the National Water Resources Policy is to take the steps needed to implement and operate the National Water Resources Management System; to award rights to use water and to regulate and monitor its uses within the sphere of Federal government competence; to create and manage the Water Resources Information System; and to promote the integration of water resource management with environmental management (NWRP, art. 29).

On July 17, 2000, Law No. 9,984 was adopted. It established the National Water Agency (ANA) as a Federal agency for implementing the National Water Resources Policy and coordinating the national water resources management system. Article 4 of the law details the responsibilities of ANA, which include, *inter alia:*

1. supervising, controlling, and assessing actions and activities deriving from compliance with Federal legislation relating to water resources;

2. granting by means of authorizations the right to use the water resources of bodies of water controlled by the Federal Government;
3. preparing technical studies on the amounts to be charged for water resources controlled by the Federal Government; and
4. planning and implementing actions intended to prevent or minimize the effects of droughts and flooding.[58]

The executive branches of the States and the Federal districts are responsible, within their areas of competence, for awarding the right to use water and for regulating and monitoring this usage; exercising technical supervision of water-supply projects; creating and managing State Water Resource Information Systems; and promoting the integration of water resource management with environmental management (NWRP, art. 30).[59]

The National Council on Water Resources (the National Council) is composed of representatives of the Presidential Ministries and Departments concerned with the management or use of water resources; representatives designated by the State Councils on water resources; and representatives of the users of water resources and of civil organizations concerned with water resources (NWRP, art. 34). Article 34 goes on to state that representatives of the Federal Executive Branch cannot exceed one half plus one of the total number of members of the National Council. The National Council is chaired by the Minister of Environment, Water Resources and Legal Amazonia (NWRP, art. 36), and its secretariat is the body within the Ministry of Environment, Water Resources and Legal Amazonia that is responsible for the management of water resources (NWRP, art. 45). The National Council's responsibilities, *inter alia,* include

1. promoting the integration of water resource planning with other planning at all levels of government;
2. arbitrating, as a last resort, conflicts between State Councils on Water Resources;
3. reviewing water resource utilization plans whose impact extends beyond the State in which they are being implemented;
4. discussing any questions that have been submitted by the State Councils on Water Resources or the River Basin Committees; and
5. reviewing proposals for amending legislation on water resources;

---

[58] For an analysis of the role of the ANA, *see* Abel Mejia, Luiz Gabriel T. de Azevedo, Martin P. Gambrill, Alexander M. Baltar & Thelma Triche, *Water, Poverty Reduction and Sustainable Development,* Brazil Water Series No. 4 (World Bank 2003).

[59] *See* José Nilson, B. Campos & Ticiana M. C. Studart, *An Historical Perspective on the Administration of Water in Brazil,* 25 Water Intl. 148 (2000).

6. establishing supplementary guidelines for the implementation of the National Water Resources Policy and the operations of the National Water Resources Management System;
7. approving proposals for the creation of River Basin Committees and monitoring the execution of the National Water Resources Plan; and
8. establishing broad criteria for the award of rights to water use and the fees to be charged thereon (NWRP, art. 35).

The National Water Resources Management System consists of the National Council of Water Resources; the State and Federal District Councils on Water Resources; the River Basin Committees; the organs at different levels of government whose competences are related to the management of water resources; and the Water Agencies (NWRP, art. 33). The system has the following objectives: to coordinate integrated water resources management; to arbitrate, at the administrative level, any conflicts related to water resources; to implement the National Water Resources Policy; to plan, regulate, and supervise the use, conservation, and recovery of water resources; and to encourage the charging of fees for water usage (NWRP, art. 32).

2.2.6.1 River Basin Authorities

The River Basin Committees are composed of representatives of the Federal Government; the States or Federal Districts in which the committees are located; the municipalities in which they are located; water users in their areas of action; and civil water resources agencies that have been active in the basin (NWRP, art. 39). If the river basin includes indigenous lands, the committee must also have representatives of the indigenous communities with an interest in the river, as well as representatives of the National Indian Foundation (FUNAI) (NWRP, art. 39, §3). Each committee elects its own chair (NWRP, art. 40).

A Water Agency whose creation is authorized by the National or State Council on Water Resources at the request of a River Basin Committee serves as executive secretariat of each Committee (NWRP, art. 41). The responsibilities of these agencies, *inter alia*, include maintaining a roster of water users, collecting fees for water use, and managing the Water Resources Information System in their area of action; arranging as needed for studies for the management of water resources in their area of action; and helping in the management of the River Basin Committees (NWRP, art. 44).

River Basin Committees act for an entire river basin, for any sub-basins therein, and for a group of contiguous river basins or sub-basins (NWRP, art. 37). Their responsibilities include: promoting discussion of issues related to water resources; coordinating the work of the entities involved in the committee;

arbitrating conflicts relating to water resources; approving the Water Resources Plan for the river basin and monitoring its execution; establishing mechanisms for receiving fees for the use of water resources; suggesting the fees to be charged; and establishing criteria for and promoting the apportionment of the cost of multiple-use projects of common or collective interest (NWRP, art. 38).[60]

2.2.6.2   Water Users' Associations and Advisory Committees

The NWRP provides for the creation of "civil water resource organizations" that include regional, local, and sectoral associations of water users (NWRP, art. 47). It does not, however, describe the responsibilities or the required composition of these bodies. It merely states, in article 48, that in order for them to participate in the National Water Resources System, these organizations must be "legally constituted." The NWRP does not contain any provisions that specifically address the issue of advisory committees.

2.2.7   Financial Arrangements

The fees charged for water use are intended to recognize that water is an economic good, to encourage rationalization of water use, and to raise revenues to finance the programs provided for in the Water Resources Plans (NWRP, art. 19).[61] In setting the fees, article 21 states, the authorities must take at least the following elements into consideration: in the case of diversions, catchments, and extractions of water, the volume of water removed, and variations in water flow caused by the use; and in the case of discharge of waste into water, the volume of the discharge being made into the water and the nature of the discharge.

In allocating the funds raised by fees, the authorities should give priority to the needs of the particular river basin from which the funds are generated. The fees should be applied to finance the studies, programs, and projects included in the relevant Water Resource Plans and to defray implementation and administrative overhead costs for the agencies and entities in the National Water Resources Management System (NWRP, art. 22). In addition, article 22 states that the funds can be used "without limit" to fund projects and public works that

---

[60] In addition, the ANA Law, in art. 4, requires ANA to ensure that its operations adhere to the objectives, guidelines, and instruments of the National Water Resources Policy and are undertaken in harmony with the public bodies and private organizations making up the National Water Resources Management System. Furthermore, the Law requires ANA to provide support to the States in creating water resources management organizations.

[61] *See* Benedito P. F. Braga, Claire Strauss & Fatima Paiva, *Water Charges: Paying for the Commons in Brazil,* 21 Intl. J. Water Resources Dev. 119 (2005).

alter the quality, quantity, and flow rate of a body of water for the benefit of the community.[62]

2.2.8   Enforcement of Regulations and Dispute Settlement

2.2.8.1   Enforcement of Regulations

Article 49 of the NWRP enumerates a number of violations related to utilization of surface or groundwater. They include diverting or using water for any purpose without having been awarded the right to use water for that purpose; beginning or undertaking any action that alters the flow rate, quality, or quantity of water without prior authorization; using water or performing works or services related thereto that contravene the terms of an award; committing fraud in measuring the volume of water used; and violating the regulations and administrative provisions established in connection with this law. These violations can result in sanctions that include fines, written censure, and temporary and permanent injunctions (NWRP, art. 50). These sanctions are imposed by the "responsible authority" and can be appealed to the "competent administrative authority" (NWRP, art. 50).

2.2.8.2   Dispute Settlement

The National Water Resources Management System is authorized to arbitrate any conflicts related to water resources "at the administrative level" (NWRP, art. 32). The River Basin Committees are authorized "as the first administrative recourse" to arbitrate conflicts relating to water resources (NWRP, art. 38). Their decisions can be appealed to the relevant State or National Council on Water Resources (NWRP, art. 38).

2.3   Cameroon

2.3.1   Statutory Framework

There are two statutes that apply to water resources law in Cameroon:

- Statute No. 98-005 of 14 April 1998, which regulates all water resources except mineral waters and spring waters (Law 98-005); and

---

[62] For discussion of water pricing in Brazil, *see Water Pricing Experiences—An International Perspective,* World Bank Technical Paper No. 386, 32 (Ariel Dinar & Ashok Subramanian, eds., World Bank 1977). *See also* Luiz Gabriel T. de Azevedo & Musa Asad, *The Political Process Behind the Implementation of Bulk Water Pricing in Brazil* in *The Political Economy of Water Pricing Reforms* 321 (Ariel Dinar, ed., Oxford Univ. Press 2000).

- Statute No. 79-10 of June 1979, amended by statute No. 90-16 of 10 August 1990, which regulates spring water (*eau de source*) and mineral water (*eau minerale*) (Law 79-10). For these purposes, "spring water" is water that is placed in commerce for human consumption, which may or may not contain minerals or gas, without mention of its therapeutic properties (Law 79-10, Art. 1), and "mineral water" is water that naturally contains either salts or gases or both and has therapeutic properties (Law 79-10, art. 1).

2.3.2 Underlying Principles and Priorities

Law 98-005 provides that water is a natural resource protected and managed by the State (Law 98-005, art. 2(1)).

2.3.3 Regulation of Water Uses

2.3.3.1 *Ownership of Water and Establishment of Water Rights*

Law 98-005 identifies the following different types of water:

1. "Surface water," which shall mean run-off water;
2. "Groundwater," which shall mean infiltration water;
3. "Spring water," which shall mean water sold as drinking water, mineralized or not, sparkling or not, without mention of its therapeutic properties; and
4. "Mineral water," which shall mean groundwater containing dissolved minerals with therapeutic properties.[63]

In addition, article 2 of Law 79-10 states that mineral and spring waters are part of the State's domain.

The State is responsible for issuing regulations that govern the use of surface or groundwater for industrial or commercial purposes (Law 98-005, art. 10(1)) and the quality of drinking water (Law 98-005, art. 12). The Minister of Energy and Water[64] can forbid the harnessing of surface and groundwater in the following situations;[65]

1. Risk of drying of the stream;
2. Obvious pollution of water;

---

[63] Law 98-005, art. 3.

[64] By Decree No. 2004/322 dated December 8, 2004, responsibility for water resources has been assigned to the Ministry of Energy and Water instead of the previous Ministry of Mines, Energy and Water.

[65] Law 98-005, art. 9.

3. Risk to public health; and
4. Public interest and utility.

2.3.3.2   Allocation of Right to Use Water

The use of water for industrial and commercial purposes requires prior authorization and the payment of a tax fixed by the law (Law 98-005, art. 10(1)), but companies that have been granted a concession to exploit or distribute drinking water are exempted from this requirement (Law 98-005, art. 10(2)). Regardless of the previous provisions, however, every use of surface or groundwater should be preceded by a study evaluating the impact of such use on the environment and the quality of life of the population (Law 98-005, art. 10(3)). There is specific authorization for the exploitation of spring and mineral water (Law 98-005, art. 13).

2.3.3.3   Transfer of Water Rights

The statutes do not contain any provisions dealing explicitly with the transfer of water rights.

2.3.3.4   Loss of Right to Use Water

The statutes do not contain any provisions that deal explicitly with how water users can lose their right to use water. Law 98-005 does, however, provide for the imposition of sanctions against those found to be violating the law.[66] Article 14 provides for automatic civil liability for anyone who has caused corporal or material damage due to the bad quality of drinking water that was distributed.

Law 79-10, art. 7, states that authorization for the use of spring and mineral water can only be modified after there has been a revision of the authorization. Article 13 provides that authorizations can be suspended by the Ministry of Energy and Water in specific situations, such as failure to exploit the source for two years and cases that present a danger to public health or pollution.

2.3.4   Protection of Water

Law 98-005 lays down detailed provisions for protection of water quality, forbidding any act, such as discharging or outflows, that is likely to:

1. alter the quality of surface and groundwater, or sea water within territorial boundaries;

---

[66] Law 98-005, title IV.

2. cause danger to public health, animal life, or aquatic or sub-marine flora; or
3. call economic and tourist development into question.[67]

However, the Ministry can authorize discharges when it has been proven after investigation that they can be done without danger (Law 98-005, art. 4(2)).

Law 79-10 stipulates that spring and mineral water is to be provided to the public as it is taken from the source. Nevertheless, under some conditions, laid out in each authorization, water can be delivered to the public after treatment and transportation through pipes or after mixing with other waters that have therapeutic properties (Law 79-10, art. 6). The Ministry of Energy and Water is responsible for examining the installations established for these purposes and for analyzing the quality of the water (Law 79-10, art. 10).

2.3.5   Regulation of Water Infrastructure

Regulation of water infrastructure is not addressed in Law 98-005. Law 79-10 provides that the Ministry of Energy and Water has the authority to inspect installations created for the commercial use of spring and mineral water.[68]

2.3.6   Institutional Arrangements

Law 98-005 does not explicitly address the issue of institutional arrangements. Law 79-10 provides that the Ministry of Energy and Water has the authority to inspect water installations (Law 79-10, arts. 10 & 12). The Ministry is also responsible for making an inventory of sources of water and for prospecting for and research of mineral and spring waters (Law 79-10, art. 4). The statutes do not provide for river basin authorities; nor do they have explicit provisions on water users' associations or advisory committees.

2.3.7   Financial Arrangements

Law 98-005 creates a special account (*Compte d'Affectation Spéciale*) within the Finances Act to guarantee financing for sustainable water development projects (Law 98-005, art. 25). That law also provides that use of water for industrial or commercial purposes is subject to charges (Law 98-005, art. 10(1)). Law 79-10 provides that the owner of rights to spring and mineral water must pay control and analysis fees, as established by decree.[69]

---

[67] Law 98-005, art. 4 (1).

[68] *See, for example,* Law 79-10, arts. 10 and 12.

[69] Law 79-10, art. 11.

2.3.8   Enforcement of Regulations and Dispute Settlement

2.3.8.1   Enforcement of Regulations

Law 98-005 stipulates that control of drinking water quality and application of the law shall be ensured by sworn controllers.[70] It also provides that anyone who, through distributing drinking water of bad quality, causes corporal harm or material damage shall be held legally responsible (Law 98-005, art. 14). Furthermore, without prejudice to the sanctions available under the Penal Code, chapter 2 of this statute provides penal sanctions, such as fines and imprisonment for violators of the law (Law 98-005, arts. 15–21).

Law 79-10 provides that authorizations can be suspended by the Ministry of Energy and Water in specific situations, such as failure to exploit the source for two years and cases that present a danger to public health or pollution (Law 79-10, art. 13). It also provides that infractions of the law are to be recorded by officers of the Police, the Administration of the Mines, and other commissioned agents (Law 79-10, art. 15). These agents have the power to investigate infractions and seize relevant documents (Law 79-10, art. 16). Those found guilty of infractions can be fined or imprisoned (Law 98-005, art. 21(1)).

2.3.8.2   Dispute Settlement

Law 98-005 provides that disputes between holders of the rights to use water can be settled by mutual consent or by arbitration (Law 98-005, art. 23). No provisions on settlement of disputes between users are included in either law; it seems that such disputes would be handled under the civil code.

2.4   China

2.4.1   Statutory Framework

Article 9 of the Constitution of the People's Republic of China states that all the waters of China are "owned by the state, that is, by the whole people."[71] It adds that the state is responsible for ensuring the rational use of natural resources and no organization or individual can appropriate or damage any natural resource.

Water resources in China are regulated by the Water Law of the People's Republic of China (the Water Law).[72] There are also a number of other statutes

---

[70] Law 98-005, arts. 12 and 19.

[71] Adopted at the Second Session of the Ninth National People's Congress and Promulgated for Implementation by the Proclamation of the National People's Congress on March 15, 1999.

[72] Adopted at the 29th Session of the Standing Committee of the Ninth National People's Congress on August 29, 2002. This law replaced the Water Law of 1988.

that are relevant to water regulation and use in China. They are:

- Environmental Protection Law of the People's Republic of China;[73]
- Fisheries Law of the People's Republic of China;[74]
- Agriculture Law of the People's Republic of China;[75]
- Water and Soil Conservation Law of the People's Republic of China;[76]
- Flood Control Law of the People's Republic of China[77] (the Flood Control Law); and
- Prevention and Control of Water Pollution Law of the People's Republic of China[78] (the Water Pollution Law).

2.4.2 Underlying Principles and Priorities

The purpose of the Water Law is to promote the development, sustainable use, management, and protection of the water resources of China in a way that contributes to economic and social development in China (Water Law, art. 1). These objectives must be achieved through comprehensive planning, with all factors taken into account and with an emphasis on using water for multiple purposes and on obtaining maximum benefits from the water used (Water Law, art. 4). In furtherance of these objectives, the Water Law requires the State to formulate a strategic plan for national water resources that provides for the use, protection, and management of water on the basis of river basins and regions (Water Law, art. 14).

The development and use of water resources must conform to the principles of promoting benefits while avoiding disasters; balancing the interests of both upstream and downstream areas and of all affected regions; promoting multiple benefits from water resources; and flood prevention (Water Law, art. 20). They should also follow the principle of the unified treatment and development of

---

[73] Adopted by the National People's Congress on December 26, 1989.

[74] Adopted at the 14th Meeting of the Standing Committee of the National People's Congress and Promulgated by Order No. 34 of the President of the People's Republic of China on January 20, 1986, and effective as of July 1, 1986.

[75] Adopted at the Second Meeting of the Standing Committee of the Eighth National People's Congress on July 2, 1993, promulgated by Order No. 6 of the President of the People's Republic of China on July 2, 1993, and effective as of July 2, 1993.

[76] Adopted at the 20th Meeting of the Standing Committee of the Seventh National People's Congress of the People's Republic of China on June 29, 1991, and promulgated by Order No. 49 of the President of the People's Republic of China and effective as of June 29, 1991.

[77] Adopted at the 27th Meeting of the Standing Committee of the Eighth National People's Congress and Promulgated by Order No. 88 of the President of the People's Republic of China on August 29, 1977.

[78] Adopted on May 11, 1984, and amended on May 15, 1996.

surface and groundwater (Water Law, art. 23). The Water Law stipulates priorities in water uses: The highest priority is assigned to the domestic needs of both urban and rural inhabitants. This is followed by, in descending order, the needs of agriculture, industry, environment, and navigation (Water Law, art. 21).

2.4.3 Regulation of Water Uses

2.4.3.1 Ownership of Water and Establishment of Water Rights

The water resources of China include both surface and groundwater (Water Law, art. 2). All water resources are owned by the State (Water Law, art. 3). The State Council exercises the rights of ownership on behalf of the State (Water Law, art. 3). Any organization or individual who uses water must do so in a way that does not infringe on the public interest or the lawful rights and interests of other people (Water Law, art. 28).[79]

2.4.3.2 Allocation of Right to Use Water

The State, acting through the Department of Water Administration under the State Council, has put in place a system of licenses for allocating the right to draw and use water (Water Law, art. 7). The Water Law does not include provisions detailing the characteristics of this system of licenses; it simply stipulates that any individual or organization that draws water directly from any river, lake, or subterranean stream must comply with the terms of the license, including payment of the necessary user fees (Water Law, art. 48). In addition, the statute provides that the precise requirements of the licensing system and the procedures for collecting fees shall be determined by the State Council (Water Law, art. 48).

There are two exceptions to the licensing scheme. The first is that agricultural collectives and their members can use the waters in ponds and reservoirs that belong to the agricultural collectives without obtaining a license (Water Law, art. 7). The second is that individuals can use a small amount of water for household use and for drinking by certain categories of livestock (Water Law, art. 48).

Article 44 states that, as part of their responsibilities for management of the national water resources, the Department of Water Administration and the Department of Development Planning Administration together shall be responsible for national mid- and long-term water planning. The article goes on to state that lower levels of government are required to develop their own mid- and long-term plans for water use, consistent with the national plan and the plans of higher levels of government. It also provides that all these mid- and long-term plans

---

[79] *See* Harald D. Frederiksen, Jeremy Berkoff & William Barber, *Water Resources Management in Asia*, 1 World Bank Technical Paper No. 212 20 (World Bank 1993).

governing the use and allocation of water must be submitted to the State Council for approval. In developing their plans, governmental authorities must use the river basin as the unit for allocation (Water Law, art. 44).[80]

The result of all these plans should be a unified system of control for the allocation and use of water (Water Law, Art. 47). Pursuant to this system, the Central Government must formulate the water quota for each activity, which is then allocated between the provinces, autonomous regions, and municipalities, subject to the central government (Water Law, Art. 47). These lower levels of government then decide how the water allocated to them shall be used (Water Law, art. 47). This means that all departments of water administration above the county level and the administrative organizations of river basins must formulate annual water allocation plans that are consistent with the overall water plans (Water Law, art. 46).

The strategic plans for river basins and regions include both comprehensive and special plans. The comprehensive plans are general plans for the development, use, management, and protection of the relevant water resources (Water Law, art. 15). The special plans that are developed in the context of the comprehensive plans are plans dealing with, *inter alia,* flood prevention, irrigation, navigation, water supply, hydropower generation, fisheries, and water resources protection (Water Law, art. 14).

In addition, departments of environmental protection at each level of government, acting under the direction of the central government, must develop water function zones for their areas that are consistent with the comprehensive plans for those rivers and lakes that are designated as "major" rivers and lakes by the State (Water Law, art. 32). The functional plans for other rivers and lakes must be drafted by the administrative department of the relevant river basin authority, together with the departments of water administration and environmental protection of the appropriate level of government (Water Law, art. 32). In both cases, the functional plan must be submitted to the State Council for review and approval (Water Law, art. 32).

Studies for these water plans are undertaken by the departments of water administration at the applicable level of government above the county level (Water Law, art. 16). Each of these levels of government is responsible for helping to build an information system of water resources and hydrology (Water Law, art. 16).

In areas of water shortage, the state must encourage the accumulation, development, and use of rainwater and slightly salty water and the desalination of seawater (Water Law, art. 24).

---

[80] *See generally China—Air, Land, and Water: Environmental Priorities for a New Millennium* (World Bank 2001).

2.4.3.3 Transfer and Loss of Water Rights

The Water Law has no provisions dealing explicitly with the transfer or loss of water rights. It seems that those issues are governed by administrative decrees.

2.4.4 Protection of Water

The Water Law stipulates that the state is responsible for protecting water resources and preventing water pollution (Water Law, art. 9). This responsibility is further described in the Water Pollution Law, which defines "water pollution" as the introduction into any water body of any substance that alters the chemical, physical, biological, or radioactive properties of the water so as to affect its use, endanger human health, damage the ecosystem, or adversely affect the quality of the water (Water Pollution Law, art. 60).

Pursuant to the Water Pollution Law, the Environmental Protection Department of the State Council is responsible for establishing national standards for the environmental quality of water; environmental protection departments at lower levels of government can supplement the national standards with local standards (Water Pollution Law, arts. 6 & 7). In addition, the departments of water administration at all levels of government must incorporate measures for the protection of the water environment into their plans and must adopt measures to prevent and control water pollution (Water Pollution Law, art. 3). However, the environmental protection departments at the various levels of government, working with water conservancy departments, public health departments, geological and mining departments, municipal administration departments, and the water sources protection agencies for major rivers, are responsible for exercising supervision over efforts to prevent and control water pollution (Water Pollution Law, art. 4).

In addition, the departments of water administration at all levels of government and the administrative departments of river basins must also pay attention in formulating their plans for the management and use of these water bodies to maintaining river flow and the quantity and quality of the water resources subject to their jurisdiction (Water Law, art. 30).[81] Consistent with this obligation, the various levels of government are required to develop and promote water-saving technology and industries (Water Law, art. 8).[82]

The Water Law also imposes on all individuals and organizations involved in the development and use of water an obligation to protect the water resources that they use (art. 6). They are also required to report the level of any pollutants that

---

[81] *See also* Water Pollution Law, arts. 9–12.

[82] *See* Edwin D. Ongley & Xuejun Wang, *Transjurisdictional Water Pollution Management in China: The Legal and Institutional Framework,* 29 Water Intl. 270 (2004).

they directly or indirectly discharge into a water body to the environmental protection department of the State Council (Water Pollution Law, art. 14). Similarly, if they engage in any activity that involves the discharge of pollutants into a water body, they must be registered with the local environmental protection department (Water Pollution Law, art. 14).[83]

The departments of water administration at all levels of government and the administrative departments of river basins are responsible for controlling the withdrawal of groundwater (Water Law, art. 36). To protect groundwater, enterprises and institutions are prohibited from discharging or dumping wastewater or pollutants into wells or pits (Water Law, art. 41). In addition, the artificial recharge of groundwater should not result in any deterioration in the quality of groundwater (Water Pollution Law, art. 45).[84]

2.4.5 Regulation of Water Infrastructure

Government at or above the county level is responsible for constructing water conservancy facilities (Water Law, art. 5). The building of all water projects must conform to the comprehensive water plan and must be reviewed by the appropriate level of government (Water Law, art. 19). If a water project involves flood prevention, it must also conform to the provisions of the Law on Flood Control (Water Law, art. 19).

Agricultural collective organizations that invest in water storage projects must obtain the approval of the department of water administration of the appropriate level of government (Water Law, art. 25). The State encourages the development of hydropower potential (Water Law, art. 26). In making decisions related to hydropower, the State must take into account the needs of flood control, water supply, irrigation, fisheries, bamboo and log rafting, and the aquatic environment (Water Law, arts. 26 & 27). Pursuant to article 29 of the Water Law, the State must also ensure that rights to compensation of people who are involuntarily resettled as a result of state-constructed water projects are respected.[85]

If any mining or construction project results in a lowering of the groundwater level or causes a loss in livelihood to any individual or organization, the construction or mining enterprise shall be responsible for taking corrective actions

---

[83] *See* Edwin D. Ongley, *Non-Point Source Water Pollution in China: Current Status and Future Prospects,* 29 Water Intl. 299 (2004).

[84] *See supra* n. 80, at 47.

[85] Some countries consider resettlement as among the larger water law issues, because most resettlement activities result from water infrastructure projects. For discussion of this issue in India, *see* Chauhan, *supra* n. 2, Part II. However, as will be discussed in chapter 3, the social and environmental issues related to water infrastructure projects are highly complex and thus they relate to a larger group of legal and policy instruments.

or paying compensation (Water Law, art. 31). Similarly, if any building project has an adverse effect on usage of water for agriculture, the construction enterprise is required to pay compensation (Water Law, art. 35).

Any structure that is built in a river must conform to the applicable standards for flood prevention and its plans must be approved by the department of water administration (Water Law, art. 38). Such a project also requires an environmental impact assessment that discusses water pollution hazards created by the project and how they will be managed (Water Pollution Law, art. 13).

2.4.6   Institutional Arrangements

The State has adopted a system of administration that combines river basin administration with administration through administrative divisions (Water Law, art. 12). This system is under the overall control of the Department of Water Administration, which is subject to the State Council (Water Law, art. 12). As discussed in section 2.4.3.2 above, this Department, together with the Department of Development Planning Administration, shall be responsible for the management of the national water resources.[86]

In addition, the Department of Water Administration is responsible for the management, protection, and inspection of all water resources. However, it must delegate these responsibilities to lower levels of government with regard to the waters within their jurisdictions (Water Law, arts. 12 & 13). It is also responsible for developing the comprehensive plans for the major river basins and lakes and for submitting these plans to the State Council for approval (Water Law, art. 17).[87] Plans for other basins and lakes must be formulated by the relevant basin's administrative department and then approved by the appropriate level of government before being submitted by the Department of Water Administration to the State Council for final approval (Water Law, art. 17).

Government at all levels must take the lead role in irrigation and conservation of water; in the areas of salinization-alkalization and waterlogging, it must take measures to regulate the groundwater level (Water Law, art. 25). It should also take measures to guarantee the safety of all water projects and to strengthen the supervision, management, and safety of these projects (Water Law, art. 42).

---

[86] For detailed discussion of the institutional arrangements *see China: Agenda for Water Sector Strategy for North China,* World Bank Report 22040-CHA, 110 (May 9, 2002).

[87] The statute does not contain a definition of "major" river basins and lakes but, as stated in art. 21 of the Flood Control Law, the term would refer to those river basins and lakes that lie across more than one province, autonomous region, or municipality.

2.4.6.1   River Basin Agencies

River basin administrative agencies must be established by the water conservancy department of the State Council (Flood Control Law, art. 8).[88] They are responsible for coordinating, supervising, and administering flood control measures in their jurisdiction (Flood Control Law, art. 8).[89] In addition, river basin administrative agencies, together with the water conservancy departments of the appropriate levels of government and under the overall authority of the central government, are responsible for managing major rivers and lakes that traverse more than one province, autonomous region, or municipality (Flood Control Law, art. 21).[90]

2.4.6.2   Water Users' Associations and Advisory Committees

The Water Law does not contain any provisions dealing with water users' associations, which are perhaps governed by administrative decrees. Nor does it contain any provisions dealing with advisory committees.

2.4.7   Financial Arrangements

The State Council is empowered to establish procedures for determining and collecting water management fees (Water Law, arts. 48 & 49). Any person who uses water provided by a water-supply project shall pay a water fee to the units that supply the water (Water Law, art. 55). These fees are set by the Department of Price Administration at the appropriate level of government in conjunction with the appropriate Department of Water Administration. Such fees shall be based on the principles of compensation of cost, reasonable profits, higher price for higher quality, and equitable sharing of costs (Water Law, art. 55).

Those who discharge pollutants into a body of water must pay a pollutant discharge fee, which is to be used exclusively to fund prevention and control of pollution activities (Water Pollution Law, art. 15). Similar fees are charged for the treatment of urban sewage (Water Pollution Law, art. 19). The Water Law provides for user fees to be charged to those who obtain licenses to use water (Water Law, art. 48).

---

[88] *See* Dajun Shen, *The 2002 Water Law: Its Impacts on River Basin Management in China,* 6 Water Policy 345 (2004). *See also* Dajun Shen, *Water-Related Risk Management in China: A Legal, Institutional, and Regulatory View,* 30 Water Intl. 329 (2005).

[89] *See* Xindeng Hu, *Integrated Catchment Management in China: An Application of the Australian Experience,* 24 Water Intl. 323 (1999).

[90] Other rivers and lakes are under the control of local governments at or above the county level.

2.4.8   Enforcement of Regulations and Dispute Settlement

2.4.8.1   Enforcement of Regulations

The departments of water administration at the appropriate level of government and the administrative organizations of the river basins are responsible for monitoring the water resources subject to their jurisdiction (Water Law, art. 16). The Department of Water Administration and the administrative organization for river basins have the authority to supervise and inspect water usage and to investigate and prosecute violations of the Water Law (Water Law, arts. 59 & 60).

Individuals and units that make outstanding contributions to the management, use, and protection of water resources in the prevention or control of water disasters may be rewarded by the government (Water Law, art. 11). Any person who violates plans for the development, use, management, and protection of water resources shall bear responsibility for the consequences of the violation (Water Law, art. 31). If water administrative authorities fail to perform their responsibilities, they shall be investigated and, if appropriate, the management of the authorities can be criminally prosecuted or subjected to disciplinary action (Water Law, art. 64). Any violation of the law can lead to fines and, when necessary, requiring the violator to repair the damage caused by the violation or to remove the unauthorized water structure (Water Law, arts. 65–72). In addition, any diversion or discharge of water that is detrimental to the public interest or the interests of other people may result in civil liability (Water Law, art. 76).

The competent authorities can also shut down or suspend activities that violate the Water Pollution Law.[91] Activities that are inconsistent with that law may also result in civil liability for the damage that they cause (Water Pollution Law, art. 55). In extreme cases, violations can result in criminal sanctions (Water Pollution Law, art. 57).

Moreover, article 78 of the Water Law reiterates a basic principle of international law that subjects domestic law to international treaties and agreements.[92] The article states that where any international treaty or agreement relating to international or border rivers or lakes concluded or acceded to by the People's Republic of China contains provisions differing from those in the laws of the People's Republic of China, the provisions of the international treaty or agreement shall apply, unless the provisions are ones on which the People's Republic of China has made reservations.

---

[91] Water Pollution Law, arts. 47, 50, 51, and 52.

[92] For a detailed discussion of this issue *see* George Schwarzenberger, *A Manual of International Law* 36 (Professional Books 1976). *See also* Antonio Cassese, *International Law* 213 (Oxford Univ. Press 2005).

2.4.8.2   Dispute Settlement

Pursuant to article 56, any dispute concerning water that arises between different administrative offices should be resolved through consultation; if this fails, the dispute should be referred to the next level of government (Water Law, art. 56). The article further states that, pending resolution of the dispute, no party may undertake any new water projects or in any way alter the existing water regime unless all parties to the dispute agree to the proposed project or alteration.

Any dispute between individuals or organizations concerning water should be resolved through consultation (Water Law, art. 57). If the consultations fail, one or both parties can request the local government at or above the county level to mediate the dispute or they can initiate civil legal proceedings in court (Water Law, art. 57). If the mediation fails, either party may initiate civil legal proceedings (Water Law, art. 57). Until the dispute is resolved, no party may unilaterally alter the existing water regime (Water Law, art. 57).

2.5   Costa Rica

2.5.1   Statutory Framework

Water in Costa Rica is regulated by the Water Law (*Ley de Agua*) of August 27, 1946, as amended in 1959, 1972, and 1974 (the Water Law).[93] In addition, there are a number of other statutes that are relevant to water resource management in Costa Rica:

- Potable Water Law, Law 1634 of October 2, 1953;
- Maritime Land Zone Law, Law 6043 of March 2, 1977 (amended February 14, 1984);
- General Health Law, Law 5395 of October 30, 1973 (amended by Law 5789 of September 1, 1975; and Law 6430 of May 15, 1980);
- Organic Environmental Law (*Ley Organica del Ambiente*), Law 7554 of October 4, 1995;[94] and
- Law Establishing the Costa Rican Institute of Aqueducts and Sewers (*Ley Constitua del Instituto Costaricense de Acueductos y Alcantarillados*), Law 2726 of April 14, 1961.

---

[93] As amended by Law 2332 of April 9, 1959; Law 5046 of August 16, 1972; and Law 5516 of May 2, 1974.

[94] Art. 50 of the Constitution of Costa Rica of 1946, as amended in 1994, provides that "Every person has the right to a healthy and ecologically balanced environment." It goes on to impose on the State the obligation to "guarantee, defend and preserve that right."

2.5.2   Underlying Principles and Priorities

The Water Law establishes priorities in potential water uses that are intended to guide the allocation of water in times of shortage (Water Law, arts. 140–42). Pursuant thereto, the highest priority is accorded to water to be used for domestic purposes, public services, drinking troughs, baths, milk production, and transportation systems. This is followed by irrigation on landholdings of less than five hectares and industrial uses and public services the disruption of which would cause serious damage to social and economic order. The next in order of priority is water for irrigation on landholdings greater than five hectares and for other industrial uses and public services. If all these uses have received the needed amount of water, any remaining water can be used for other necessary purposes.

2.5.3   Regulation of Water Uses

2.5.3.1   Ownership of Water and Establishment of Water Rights

The Water Law provides that certain water resources are considered national property over which the federal government exercises dominion. They include waters of lakes and estuaries that are connected either permanently or intermittently to the sea; water of natural internal lakes; waters of rivers and their tributaries, from their source to the point of their discharge into the sea, lake, pond, or estuary; and water that flows, either intermittently or constantly (Water Law, arts. 1 & 2). The law also provides that much of the riparian lands next to these publicly owned water resources is state property (Water Law, art. 3).

The Water Law recognizes certain water resources as being subject to private dominion by the owner of the land on which the resource is found. These include rainwater that falls on privately owned land and is stored on that land; lakes or puddles that form naturally on private land; groundwater that the land owner can access through wells on the property; and mineral and thermal waters where they come to the surface (Water Law, art. 46). Property owners who have dominion over water resources can freely and without a concession open wells for domestic and everyday use (Water Law, art. 6).

2.5.3.2   Allocation of Right to Use Water

The State, through the grant of concessions, gives individuals and entities the right to use public water resources (Water Law, art. 18). The length of these concessions, which are issued by the National Electricity Service, may vary up to a maximum of 30 years (Water Law, art. 19). The concession specifies the use to which the water will be put, the amount of water that can be used for the stated purpose, and, if applicable, the land to be irrigated by the water (Water Law, art. 21). If there is not enough water to meet all demands, the concessionaire may be limited to using water during specified times during the day (Water Law, art. 21). Concessionaires who do not comply with the time periods within which they are able to use water can be sanctioned (Water Law, art. 21).

One qualification on all concessions is that if the population is unable to obtain access to an amount of water equal to 50 liters per day per person, of which 20 liters are potable, they can take the remaining balance from public water resources even if these resources are intended for other uses (Water Law, arts. 34–36). In addition, if public water resources have been artificially deviated from their natural course, the public can access the water in the deviation and withdraw the amounts that can be withdrawn without machines or other apparatus even if the resource is subject to a private concession (Water Law, art. 12).

2.5.3.3 Transfer of Water Rights

The Water Law does not contain any provisions that explicitly deal with the issue of transferring water rights but it implicitly allows concessionaires to transfer their concessions.

2.5.3.4 Loss of Right to Use Water

Concessions to use water are terminated at the end of the concession period unless they are renewed. In addition, a person can lose a concession if the purpose for which the concession was granted is no longer applicable, or if, after a hearing, the National Electricity Service concludes, *inter alia,* that the concessionaire has failed to use the concession for a period of three to five years, is using the waters for a different purpose than the one for which the concession was granted, or there was an unauthorized transfer of the concession. Concessions can be modified by the National Electricity Service but such modifications must be officially published three consecutive times before they can become effective (Water Law, arts. 137–39).

2.5.4 Protection of Water

The Water Law includes a number of provisions on the issue of protection of water. Municipalities cannot alienate or mortgage land where this may cause adverse effects on water resources (Water Law, art. 154). If downstream lands are damaged by water flows that are not produced naturally, the downstream landowner is entitled to compensation (Water Law, art. 94). The cutting of trees that can lead to adverse effects on water is regulated by the authorities (Water Law, arts. 145–46).

2.5.5 Regulation of Water Infrastructure

Construction of water infrastructure requires the permission of the Ministry of the Interior (Water Law, art. 99). This permission can be given after a hearing in which those who object can participate (Water Law, arts. 100–03).

The construction of hydroelectric facilities requires a concession, which can only be issued after all applicable legal requirements, including those not directly related to water resources management, have been met (Water Law, art. 46). Private companies can be authorized to construct and operate canals in order to facilitate water transportation for periods of up to ninety-nine years (Water Law, arts. 58–62).

2.5.6 Institutional Arrangements

The primary regulator of water in Costa Rica is the National Electricity Service, operating through its Department of Water (Water Law, arts. 175–85). It has authority over public waters and decides whether to grant or deny all concession applications. In evaluating concession applications, the National Electricity Service will pass the application to the Cantonal Water Inspectorate, which is part of the National Electricity Service (Water Law, art. 194), to make the actual investigation of the concession applicant and the proposed use of the water (Water Law, art. 181).

2.5.6.1 Water Users' Associations

The Water Law allows for the formation of water users' associations (Water Law, arts. 131–36). These associations must register with the Ministry of Environment and Energy and their founding documentation must be published in the Official Register. Associations are eligible to obtain concessions to use water and to construct works for irrigation and other purposes. The Water Law does not contain any provisions on river basin authorities or advisory committees.

2.5.7 Financial Arrangements

Concession holders are required to pay for the concession. The fees paid can be a mix of a lump sum and an amount that varies according to the amount of water used by the concession holder (Water Law, arts. 169–74). Depending on the nature of the concession, payment is made to the National Electricity Service or the local municipality (Water Law, arts. 169–74).

2.5.8 Enforcement of Regulations and Dispute Settlement

2.5.8.1 Enforcement of Regulations

Violations of the Water Law can result in fines and prison sentences (Water Law, arts. 162–63). Persons who fail to cooperate with the inspectors of the National Electricity Service can be liable for fines and, if applicable, the loss of their concessions (Water Law, art. 168).

2.5.8.2 Dispute Settlement

Any disputes relating to the granting, modification, or revocation of concessions are to be resolved by the Inspectors of the National Electricity Service (Water Law, arts. 186–87). If they fail to resolve the matter, it can be referred to the National Electricity Service (Water Law, arts. 192–93). Thereafter, if necessary, the matter can be referred to the courts of Costa Rica (Water Law, Art. 182).

2.6 European Union (EU)*

2.6.1 Statutory Framework

European Directive 2000/60/EC of 23 October 2000 establishes the framework for Community action relating to water policy (the EC Directive).[95] This framework sets forth an integrated approach to the protection, improvement, and sustainable use of Europe's rivers, lakes, estuaries, coastal waters, and groundwater. Each Member State is obliged to adapt its domestic laws relating to water to conform to this Directive.[96]

---

* Although it is not a country, the European Union (EU) has been included in this study because its Directives on water must be incorporated into the domestic law of its Member States. Consequently, its Directives offer an excellent indication of future developments in national water law in EU Member States.

NOTE: In keeping with official EU citations, references to dates with respect to Directives in this part of the study are written in the format of Day.Month.Year.

[95] OJ L 327, 22.12.2000, p. 1.

[96] For an overview and analysis of the Water Framework Directive, *see* Götz Reichert, *The European Community's Water Framework Directive: A Regional Approach to the Protection and Management of Transboundary Freshwater Resources?* in *Water Resources and International Law* 429 (Laurence Boisson de Chazournes & Salman M. A. Salman, eds., Martinus Nijhoff Publishers 2005). *See also* H. Blöch, *The European Community Water Framework Directive,* in *Management of Transboundary Water in Europe* 25 (Malgorzata Landsberg-Uczciwek, Martin Adriaanse & Rainer Enderlein, eds., Ministry of Environment Protection, Natural Resources and Forestry, Poland 1998).

EU water legislation dates as far back as the 1970s. Council Directive 80/778/EEC of 15 July 1980, as amended,[97] deals with the quality of water intended for human consumption. This Directive is but one of many regulating the use and protection of water resources in the EU. Other important ones are

- the Dangerous Substances Directive,[98] which serves as a general framework for the control of discharges and water quality of surface waters;
- the Urban Wastewater Treatment Directive;[99]
- the Nitrates Directive,[100] which aims to control and limit nitrate pollution by diffuse agricultural sources; and
- the Surface Water Directive, which deals with the quality required of surface waters intended for drinking.[101]

2.6.2   Underlying Principles and Priorities

The preamble to the EC Directive states that "water is not a commercial product like any other" but is "a heritage, which must be protected, defended and treated as such."[102] It goes on to state that EU environmental policy is aimed at "preserving, protecting and improving the quality of the environment" and at "prudent and rational utilization of natural resources."[103] The policy is based on the precautionary principle and on the principles of prevention that environmental damage should, as a priority, be rectified at the source and that the polluter should pay.

The EC Directive also stipulates that planning and implementation of measures to ensure the protection and sustainable use of water is undertaken within the framework of the river basin.[104] However, decisions should be taken "as close as

---

[97] OJ L 229, 30.8.1980, p. 11. Last amended by Council Directive 98/83/EC of 3 November 1998 on the Quality of Water Intended for Human Consumption, OJ L 330, 5.12.1998, p. 32.

[98] Council Directive 76/464/EEC of 4 May 1976 on Pollution Caused by Certain Dangerous Substances Discharged into the Aquatic Environment of the Community, OJ L 129, 18.5.1976, p. 23.

[99] Council Directive 91/271/EEC of 21 May 1991 concerning Urban Waste-water Treatment, OJ L 135, 30.5.1991, p. 40.

[100] Council Directive 91/676/EEC of 12 December 1991 concerning the Protection of Waters Against Pollution Caused by Nitrates from Agricultural Sources, OJ L 375, 31.12.1991, p. 1.

[101] EC Directive 75/440/EEC (O.J. 145, 13.6, 1977).

[102] EC Directive Preamble, recital 1.

[103] *See id.* recital 11.

[104] EC Directive Preamble, recital 13. Art. 2(13) of the EC Directive defines "river basin" as "the area of land from which all surface run-off flows through a sequence of streams, rivers, and possibly lakes into the sea at a single river mouth, estuary or delta."

possible to the locations where water is affected or used."[105] Moreover, in order to ensure the participation of the general public, including water users, in the establishment and updating of river basin management plans, "proper information of planned measures" should be made publicly available "before final decisions on the necessary measures are adopted."[106]

Based on these principles, the EC Directive is designed to create a "framework for the protection of inland surface waters, transitional waters,[107] coastal waters and groundwaters" (EC Directive, art. 1). This framework should, *inter alia*, prevent further deterioration of aquatic systems; promote sustainable water use; reduce pollution of water bodies, including groundwater;[108] and contribute to the provision of a sufficient supply of good quality water (EC Directive, art. 1). Water policy in the EU needs to be integrated with EU policy in such areas as energy, transportation, agriculture, regional policy, fisheries, and tourism.[109]

2.6.3 Regulation of Water Uses

2.6.3.1 Ownership of Water and Establishment of Water Rights

The EC Directive does not contain any provisions dealing with the ownership of water or the establishment of water rights. Since it is intended as a framework for EU action, it leaves these matters to the domestic law of each Member State. For the same reasons the EC Directive does not contain any provisions dealing with the allocation, loss, or transfer of rights to use water.

2.6.4 Protection of Water

The EC Directive and its eleven annexes deal extensively with the issue of protection of water.[110] Article 4 of the EC Directive establishes the environmental objectives that are to be achieved for each category of water in the river basin management plan. For example, it requires Member States to "protect, enhance and

---

[105] *See id.*, recital 13.

[106] EC Directive Preamble, recital 46.

[107] "Transitional waters" are defined in art. 2(6) as "bodies of surface waters in the vicinity of river mouths which are partly saline in character as a result of their proximity to coastal waters but which are substantially influenced by freshwater flows."

[108] The emphasis on groundwater in the European Framework Directive is understandable given the fact that about 75 percent of drinking water comes from groundwater. *See* Gabriel Eckstein & Yoram Eckstein, *A Hydrogeological Approach to Transboundary Ground Water Resources and International Law,* 19 Am. U. Intl. Law Rev. 201 (2003).

[109] EC Directive Preamble, recital 16.

[110] For a compilation of legislation, *see European Community Environment Legislation— Volume 7—Water* (Office of Official Publications of the European Communities 1992).

restore all bodies of surface water" (EC Directive, art. 4(1)(a)(ii)) and to "implement the measures necessary to prevent or limit the input of pollutants into groundwater" (EC Directive, art. 4(1)(b)(i)). Article 4 also establishes deadlines as to when the relevant category of water must have achieved "good" surface or groundwater status.[111] More extensive details on pollution controls and on the acceptable levels of pollutants in water bodies are laid out in the annexes to the EC Directive.

The EC Directive also requires each Member State to undertake a study of each river basin district within its territory (EC Directive, art. 5). The terms "river basin" and "river basin district" are not synonymous. A "river basin" is defined in article 2(13) of the EC Directive as an area of land that forms a natural basin. A "river basin district" refers to the administrative unit, which may comprise more than one river basin (EC Directive, art. 2(15)). The study undertaken by the Member State should analyze the characteristics of the river basin district and the impact of human activity on the surface and groundwater in the basin, and do an economic analysis of its water use (EC Directive, art. 5). The study is to be updated every six years (EC Directive, art. 5). Member States are also required to establish a register of all areas lying within each river basin that have been designated as requiring special protection under EU legislation dealing with the protection of water or the conservation of habitats and species dependent on water (EC Directive, art. 6).

Member States are required to identify, within each river basin district, all bodies of water used for the abstraction of water for human consumption and to monitor these bodies to ensure that they meet certain stipulated water quality standards (EC Directive, art. 7). In addition, Member States are required to establish programs for monitoring water quality in each river basin district. Those programs should cover such issues as flow rates, ecological and chemical status, and quantitative status (EC Directive, art. 8).[112]

The EC Directive requires each Member State to develop a program of measures and a management plan for each river basin district within its territories that,

---

[111] Art. 2(18) of the EC Directive defines "Good surface water status" as "the status achieved by a surface water body when both its ecological status and its chemical status are at least 'good'." and art. 2(20) defines "Good groundwater status" as "the status achieved by a groundwater body when both its quantitative status and its chemical status are at least 'good'."

[112] In this connection *see* The Protocol on Water and Health to the 1992 Convention on the Protection and Use of Transboundary Watercourses and International Lakes (concluded in June 17, 1999, and entered into force on August 4, 2005). The objective of the Protocol, as stated in art. 1, is "to promote at all appropriate levels, nationally as well as in transboundary and international contexts, the protection of human health and well-being, both individual and collective, with a framework of sustainable development, through improving water management, including the protection of water ecosystems, and through preventing, controlling and reducing water-related diseases."

inter alia, protects the water in the basin, promotes efficient and sustainable water use, and controls pollution discharges into the water bodies in the river basin.[113]

Each Member State is also required to "encourage the active involvement of all interested parties" in the implementation and updating of the pertinent river basin management plans (EC Directive, art. 14). This imposes on each Member State an obligation to "publish and make available for comments to the public," *inter alia*, a timetable and work program for producing the plan, including a period of at least six months for public consultations as well as draft copies of the river basin management plan (EC Directive, art. 14). The Member States are also required to send copies of the river basin management plan, as well as any updates, to the EU Commission and to any other Member States that may have an interest in the particular river basin district (EC Directive, art. 15).[114]

As discussed in section 2.6.1, this Directive is one of many regulating the use and protection of water resources in the European Union.[115] Some of the other important ones include the Dangerous Substances Directive, the Urban Wastewater Treatment Directive, the Nitrates Directive,[116] and the Surface Water Directive.[117]

2.6.5 Regulation of Water Infrastructure

The EC Directive has no provisions dealing explicitly with the regulation of water infrastructure.

2.6.6 Institutional Arrangements

The European Parliament and the Council shall adopt special measures against pollution of water by individuals or groups. The EU Commission shall prepare a list of priority substances that present significant risks to, or via, the aquatic environment (EC Directive, art. 16). The list that is developed by the Commission is to take into account the recommendations of a number of official technical

---

[113] EC Directive, arts. 11, 13, and Annex VII.

[114] *See* Klaus Lanz & Stefan Scheuer, *EEB Handbook on EU Water Policy Under the Water Framework Directive* (European Env. Bureau 2001).

[115] *See supra* nn. 97–100.

[116] For discussion and analysis of this Directive *see* Stephen Merrett & Nick Walton, *Nitrate Pollution on the Island of Jersey—Managing Water Quality Within European Union Community Directives,* 30 Water Intl. 155 (2005).

[117] This comprehensive coverage of water quality by the European Union is comparable to the way the United States of America dealt with the issue of water quality. As discussed earlier, water quality issues in the United States are under the authority of the Federal government and are addressed in a comprehensive manner in the Clean Water Act, 1972. *See also supra* n. 2.

environmental bodies, as well as the Member States, business and environmental groups, and international organizations to which the EU is a party (EC Directive, art. 16(5)). Those bodies include the Scientific Committee on Toxicity, Ecotoxicity and the Environment and the European Environment Agency.

The EU Commission is required to publish a periodic report reviewing, *inter alia*, both progress made in implementing the EC Directive and the status of surface and groundwater in the EU and summarizing proposals, control measures, and strategies for dealing with pollutants (EC Directive, art. 18). The EU Commission shall be assisted in its responsibilities under the Directive by a regulatory committee (EC Directive, art. 21).[118]

2.6.6.1   River Basin Authorities

Member States are required to identify the appropriate competent authority for each river basin within their territory and to adopt appropriate administrative arrangements for the river basin district (EC Directive, art. 3). The EC Directive has no provisions on water users' associations or on advisory committees.

2.6.7   Financial Arrangements

Member States shall take account of the principles of cost recovery, including environmental and resource costs and the polluter-pays principle, in their water pricing policies (EC Directive, art. 9). Pricing policies shall also provide incentives for users to use water efficiently, thereby contributing to the environmental objectives of the EC Directive, and must ensure adequate contribution from different water users to the recovery of the cost of providing water services (EC Directive, art. 9).[119]

2.6.8   Enforcement of Regulations and Dispute Settlement

2.6.8.1   Enforcement of Regulations

Each Member State is required to determine "effective, proportionate and dissuasive" penalties that will be applicable to breaches of the national laws adopted pursuant to the EC Directive (EC Directive, art. 23). Each Member State is

---

[118] The composition of the committee and its powers and responsibilities are set out in arts. 5–7 of Council Decision 99/468/EC of 28 June 1999, which lays down the Procedures for the Exercise of Implementing Powers Conferred on the Commission, OJ L 184, 17.7.1999, p. 23.

[119] *See* R. Milaszewski, *Economic Instruments Used in Water Management*, in Landsberg-Uczciwek *et al.*, eds., *supra* n. 96, at 85.

expected to adopt the laws and regulations needed to bring its national legislation and regulatory framework into compliance with this EC Directive (EC Directive, art. 23).

2.6.8.2   Dispute Settlement

The EC Directive does not establish or refer to any dispute settlement bodies that are specifically dedicated to resolving disputes related to water. However, a number of cases have been decided by the European Court of Justice under other EC Directives, such as the cases against France and the United Kingdom under the Surface Water Directive.[120]

With regard to international water disputes, the EC Directive stipulates that if transboundary effects might occur within a river basin, the requirements for achievement of the environmental objectives established under article 4 and, in particular, all programs of measures pursuant to article 11, should be coordinated for the whole of the river basin district.[121] The pivotal provision in this regard is article 3(3). It requires that in the case of a river basin covering the territory of more than one Member State, an "international river basin district" has to be established (EC Directive, art. 3(3)). At the request of the Member States involved, the Commission of the European Community shall act to facilitate the assigning to such international river basin districts (EC Directive, art. 3(3)). Member States are obliged to ensure together that the requirements of the EU Directive are coordinated for the whole of the international river basin district.

---

[120] *See* Case C-266/99 (1999/C-281/06), *Commission v. French Republic,* where the European Court of Justice found France to have failed in its obligations under Directive 75/440/EEC (OJ L 145, 13.6.1977, p. 1) concerning the quality required of surface waters intended for the abstraction of drinking water in Member States (also known as the Surface Water Directive), and in particular art. 4 thereof. The Commission's principal contention centered on France's failure to take necessary measures to ensure that water intended for abstraction of drinking water conform with the values laid down in art. 3, and the degradation of the quality of surface water by pollution caused by nitrates. Similarly, in Case 69/99 (1999/C 1999/069), *Commission v. United Kingdom,* the European Court of Justice found that the UK had failed to fulfill its obligations under Directive 91/676/EEC (OJ L 375, 31.12.1991, p. 1) concerning protection of waters against pollution caused by nitrates from agricultural sources and the identification of waters affected by pollution. The UK had in fact omitted from consideration all surface and groundwaters not being used for the extraction of drinking water, thus inappropriately limiting the areas. Since the decision, designation processes that have been relaunched in England, Scotland, and Wales could lead to around 80 percent of England being designated as Nitrate Vulnerable Zones (NVZ), which would require that action programs be put in place. For more on this case *see* http://europa.eu.int/comm/secretariat_general/sgb/droit_com/index_en.htm#infractions.

[121] EC Directive Preamble, recital 35.

The EC Directive provides the option of using existing structures stemming from international agreements (EC Directive, art. 3(4)). Accordingly, Member States may identify an existing international body as a competent authority for applying the rules of the EC Directive within the international river basin district (EC Directive, art. 3(6)). Thus, any "joint body" established under international law may be entrusted with the task of implementing the supranational requirements of the EC Directive.[122]

2.7   France

2.7.1   Statutory Framework

Water in France is governed by the Statute of January 3, 1992, amended by the Ordinance of September 18, 2000, which is incorporated as articles L. 210-1 to L. 217-1 into the Environment Code. As discussed in the previous section, all EU Member States were expected to incorporate the Water Framework Directive 2000/60/CE (EC Directive)[123] into their domestic law by December 31, 2003. Accordingly, France's 1992 Statute was amended by Law 2004-332 of April 21, 2003[124] to conform to the Directive.

The 2003 Law addresses some basic water resources issues. It focuses on planning and management of water and on the responsibilities outlined in the *schéma directeurs d'aménagement et de gestion des eaux* (SDAGE, the water management master plan). It strengthens the principles of transparency and participation to satisfy consumer and user expectations in terms of justice and equity in water pricing. The law reinforces the polluter-pays principle by reforming the whole system of cost recovery of water basin agencies. It also enhances Government control and monitoring of water resources management by empowering the Parliament with greater oversight over water pricing practices and planning and the

---

[122] In this connection *see* the 1992 Convention on the Protection and Use of Transboundary Watercourses and International Lakes, which entered into force in October 1996; 31 ILM 1312 (1992), and which recital 35 of the EC Directive Preamble specifically highlights. For an analysis of this Convention *see* Branko Bosnjaovic, *UN/ECE Strategies for Protecting the Environment with Respect to International Watercourses: The Helsinki and Espoo Conventions,* in *International Watercourses—Enhancing Cooperation and Managing Conflict,* World Bank Technical Paper No. 414, 47 (Salman M. A. Salman & Laurence Boisson de Chazournes, eds., World Bank 1998).

[123] Council Directive 2000/60/CE of 23 October 2000 establishing a Framework for Community Action in the Field of Water Policy, OJ L 327, 22.12.2000, p. 1. *See supra* section 2.6 of this study.

[124] OJ 95, 22.04.2005, p. 7327.

capacity of the administration to police water uses. It was implemented in Decree No. 2005-475 of May 1, 2005.[125]

2.7.2 Underlying Principles and Priorities

Water is part of the nation's common heritage; its protection, enhancement, and development as a usable resource must be managed accordingly, with due respect to natural equilibriums (Environment Code, art. L.210-1). This means that water management must seek to reconcile the water needs associated with, *inter alia*, public health, aquatic ecosystems, protecting the quality and quantity of available water, protecting against flooding, and such human activities as agriculture, fishing, industry, energy, and transportation (Environment Code, art. L.211-1).

2.7.3 Regulation of Water Uses

2.7.3.1 Ownership of Water and Establishment of Water Rights

The law provides that the State manages the water on behalf of the nation and that rights to use water are determined according to the regulatory scheme illustrated in the law. The law also provides that riparian landowners own half the water in rivers flowing across their land (Environment Code, art. L.215-2). However, groundwater is publicly owned, and the owners of the land overlying the ground-water only have the right to use the groundwater.[126]

2.7.3.2 Allocation of Right to Use Water

The regulatory scheme establishes rules for the allocation of both surface and groundwater. In the case of surface water, the law provides that riparian landown-ers can use the water that borders or crosses their land, provided they do so in a way that complies with the law (Environment Code, arts. L.215-1–215-5). This means that they can use the water in any way that does not modify the flow of the water. In addition, the State allows each natural or legal person to draw off up to 40 cubic meters per day for domestic use without prior State authorization. Finally, the law recognizes that rights to water previously acquired by riparians or third parties are preserved and are not affected by the regulatory scheme.

The regulatory scheme also provides that half the water flowing in a river belongs to the owners of the land on each side of the river. This principle does not change if the river changes the direction of its flow due to either natural causes or the construction of works on the river.

---

[125] OJ 113, 17.05.2005, p. 8552.

[126] This principle derives from a cross-reading with the Civil Code, which deals with ownership and the law on public domain.

In the case of groundwater, the rights of landowners to use the groundwater under the surface of their land are granted by the State and must be approved at the regional level by the Prefect for the district. Rights to pump groundwater for nondomestic purposes are subject to the requirements (i) to use instrumentation that can evaluate and measure water use, and (ii) to carry out an environmental impact assessment of the proposed groundwater extraction (Environment Code, art. L.214-8).

In order to draw off natural mineral waters, a natural or legal person who wishes to use the water must apply for authorization from the Prefect in the relevant department. The Health Code governs the definition of mineral waters, and authorizations are granted only after the Ministry of Health issues a regulation describing the content of the water especially its biochemical content. The authorization, which is renewable, is granted after a public investigation and for a stipulated period subject to specified conditions (Environment Code, arts. L.214-2 & L.214-4). Similar authorization is required in the case of waterworks that may present a danger to public health, impact the flow of water in the relevant water resource, or increase the risk of flooding. In order to transport, distribute, or modify natural mineral waters, the proponent of such activity must seek a declaration from the Prefect in the relevant department (Environment Code, art. L.214-9).

2.7.3.3   Transfer and Loss of Water Rights

Article L.213-3 of the Environment Code gives regional authorities the role of coordinating the National Policy related to management of water resources. The statute has no provisions dealing explicitly with the loss of rights to use water.

2.7.4   Protection of Water

Pursuant to the Water Law, the Prefect in charge of coordination of the water basin, working with the water basin agency, is required to develop an SDAGE (Environment Code, art. L.212-2). The SDAGE focuses on the planning and management of water resources at the basin level, subject to the committee's jurisdiction. It must include a program for monitoring the condition of these water resources (Environment Code, art. L.212-2-2). The SDAGE, which must comply with the requirements of the EC Directive, is to be updated every six years (Environment Code, art. L.212-2).

2.7.5   Regulation of Water Infrastructure

The proponent of waterworks that may present a danger to public health, impact the flow of water in the relevant water resource, or increase the risk of flooding must obtain an authorization from the Prefect in the relevant department. The authorization, which is renewable, is granted after a public investigation and for a stipulated period subject to specified conditions (Environment Code, art. L.214-4). These authorizations can be granted to both government-owned companies and private corporations acting as concessionaires in the public domain.

2.7.6 Institutional Arrangements

The High Council on Water Public Services and Water Treatment (*Haut Conseil des services publics de l'eau et de l'assainissement* – the Council) regulates water services. It is responsible for establishing prices, the distribution of water, and provision of information to water users. It is composed of six members who are appointed based on qualifications relating to water matters (economics, legal, and technical). Three of the members are appointed by the Government and the remaining three are appointed by the President of the National Assembly, the Senate, and the Social and Economic Council. In addition to the responsibilities mentioned, the Council also makes recommendations to courts and it can summon parties to water agreements that are inconsistent with the Water Law. The Prefects in each department are responsible for issuing authorizations and declarations that allow specified water uses.[127]

A local water committee, which is established by the Prefect of that department, is responsible for the development, revision, and control of the application of the *schémas d'aménagement et de gestion des eaux* (SAGE or water management scheme) (Environment Code, art. L.212-4). Half its membership is selected by the Prefect to represent the local department, another quarter is chosen by the central government, and the remaining quarter is chosen by local water users in the department.

The SDAGE is developed in conjunction with the relevant water basin committees (Environment Code, art. L.212-2) and must be submitted to the relevant local and regional councils (Environment Code, art. L.212-6). Decree No. 2005-636 of May 30, 2005,[128] gives to the Minister in charge of the environment the role of coordinating the actions of the various ministries dealing with water and the execution of decisions taken by these ministries.

2.7.6.1 River Basin Authority

The administrative authority delimits the boundaries of each water basin (Environment Code, art. L.212-1). The Prefect appoints a local water committee to

---

[127] *See supra* section 2.7.3.2.

[128] OJ 125, 31.05.2005.

assist local authorities in regulating the use of water resources in the basin (Environment Code, art. L.212-4). This committee consists of representatives of water users (one third); the general council and regional representatives (one third); and representatives of the local chambers of commerce and local state-owned companies (one third) (Environment Code, art. L.212-4).

One responsibility of the committee is to develop the SDAGE for the basin or group of basins under its jurisdiction. The SDAGE must establish the guidelines for good management of the water resources in the basin and quality and quantity objectives for the water resource (Environment Code, art. L.213-2). In developing the SDAGE, the committee must seek the views of the public (Environment Code, art. L.212-2).

2.7.6.2   Water Users' Associations and Advisory Committees

People or organizations that have an interest in water management in a particular area can participate in a local water community (*les communautés locales de l'eau*).[129] The National Committee on Water provides its opinion on water management at the national and regional levels (Environment Code, art. L.213-1).

2.7.7   Financial Arrangements

The general principle is that the costs of water use must be paid by the users (Environment Code, art. L.210-1). Consequently, the law provides for a variety of different fees. Each water user is billed for its water use and charged fees based on use. All fees are collected by the administrator of the water agency based on public collection procedures and rules. It should be mentioned that provision of waters for the poor is mentioned explicitly in the law and a subsidy system is in place to assist the poor to access clean and potable water.[130]

2.7.8   Enforcement of Regulations and Dispute Settlement

2.7.8.1   Enforcement of Regulations

Public officials have the authority to inspect waterworks and installations and to check the owner's compliance with regulations. Authorizations and declarations must be used within five years of their issuance or a new application must be submitted to the appropriate authorities. Individuals and entities that fail to comply with the regulations or the terms of authorizations or decrees are subject to either fines or imprisonment (Environment Code, Chapter VI).

---

[129] *See* Environment Code, arts. L.213-2, L.213-5, and L.213-9.

[130] For a discussion of water pricing policies in France *see* Dinar & Subramanian (eds.) *supra* n. 62, at 46.

2.7.8.2   Dispute Settlement

There is no special water law court or administrative tribunal. Disputes regarding water management, policy, or regulation are handled by administrative courts (*Tribunal administrative* and *Conseil d'Etat*). However, if the dispute can result in a violation of the law and the penal code that may be sanctioned by imprisonment and fines, it can be referred to the civil courts (*Tribunal d'instance*) (Environment Code, art. L.216-9).

2.8   Germany

2.8.1   Statutory Framework

There are no provisions in the Federal Constitution of Germany[131] that directly regulate the use or protection of water. There are, however, fairly new "soft law" provisions, formulating a mere "aim," that deal with the protection of "natural resources."[132] Furthermore, the Federal Constitutional Court[133] in 1981 rendered a decision that upheld a federal law regulating the use of groundwater.[134] The Court in its decision acknowledged groundwater as a public good. According to the Court, an individual's property rights are not violated if Federal law restricts the use of groundwater.

Germany is a Federal State composed of sixteen States or *Länder*. The Basic Law allocates responsibilities and authority between the Federation and the *Länder* with regard to the regulation of water uses and water protection. Pursuant to article 75, no. 4 of the Basic Law, water resources are subject to federal framework legislation. Therefore the responsibility for setting up regulatory frameworks lies with the Federal Government, while the *Länder* are responsible for implementing and supplementing the Federal regulations and enforcing all statutory provisions in the field of water pollution control.

There are a number of statutes that regulate water in Germany. The most significant is the Act on the Regulation of Matters Pertaining to Water (Federal Water Act) of 19 August 2002,[135] which implements Directive 2000/60/EC of the European Parliament and of the European Council of 23 October 2000.[136] As

---

[131] Basic Law, or *Gundgesetz (GG)*.

[132] Basic Law, art. 20a.

[133] *Bundesverfassungsgericht (BverfG)*.

[134] The "Nassauskießung" Case, Bundesverfassungsgericht, Decision of July 15, 1981, BVerfGE 58, 300 ff.

[135] Act on the Regulation of Matters Pertaining to Water of 1957 (Federal Water Act [*Wasserhaushaltsgesetz – WHG*]), modified version of August 19, 2002, promulgated in the Federal Law Gazette I 2002 [BGBl. I 2002], p. 3245.

[136] Council Directive 2000/60/CE of 23 October 2000 establishing a Framework for Community Action in the Field of Water Policy, OJ L 327, 22.12.2000, p. 1.

discussed earlier, this Directive establishes a framework for Community action in the field of water policy. The Federal Water Act also refers to a number of other statutes and ordinances that are relevant to the regulation of water, which include

- Act Amending the Environmental Audit Act of 16 August 2002;[137]
- Federal Nature Conservation Act;[138]
- Environmental Impact Assessment Act;[139]
- Council Directive 96/61/EC of 24 September 1996 concerning integrated pollution prevention and control (IPPC Directive);[140] and
- Ordinance of 10 February 1945 on the Simplification of Water Legislation and Legislation Relating to Water Associations.[141]

The following statutes and ordinances also apply to specific aspects of water regulation:

- Waste Water Charges Act;[142]
- Waste Water Ordinance;[143]
- Washing and Cleansing Agents Act;[144] and
- Federal Soil Protection Act.[145]

---

[137] *Veranderungdes Umweltauditgesetzes* BGBl. I 2002 S.3167.

[138] Federal Nature Conservation Act of March 25, 2002, [*Gesetz über Naturschutz und Landschaftspflege (Bundesnaturschutzgesetz – BnatSchG)*], promulgated in the Federal Law Gazette I 2002 [BGBl. I 2002], p. 1193.

[139] Environmental Impact Assessment Act of 1990 [*Gesetz über die Umweltverträglichkeitsprüfung (UVPG)*, modified version of September 5, 2001, promulgated in the Federal Law Gazette I 2002 [BGBl. I 2002], p. 2350.

[140] OJ L 257,10.10.1996, p. 26.

[141] Ordinance on the Simplification of Water Legislation and Legislation Relating to Water Associations [*Verordnung über Vereinfachungen im Wasser- und Wasserverbandsrecht*] of 1945, promulgated in the Law Gazette of the German Reich I 1945 (RGBl. I 1945), p. 29.

[142] Waste Water Charges Act [*Gesetz über Abgaben für das Einleiten von Abwasser in Gewässer (AbwAG)*] of 1976, modified version of November 3, 1994, promulgated in the Federal Law Gazette I 1994 (BGBl. I 1994), p. 3370.

[143] Waste Water Ordinance [*Verordnung über Anforderungen an das Einleiten von Abwasser in Gewasser (AbwV)*] of 1997, modified version of October 15, 2002, promulgated in the Federal Law Gazette I 2002 [BGBl. I 2002], p. 4047.

[144] Washing and Cleansing Agents Act [*Gesetz über die Umweltverträglichkeit von Wasch- und Reinigungsmitteln (WaschMG)*] of 1975, modified version of March 5, 1987, promulgated in the Federal Law Gazette I 1987 (BGBl. I 1987), p. 875.

[145] Federal Soil Protection Act, [*Gesetz zum Schutz vor schädlichen Bodenveränderungen und zur Sanierung von Altlasten – Bundesbodenschutzgesetz (BBodSchG)*], modified version of September 9, 2001, promulgated in the Federal Law Gazette I 2001 [BGBl. I 2001], p. 2331.

2.8.2 Underlying Principles and Priorities

The Federal Water Act is applicable to surface waters, coastal waters, and ground-water.[146] According to the act, water is an integral part of the natural environment and must be protected (Federal Water Act, pt. I, art. 1a(1)). It must be managed to serve the public interest, benefit individual water users, and avoid impairments in its ecological functions and to ecosystems and wetlands (Federal Water Act, pt. I, art. 1a(1)). When activities do have an impact on a body of water, "every-one shall be obliged to exercise all due required caution under the circumstances" to prevent pollution of or any other detrimental changes in the water and to ensure that the water is used economically (Federal Water Act, pt. I, art. 1a(2)).

Länder (State) law requires that the public water supply be met primarily from local water sources unless this is contrary to the overriding public interest (Federal Water Act, pt. I, art. 1a(3)).

2.8.3 Regulation of Water Uses

2.8.3.1 *Ownership of Water and Establishment of Water Rights*

Ownership of land does not bestow any entitlement to the use of any water, which requires a permit or a license (Federal Water Act, pt. I, art. 1a(4)). Article 2(1) of the Federal Water Act requires all users of water to have an official permit or license, except where the provisions of the Act or a regulation issued by a *Länder* specifically provide that they do not have to. The article further states, in subsec-tion 2, that this permit or license is merely a right to use water and does not give the holder title to water in any specific quantity or quality.

There are only certain circumstances in which the right to use water can be established without having to obtain a permit or license. For example, surface waters may be used without a permit by property owners and riparian owners or by those authorized by these owners, provided that this does not harm others and does not lead to detrimental changes in the properties of the water (Federal Water Act, pt. II, art. 24(1)). Permits are also not required, *inter alia,* for the use of groundwater for domestic or farming purposes (Federal Water Act, pt. IV, art. 33(1)) and where there was an existing right or authorization to use the water, arising, for example, under other legislation (Federal Water Act, pt. I, arts. 15 & 17).

The uses to which the Federal Water Act is applicable include, *inter alia,* the withdrawal or diversion of surface water; damming of surface water; introduction or discharge of substances into surface water, groundwater, or coastal water; and

---

[146] Federal Water Act, Introductory Provision, art. 1.

any measures that are likely to cause permanent changes to the physical, chemical, or biological properties of the water (Federal Water Act, pt. I, art. 3).

2.8.3.2   Allocation of Right to Use Water

Allocation of the right to use water is by permit or license, except in the limited circumstances described above. Permits and licenses are issued subject to conditions that are designed, *inter alia,* to prevent detrimental effects on other persons or, if this is not possible, to compensate them for these detrimental effects and for impairments in the ecological or chemical status of the water (Federal Water Act, pt. I, art. 4). A permit or license can be refused if the proposed use is likely to be detrimental to the public interest (Federal Water Act, pt. I, art. 6).

A permit gives the holder a revocable right to use a body of water for a particular purpose, in a specific way, and for a stipulated period of time (Federal Water Act, pt. I, art. 7). A license gives the holder the right to use a body of water for a particular purpose and to a specified extent, but in fulfilling the purpose of the license the holder does not have the right to utilize objects, including land, belonging to another person or installations in the possession of another person (Federal Water Act, pt. I, art. 8). In addition to these conditions, a license is only granted if the holder can be expected to carry out the project with a secure legal position (Federal Water Act, pt. I, art. 8). Licenses are granted for a specific period of time, which in special circumstances may exceed thirty years (Federal Water Act, pt. I, art. 8(5)).

Licenses and permits can only be issued in a procedure that affords affected persons and authorities the opportunity to raise formal objections and, if applicable, only after compliance with the provisions of the Environmental Impact Assessment Act (Federal Water Act, pt. I, art. 9).[147] The procedure for issuing licenses and permits allows the responsible agencies to authorize the applicant to commence using the water prior to the permit or license being issued, provided that (i) the final decision is likely to favor the applicant, (ii) the early commencement is in the public interest, and (iii) the applicant promises to pay compensation for any damage caused before the final decision on the permit or license is taken and to restore the site to its former state if the license or permit is refused (Federal Water Act, pt. I, art. 9a). These proceedings also provide that after the license or permit is granted, it may be modified if subsequent conditions that could not be adequately ascertained at the time of issuance so warrant (Federal Water Act, pt. I, art. 10). Furthermore, the permit or license can be issued subject to a reservation that requirements can be added to the license or permit later (Federal Water Act, pt. I, art. 5).

---

[147] *See also supra* n. 139.

It is important to note that, in addition to individuals, water and soil associations and special purpose associations of local authorities also need to obtain permits or licenses if they wish to use water for a purpose that requires a license or permit (Federal Water Act, pt. I, art. 13).

2.8.3.3   Transfer of Water Rights

Unless otherwise specified at the time the permit is granted, both a permit (Federal Water Act, pt. I, art. 7) and a license (Federal Water Act, pt. I, art. 8) can be passed to any legal successor, including, where applicable, with the transfer of the title to the land to which the permit applies.

2.8.3.4   Loss of Right to Use Water

A license can be revoked, completely or in part, against payment of compensation, if the unrestricted continued use of water is "likely to cause considerable impairment to the public interest, in particular the public water supply" (Federal Water Act, pt. I, art. 12). In addition, a license can be revoked if the holder fails to start using the water within the period specified in the license; has not used it for an uninterrupted period of three years; is using "considerably less" water than anticipated; or exceeds the limits of the license or exercises it in a way that does not conform to the original plan (Federal Water Act, pt. I, art. 12).

2.8.4   Protection of Water

The Federal Water Act stipulates that disposal of wastewater that requires a permit (Federal Water Act, pt. I, art. 7a) must take place in a manner that does not impair the public interest (Federal Water Act, pt. I, art. 18a). The Federal Water Act further requires that any individual who uses a body of water must accept official supervision of the installations, equipment, and processes that are important to the use of the water (Federal Water Act, pt. I, art. 21).

The authorities can establish water protection areas "where the public interest so requires" in order to, *inter alia,* protect bodies of water against detrimental effects on the public water supply, recharge groundwater, and prevent the harmful effects of rainwater run-offs (Federal Water Act, pt. I, art. 19). The authorities can restrict or prohibit certain activities in these areas and can impose certain requirements on the owners and authorized users of land within these areas (Federal Water Act, pt. I, art. 19).

The Federal Water Act requires that users of water who are permitted to discharge more than 750 cubic meters of wastewater in one day must appoint officers for water pollution control (Federal Water Act, pt. I, art. 21a). The responsibilities of these officers include supervising compliance with water regulations, conducting inspections of wastewater installations, promoting suitable waste water treatment procedures, and submitting an annual report to the water user (Federal Water Act, pt. I, art. 21b).

Except when bodies of surface water are classified as artificial or heavily modified, they must be managed in such a way as to preserve or attain a good ecological or chemical status and avoid any adverse changes in this status (Federal Water Act, pt. II, art. 25a). Artificial or heavily modified bodies of surface water are those bodies for which the changes in hydromorphological characteristics that would be necessary to achieve a good ecological status would have adverse effects on, *inter alia,* the environment, navigation, recreation, and other important "sustainable human development activities" (Federal Water Act, pt. II, art. 25b). These bodies of surface water should be managed so as to avoid adverse changes in their ecological and chemical status (Federal Water Act, pt. II, art. 25b).

Unless responsibility for maintaining and developing a water body is the function of regional authorities, water and soil associations, or associations of local authorities, it is the responsibility of the owners of waters, riparian owners, and owners of land and facilities who either benefit from the maintenance of water or who make maintenance more difficult (Federal Water Act, pt. II, art. 29).

The Federal Water Act requires that bodies of water that are in a natural or near-natural condition should be preserved in that condition provided this does not conflict with "overriding concerns of public interest" (Federal Water Act, pt. II, art. 31). If such bodies of water are to be developed, plans for their development must be approved by the competent state authority (Federal Water Act, pt. II, art. 31).

The Federal Water Act provides, in article 32b, for the maintenance of coastal waters by prohibiting the disposal of solid matter into such waters and by allowing substances to be stored or deposited near coastal waters only in ways that do not create a "reason to fear pollution . . . or any other detrimental changes" in the water.

Pursuant to article 33a, groundwater must be managed to avoid adverse changes in the quantitative and chemical status of the water. Moreover, substances can only be discharged into the groundwater if there are "no grounds to fear harmful pollution of the groundwater or any other detrimental change in its properties" (Federal Water Act, pt. IV, art. 34).

2.8.5 Regulation of Water Infrastructure

The construction, operation, and modification of wastewater installations that must conform to the requirements for the discharge of waste water and to the "generally accepted state-of-the-art" (Federal Water Act, pt. I, art. 18b) are subject to mandatory environmental impact assessments, pursuant to the Environmental Impact Assessment Act (Federal Water Act, pt. I, art. 18c).[148]

The construction, operation, and modification of pipelines for the conveyance of substances constituting a hazard to water require a license (Federal Water Act, pt. I, arts. 19a & 19b), which may be revoked, pursuant to art. 19c, if it is feared that continued operation of the pipeline may lead to pollution of or detrimental change in a body of water. The operators of pipelines are required to monitor them for leaks and the effective functioning of safety equipment (Federal Water Act, pt. I, art. 19i). In addition, the Federal Water Act requires operators of installations on water to commission specialist firms to install, maintain, and repair the installations (Federal Water Act, pt. I, art. 19i). Article 19k of the Federal Water Law stipulates that any person who fills or empties a water storage installation that may be a hazard to water must carefully supervise the filling or emptying and must ensure that all safety equipment functions properly.

2.8.6 Institutional Arrangements

2.8.6.1 River Basin Authorities

Germany is divided into ten river basin districts (Federal Water Act, pt. I, art. 1b). In order to ensure coordination of the management of these districts, they are regulated by State law (Federal Water Act, pt. I, art. 1b). Each of the States within Germany, through the competent State authority, is required to assign the river basins within its boundaries to one of the river basin districts (Federal Water Act, pt. I, art. 1b).

The Federal Water Law stipulates that State law must require each of these river basin districts to prepare a program of measures to achieve the objectives set out in the Federal Water Act (Federal Water Act, pt. V, art. 36). The river basin district, pursuant to State law, is also required to prepare a management plan for the district that describes, *inter alia,* the characteristics of the waters in the river basin and the management objectives for the waters; gives an economic analysis of water use in the basin district; and designates the bodies of surface water in the district that are either artificial or heavily modified (Federal Water Act, pt. V, art. 36b). The Federal Water Act requires the authorities to maintain a register of all bodies of water covered by the law (Federal Water Act, pt. V, art. 37). There is no information in the Federal Water Act on water users' associations or on advisory committees, and it is likely that those aspects are covered under other regulations.

---

[148] *See also supra* n. 139.

2.8.7   Financial Arrangements

The Federal Water Act contains no information on user fees or licensing fees, as those issues are regulated by the states.

2.8.8   Enforcement of Regulations and Dispute Settlement

2.8.8.1   Enforcement of Regulations

All individuals who use a body of water or who have filed an application for a permit or license must allow official supervision of the installations, equipment, or processes they utilize in their use of the body of water (Federal Water Act, pt. I, art. 21). Any person who "willfully or negligently," *inter alia,* uses water without the required permit or license; contravenes a condition of the license or permit or the provisions of the Federal Water Act; or fails to comply with good technical practice in the installation, maintenance, or operation of a water installation has committed an administrative offense and is liable for a fine of up to €50,000 (Federal Water Act, pt. VI, art. 41(2)). In addition, article 20 stipulates that compensation is payable for any damage caused to property as a result of water use, or if water use is impaired in some way.

2.8.8.2   Dispute Settlement

The Federal Water Act provides in article 10 that an affected party that raises objections to the granting of a license, but cannot ascertain the extent of the detrimental effects the granting of the license will have, can demand that protective conditions be incorporated into the license and that they receive any compensation that may be due to them.

2.9   Republic of Kazakhstan

2.9.1   Statutory Framework

Article 6 of the Constitution of the Republic of Kazakhstan states that "[t]he land and underground resources, water, flora, fauna and other natural resources shall be owned by the state. The land may also be privately owned on terms, conditions and within the limits established by legislation."

Water legislation in the Republic of Kazakhstan (Kazakhstan) is based on the powers implicit in this provision of the Constitution (Water Code, art. 2). The primary statute is the Water Code of the Republic of Kazakhstan, No. 481-II of

July 9, 2003 (Water Code). Other relevant statutes are

- Law of the Republic of Kazakhstan on Environmental Protection (July 15, 1997); and
- Law of the Republic of Kazakhstan on Specifically Protected Natural Territory (July 15, 1997).

2.9.2 Underlying Principles and Priorities

The principles on which the Water Code is based are outlined in article 9; they include an acknowledgement of the national importance of water as the basis for life and the activities of the population; equitable access to water; rational water use that incorporates up-to-date technologies; balancing the use of bodies of water with their protection; charging for special uses of water; public participation in water use and water protection; and the availability of information on the status of the water fund.

The principles on which public administration of the water fund is based include state regulation and control of the use and protection of the water fund; sustainable use of water; creation of optimal conditions for water use, preservation of environmental sustainability, and public health; and basin administration (Water Code, art. 34).

Based on these principles, the Water Code has a number of goals. First, it seeks to achieve and maintain an ecologically and economically optimal level of water resource use; protection of the water fund; and improvement in the living conditions of the population (Water Code, art. 3). The "water fund," as described in article 4, includes all bodies of water in the territory of Kazakhstan included in the National Water Cadastre.[149] Water resources in Kazakhstan include both surface and groundwater (Water Code, art. 6).

Second, the Water Code establishes a State policy in favor of sustainable water use and protection of the water fund, including the principles that regulate use and protection of the water fund (Water Code, art. 3).

Third, the Water Code deals with the relationship between land and water use and transboundary water use and protection (Water Code, art. 10).

2.9.3 Regulation of Water Uses

2.9.3.1 Ownership of Water and Establishment of Water Rights

Water resources are an exclusive State property and the rights of ownership, use, and disposal for the water fund are exercised by the government of Kazakhstan (Water Code, art. 8). Drinking-water supply systems can be the property of the

---

[149] *See* Water Code, arts. 58–59, for more details on State records and the State Water Cadastre.

State, community, or legal or natural persons (Water Code, art. 28). Similarly, pursuant to article 29, water facilities intended for agricultural water users can be State-owned or private property.

All water bodies are for general/common use unless otherwise provided for in legislation (Water Code, art. 16). Water bodies that are not for general/common use are classified, in article 11, into water bodies for joint use, water bodies for isolated use, water bodies for wildlife sanctuaries or reserves, and water bodies of special State importance. Their use is regulated by the Water Code (Water Code, arts. 17–21).

Article 23 states that any person can use water bodies that are for general/common use. This means that a "public water servitude" is integral to the right to use water bodies of general/common use. Legislation can also create public water servitudes over other categories of water bodies (Water Code, art. 23). Private servitudes, which mean that a water body is restricted for the benefit of a private party, can be created by court decision (Water Code, art. 23). No license or special permission is required to exercise these servitudes (Water Code, art. 23). Both public and private servitudes are established for the following purposes: withdrawing water without special technical means or devices, livestock watering, and the use of water bodies for transport (Water Code, art. 23).

The right to use water bodies can be granted to natural and legal persons by local executive authorities with the approval of the "authorized body for use and protection of the water fund" (Water Code, art. 22).[150] The right to use water is deemed permanent if it is granted without a fixed term (Water Code, art. 70). However, the right to use water can be for short- or long-term use, with the former being for periods of up to five years and the latter for periods from five to forty-nine years (Water Code, art. 22).

Water uses can be divided into general, special, isolated, joint, primary, secondary, permanent, and temporary (Water Code, art. 64). "General" use, as defined in article 65, includes using water without application of facilities or technical devices having an impact on water conditions. The right to general use accrues to citizens from the moment of their birth and cannot be assigned (Water Code, art. 64). "Special" use includes uses that require application of facilities or technical devises. The right to a special use can only be acquired by obtaining a license or a permit (Water Code, art. 76) and the use is limited by the terms of the license or permit (Water Code, art. 64). "Isolated" water uses arise where only one person uses a particular water body. These uses require the permission of the local representative authority (Water Code, art. 67). "Joint" water uses arise when several people use one water body pursuant to the terms established by the local representative authority (Water Code, art. 68).

---

[150] Art. 62 of the Water Code lays out in detail the rights and obligations of legal persons.

"Primary" water uses are those uses that are undertaken to meet the user's own needs or to deliver water to "secondary" users pursuant to the terms of a contract (Water Code, art. 69).

The law establishes some limits on water use. These limits are set by the authorized body for use and protection of the water fund with the approval of the central executive for environmental protection. The limits, which are adjusted annually, are based on existing water basin plans, the norms for determining the allowable negative impact on water, and the declared needs of all water users (Water Code, art. 82).

The rights of water users, as listed in article 71, include, *inter alia,* the right to establish organizations and associations of water users and to protect their right to use water. Their obligations include compliance with all applicable limits and regulations, maintaining any facilities and technical devices having an impact on water, making the required payments, and providing the required information (Water Code, art. 72).

Natural and legal persons who wish to undertake water supply and related services must, pursuant to article 79, establish "non-governmental hydroeconomic organizations."[151] These organizations are required to comply with all applicable laws and contracts (Water Code, art. 80).

2.9.3.2   Allocation of Right to Use Water

The State plan for the protection and use of the water fund is designed to ensure a "scientifically justified" distribution of water use between users and the protection of water resources. This plan is part of the scheme for the development and allocation of the country's productive forces (Water Code, art. 44).[152] The Water Code includes some general rules applicable to the allocation of water to different uses, such as drinking, sanitation and recreation, agricultural needs, industrial and power system needs, transportation, timber rafting and fire-fighting, and the fishing and hunting industry, and for use of water bodies in nature reserves (Water Code, arts. 90–111).

2.9.3.3   Transfer of Water Rights

The natural or legal persons who hold the right to use water bodies cannot, pursuant to article 22(4), dispose of this right.

---

[151] Water Code, art. 1(25), defines hydroeconomic organizations as organizations that undertake activities related to the regulation, supply and reproduction of water, water treatment, wastewater drainage, and operation of water bodies.

[152] *See also* Water Code, arts. 45–47 and 81.

2.9.3.4 Loss of Right to Use Water

Rights to use water can be restricted in accordance with the procedures established in law in order to protect the public interest (Water Code, art. 74). Special water rights can be terminated if the holders of a right transfer it, if the right is not used for up to three years, and in cases of noncompliance with the law (Water Code, art. 75).

2.9.4 Protection of Water

All actors that can affect water conditions are required to observe the regulations dealing with environmental protection, subsoil protection, public health and industrial safety, and the conservation of water resources (Water Code, art. 55). In this regard, the Water Code includes standards applicable to the treatment and quality of discharged water (Water Code, art. 56) and to controlled flows of water for health and environmental purposes (Water Code, art. 57). In addition, the State is also required to develop a uniform system of normative, technical, public health, and metrological standards for protecting the quality and quantity of water resources and for measuring water parameters (Water Code, arts. 83–89).

The Water Code stipulates that water bodies must be protected from a variety of pollutants by requiring that common requirements for the protection of water bodies be developed by central and local executive authorities.[153] It also establishes requirements for the protection of small water bodies (Water Code, arts. 121–122), for the construction and operation of waterworks in water bodies (Water Code, arts. 125–26), and for the management of water bodies of special State significance (Water Code, arts. 127–131).

2.9.5 Regulation of Water Infrastructure

In general, water facilities can be either public or private property (Water Code, art. 24). However, the President of Kazakhstan can designate a water facility as having special strategic importance, in which case the facility is deemed public property that cannot be assigned for asset management or leased and cannot be privatized (Water Code, art. 25). Otherwise, State-owned water facilities are assigned to State water organizations but can be leased or privatized (Water Code, art. 26). The classification of a facility as State-owned is established by the government on the basis of a recommendation from the "authorized body for use and protection of the water fund and authorized body for use and protection of the subsoil reserves" (Water Code, art. 26). Communal water facilities are managed by public utility companies and can be used free of charge (Water Code, art. 27).

---

[153] Water Code, arts. 112–20 and 123–24.

Rights to water facilities and transactions regarding these rights must be registered with the state as stipulated in article 31 of the Water Code. The owners of water facilities are responsible for ensuring safe technical conditions at the facilities (Water Code, art. 32). The authorized bodies for use and protection of the water resources oversee these facilities (Water Code, art. 32).

2.9.6 Institutional Arrangements

The Government is responsible for the public administration of water resources, together with the "authorized body for administration of use and protection of the water fund," local representative and executive agencies, and other State agencies that are established by legislation (Water Code, art. 33). The Government also establishes State hydroeconomic organizations to, *inter alia*, monitor water bodies, draw up the State cadastre, develop hydroeconomic norms, and maintain and operate hydroeconomic bodies and facilities that are owned by the State (Water Code, art. 77).

The main tasks of State administration include: analysis and assessment of water supply; assessment of the available water resources, their quality, and the availability of rights to use them; the development of new technologies for water consumption, drainage, and protection; management of water use; controlling the qualitative and quantitative conditions of water bodies; management of State-owned water bodies and facilities; and the development of a market in water services (Water Code, art. 35).

In fulfilling these tasks, the Government is responsible for, *inter alia*, developing the main policies for the use and protection of the water resources; establishing the administration of State-owned water facilities; determining the procedures for maintaining water reserves and their uses and the State water cadastre; determining procedures for developing master and basin water use plans; determining procedures for entering into leases and asset management agreements for water facilities; and approving fees for surface water resources (Water Code, art. 36).

The State's authority over the use and protection of water resources is exercised by a number of different bodies, each acting within its own specific terms of reference. They include the authorized body for use and protection of the water fund; the centralized body of environmental protection; and local executive bodies, with the authorized body for use and protection of the water fund acting as the coordinating authority (Water Code, art. 49).

The responsibilities of the authorized body for the use and protection of the water resources include participating in the development and implementation of State policies with regard to the use and protection of the water fund; developing programs for the use and protection of river basins and other water bodies; approving water consumption rates for economic sectors; approving standard regulations for water use; issuing and suspending licenses and permits for water use; exercising control over the use and protection of water resources; creating a database on water bodies; arranging for research related to water resources; trying administrative cases of infractions with regard to water legislation; developing and implementing water investment projects; and developing fees for surface water use (Water Code, art. 37).

The responsibilities of local representative bodies include establishing regulations for general water use on the basis of the regulations approved by the authorized body for the use and protection of the water fund; approving local budgets for the use and protection of water bodies; approving regional programs for water use and protection; and establishing procedures for the allocation of water facilities that are communal property (Water Code, art. 38).

The responsibilities of local executive bodies include administering communal property and implementing measures for protecting water bodies and facilities; participating in the activities of basin authorities; developing and implementing regional programs for water use and protection; and informing the public about the condition of water bodies in their area of responsibility (Water Code, art. 39). Local executive bodies are also required to establish municipal hydroeconomic organizations to maintain and operate hydroeconomic facilities owned by municipalities; supply water to water users from water bodies; and deal with used, waste, and drainage waters (Water Code, art. 78).

The responsibilities of territorial bodies of the central executive body for environmental protection include participating in the approval of plans for the use and protection of water bodies, monitoring water bodies, State control over the use and protection of the water fund, and developing and implementing basin agreements (Water Code, art. 41).[154]

2.9.6.1   River Basin Authorities

Basin authorities are territorial departments of the authorized body for the use and protection of the water fund (Water Code, art. 40). Their functions can include administration of the water resources in the basin; implementation of State control over the use and protection of the water fund; maintenance of State records relating to water bodies; issuing and suspending licenses for all types of special water uses; approving schemes for the use and protection of the water in the basin; reporting violations of water legislation; and disseminating information on activities related to the rational use and protection of water resources (Water Code, art. 40).

They are also responsible for concluding basin agreements dealing with the rehabilitation and protection of water bodies (Water Code, art. 42). These

---

[154] *See generally*, Branscheid, *supra* n. 46.

agreements can provide for the establishment of a basin council to examine topical issues on the use and protection of water resources and to make suggestions and recommendations to the participants in the agreement (Water Code, art. 43). This council is chaired by the head of the basin authority and consists of the heads of the local representative and executive bodies and representatives of water users' associations; it may include representatives of nongovernmental organizations (Water Code, art. 43).

2.9.6.2   Water Users' Associations and Advisory Committees

The Water Code makes a number of references to water users' associations but does not have any provisions that deal specifically with the composition or rights and responsibilities of such associations.[155]

2.9.7   Financial Arrangements

The general use of water is free of charge; special uses are subject to fees established in the tax legislation (Water Code, art. 133). All services related to the taking of water, its distribution, and its purification must be paid for (Water Code, art. 134). These fees are established in the antimonopoly law and in the terms and conditions of the agreements for the provision of water services (Water Code, art. 134).

The State also provides various types of financial support to the water economy. Such financial support includes financing the construction and maintenance of water facilities, subsidizing the cost of water to farmers, subsidizing the cost of drinking water to a certain category of users, and extending credit to certain participants in the water economy (Water Code, art. 135).

The Water Code also deals with additional economic issues, such as the financing of approved programs for the use and protection of water bodies, providing credit and other benefits to persons involved in the protection and use of water resources, and the creation of public funds for the restoration and protection of water bodies (Water Code, art. 132).

2.9.8   Enforcement of Regulations and Dispute Settlement

2.9.8.1   Enforcement of Regulations

Authorized public officers have the right to enforce observance of water legislation; make suggestions on the suspension or annulment of licenses or permits for

---

[155] In this connection, *see* Vilma Horinkova & Iskandar Abdullaev, *Institutional Aspects of Water Management in Central Asia: Water Users' Associations*, 28 Water Intl. 237 (2003).

water use; make inspections; obtain information on water use; make reports of infractions; and make suggestions on sanctions for perpetrators of the infractions.[156]

Uses of water that intentionally violate the regulations applicable to water use or to pollution of surface and groundwater are subject to sanctions. In addition, persons who fail to comply with the provisions of the Water Code and the rules applicable to the utilization of water facilities or who falsify data must be reported to the State authorities (Water Code, art. 139). They will be held responsible for their actions in accordance with the law of Kazakhstan (Water Code, art. 140).

2.9.8.2 Dispute Settlement

Water disputes are settled by negotiation between the interested parties, by the relevant administrative body, or by the courts (Water Code, art. 137).

2.10 Mexico

2.10.1 Statutory Framework

Article 27 of the 1917 Constitution of Mexico (as amended)[157] mandates the federal government to regulate the distribution of water, the extraction and utilization of groundwater, concessions, riparian rights, national reserves, and communal possession of water rights, and to establish government bodies for dealing with these issues.[158] The Constitution also imposes on the Federal Government the responsibility to protect the environment, including water resources.[159]

Pursuant to this mandate, the Federal Government has adopted a number of statutes. The most pertinent is the National Water Act of December 1992, as amended in 2004 (Water Act).[160] Other statutes relevant to the management of water are

- 1971 Law of Prevention and Control of Pollution;
- 1982 Law for Protection of the Environment;

---

[156] Water Code, arts. 50–53.

[157] Political Constitution of the United Mexican States (as amended to August 2, 2004), published in the *Official Journal of the Federation*, February 5, 1917.

[158] *See* Cecilia Tortajada, *Legal and Regulatory Regime for Water Management in Mexico and its Possible Use in Other Latin American Countries*, 24 Water Intl. 316 (1999).

[159] Constitution of 1917, arts. 25, 73, and 115.

[160] National Water Act (as amended to April 29, 2004), published in the *Official Journal of the Federation*, December 1, 1992. For an analysis of the 1992 Act, *see* Héctor Garduño Velasco, *Modernization of Water Legislation: The Mexican Experience*, in *Issues in Water Law Reform*, 67 FAO Legislative Studies 83 (FAO 1999).

- 1988 General Law on Ecological Equilibrium and Environmental Protection;
- 1992 Federal Law of the Sea; and
- 1992 Fishery Law.

2.10.2   Underlying Principles and Priorities

The Water Act is applicable to all national waters, whether surface water or groundwater (Water Act, art. 2). The Federal Government must approve a national water program that integrates specific regional, basin, State, and sectoral subprograms. The act also requires the creation of an inventory of national waters; the formulation of strategies and policies for regulating water use; and the implementation of water use programs that involve all relevant users and their organizations and all levels of government and that are based on the natural replenishment levels of water (Water Act, art. 15).[161]

Article 7 of the Water Act identifies water-related matters that are deemed to be in the public interest. They include the protection, conservation, and improvement of basins, aquifers, river beds, enclosed bodies of water, and other nationally owned water bodies; the use of water to generate electricity; restoring the hydrological balance between surface and groundwater; wastewater treatment facilities; the construction, operation, maintenance, and development of public waterworks and related services; establishment of irrigation districts and drainage units; flood prevention; monitoring of the quantity and quality of national waters; and effective efforts to modernize the domestic services of urban and public waters.

Article 7 *bis* adds into the law public interest considerations as a goal. To achieve this goal, the Federal Government decentralizes water resources management to the Commissions and the *Organismos de Cuenca* (Basin Organizations) at the State level. In addition, the prevention, conciliation, arbitration, mitigation, and solution of conflicts related to water are also considered to be in the public interest.

2.10.3   Regulation of Water Uses

2.10.3.1   Ownership of Water and Establishment of Water Rights

Article 27(5) of the Constitution of Mexico specifies that "national waters" are waters that are owned by the nation. Individuals and corporations can obtain the right to use national waters by obtaining a concession from the National Water

---

[161] *See* Fernando Gonzalez-Villareal & Héctor Garduño Valesco, *Water Resources Management and Planning in Mexico*, 10 Intl. J. Water Resources Dev. 239 (1994).

Commission, *Comisión Nacional del Agua* (the Commission, or CNA), through the *Organismos de Cuenca* in accordance with the rules and procedures established in the Water Act (Water Act, art. 20). State and municipal departments or agencies and Federal agencies can obtain the right to use water through a grant from the Commission (Water Act, art. 20). The Commission maintains a Public Registry of Water Rights in which it records all concessions and grants as well as final decisions of judicial and administrative tribunals concerning disputes of concessions, grants, and regulated zones and their status (Water Act, art. 30).[162]

The Water Act provides that a user can establish a right to use national waters for agricultural, fish farming, tourism, and other productive activities, provided the user has obtained a concession from the Commission in coordination with Mexico's *Secretaría de Agricultura, Ganadería, Desarrollo Rural, Pesca y Alimentación* (SAGARPA; Secretary of Agriculture) (Water Act, art. 82). In addition, surface water can be freely used "by manual means" for residential or stock-raising purposes, provided that these uses do not cause significant changes in the flow of the water or in its quality or quantity (Water Act, art. 17).

Groundwater can be freely extracted by artificial works unless the Federal Government in the public interest regulates their extraction and utilization (Water Act, art. 18).[163]

2.10.3.2   *Allocation of Right to Use Water*

Any legal or natural person can apply to the Commission for a concession, which may only be granted after a competitive bidding process (Water Act, art. 22), that gives the person the right to exploit, use, or develop the national water for the duration of the concession (Water Act, art. 25). The application should include information on the site from which the water will be drawn, the volume of water to be consumed, the use to which the water will be put, the period for which the concession is sought, and the waterworks, if any, that the applicant is planning to construct (Water Act, art. 21). In addition, the following documentation must be attached to the application: documents that accredit the ownership property or possession of the building from which the water will be extracted, disclosure of the environmental impact pursuant to the Law of Ecological Equilibrium and Environmental Protection, the construction project to be carried out, technical documents, and a map of the location of the site

---

[162] *See* Simas, *supra* n. 55, at 149.

[163] *See* Karin Kemper, *Groundwater Management in Mexico: Legal and Institutional Issues,* in *Groundwater: Legal and Policy Perspectives*, World Bank Technical Paper No. 456, 117 (Salman M. A. Salman, ed., World Bank 1999).

(Water Act, art. 21 *bis*). The Commission, which must respond to the applicant within 60 days, takes into account the availability of water in accordance with the water resource program; existing rights to use water; and restrictions on the right to use water from the identified water resource (Water Act, art. 22). In cases where there is not enough water for irrigation purposes, the water shall be distributed according to the regulations established by the irrigation district (Water Act, art. 69).

Concession holders and grantees have the right to exploit, use, or develop national waters in accordance with the terms of their concession or grant and to carry out the works necessary for exercising this right (Water Act, art. 28). In the case of corporate concession holders, these rights can include the right to manage or operate an irrigation system (Water Act, art. 51). In return they are required to comply with the provisions of the Water Act and the terms of their concession or grant, make the necessary payments, allow inspections by the Commission and/or personnel of the *Procuraduría Federal de Protección al Ambiente* (Federal Bureau of Environmental Protection—PROFEPA) and provide the necessary information to the Commission to verify compliance with the law and the terms of the concession or grant (Water Act, art. 29).

Concessions are granted for periods of between five and thirty years (Water Act, art. 24). The concessions should contain information similar to that contained in the application (Water Act, art. 23). Once the concession or grant has been issued, the concession holder or grantee, after notifying the Commission, can change the use to which it puts the water (Water Act, art. 25). The Commission shall allocate to states and municipalities national water for use in potable water and sewerage systems (Water Act, art. 44).

2.10.3.3   Transfer of Water Rights

Transfers of concessions or grants that involve merely changes of title holder must be made by application to the Commission for approval as well as incorporation in the Public Registry of Water Rights (Water Act, art. 33). However, the prior permission of the Commission is required if the transfer may affect the rights of third parties or can affect the conditions of the pertinent water basin (Water Act, art. 33). In this case, the rights of concession holders or grantees can only be assigned for specified causes and, in some cases, with substantiated justifications for the assignment (Water Act, art. 25).[164]

The right to use groundwater is usually transferred with the transfer of the ownership of the pertinent land but can be done separately (Water Act, art. 35).

---

[164] *See also* Water Act, arts. 33–37.

2.10.3.4 Loss of Right to Use Water

Concessions or grants can be terminated in one of three ways: (i) suspended, if the concession holder or grantee fails to make the payments required by law, refuses to allow required inspections, discharges waste waters, or does not comply with the terms of the concession or grant (Water Act, art. 29 *bis* 2); (ii) extinguished, if, *inter alia,* the holder dies, renounces the concession or grant, fails to utilize the rights granted under the concession for a period of two consecutive years, the competent authority declares the concession or grant invalid, the period of the concession or grant expires and is not extended, it is in the public interest, or by a ruling of the courts (Water Act, art. 29 *bis* 3); and (iii) revoked, if the holder uses a greater volume of water than is authorized; fails to pay the requisite fees; fails to comply with the provisions of the Water Act dealing with the exploitation, use, development, or preservation of the quality of national water; assigns the concession in violation of the terms of the Water Act; or harms the ecosystem (Water Act, art. 29 *bis* 3). The rights of concession holders or grantees can only be assigned for specified causes and, in some cases, with substantiated justifications for the assignment (Water Act, art. 25).[165]

2.10.4 Protection of Water

The Commission is responsible for promoting and, where pertinent, building and operating the Federal infrastructure and services needed to conserve and improve the quality of national waters (Water Act, art. 86). It is also in charge of developing comprehensive programs for protecting national waters and monitoring their implementation. The Commission must keep up to date the Information System about national water in coordination with the National Information Systems (NIS) concerning quality, quantity, use, and conservation of national waters and give all support necessary to the Federal Bureau of Environmental Protection (Water Act, art. 86).[166] These programs should include regulation of the discharge of wastewater and sewerage (Water Act, arts. 88–95).

The Commission, with the aid of the Basin Organizations, is required to promote among the population, authorities, and mass media the use, culture, and availability of water of the country and its regions. To this end, the Commission will, *inter alia,* coordinate with Federal and State educational authorities to have information

---

[165] *See id.*

[166] *See* Cecilia Tortajada, *Environmental Impact Assessment of Water Projects in Mexico,* 16 Intl. J. Water Resources Dev. 73 (2000). *See also* Cecilia Tortajada, *Water and Environment Policies and Institutions in Mexico,* in *Water Policies and Institutions in Latin America,* Water Resources Management Series 126 (Cecilia Tortajada, Benedito P. F. Braga, Asit K. Biswas & Luis E. Garcia, eds., Oxford Univ. Press 2003).

on water, especially with respect to availability, incorporated into academic programs; initiate regular advertising campaigns; and promote the rational use and conservation of water as a matter of national security (Water Act, art. 84 *bis*).

2.10.5 Regulation of Water Infrastructure

The concession or grant of the right to exploit, use, or develop water can also authorize the construction of the works necessary for this purpose (Water Act, art. 23). Permits may be required from the Commission in order to construct these works (Water Act, art. 98), which may be carried out by the public or the private sector. In this regard, article 7 of the Water Act states that it is in the public interest to promote private participation in the financing, construction, and operation of federal water infrastructure, and, pursuant to article 108, in the supply of water and electricity.[167]

The Commission is responsible for building and operating the federal water infrastructure needed to preserve, conserve, and improve water quality in watersheds and aquifers (Water Act, arts. 86 & 101). However, the Federal Executive Branch decides if water infrastructure for the hydroelectric system is to be built by the Commission or the Federal Electricity Commission (Water Act, art. 79). In the latter case, both Commissions cooperate in administering the infrastructure (Water Act, art. 113).

Water users and their associations can build whatever water infrastructure they require and are responsible for the operation and management of these structures (Water Act, art. 97). Permits from the Commission may be required in order to construct these works (Water Act, art. 98).

The Federal Executive Branch, through the Commission, is responsible for the development necessary for public constructions. Public constructions are those that expand and improve the knowledge of the availability of water resources; guarantee such availability and the use of the waters in the basins; and control and serve for the defense and protection of national waters, as well as those that are necessary to prevent floods, droughts, and other exceptional situations; allow the supply, purification, and desalination of water when the execution affects two or more States; have strategic importance in a hydrologic region by their dimensions or cost of investment; and are necessary for the execution of national plans or programs related to water (Water Act, art. 96 *bis* 2).

2.10.6 Institutional Arrangements

The Federal Executive Branch, acting through the Secretary of the Environment and Natural Resources (Water Act, art. 8), promotes coordination of all actions

---

[167] *See also* Water Act, arts. 103–108.

dealing with national waters with the governments of federative entities and municipalities; promotes the involvement of users and private parties in the construction and administration of waterworks and services; and signs international instruments that according to the law are within the competence of the office, in coordination with the Secretary of Foreign Affairs (Water Act, art. 8). It is also responsible for approving the national water program developed by the Commission (Water Act, art. 15).

The Commission, which is under the Secretariat of the Environment and Natural Resources, is headed by a Director General, who is appointed by the Federal Executive (Water Act, art. 12). It has the authority to formulate, revise, and oversee the implementation of the national water plan and to promote the development of water supply and sewerage systems (Water Act, art. 9). It is also responsible,[168] *inter alia,* for safeguarding national water resources, including their quality; issuing concessions, grants, and permits; promoting the efficient use of water; collecting all water-related fees and taxes; developing standards for water; concluding agreements with foreign organizations or institutions and compatible organizations in order to attain technical cooperation; keeping up to date and making public periodically the inventory of national waters; integrating into the NIS the quantity, quality, uses, and conservation of the water; and monitoring compliance with the Water Act.[169] It is also responsible for administering national properties that are adjacent to national waters and the water-related infrastructure on this land (Water Act, arts. 113–18). The Commission, in conjunction with State and municipal governments and individuals and corporations, is involved in flood prevention activities (Water Act, arts. 83 & 84). It also works with the Federal Electricity Commission in developing the program for water that can be used for hydroelectric purposes (Water Act, art. 78).

The Technical Council of the Commission is composed of the Federal Controller and the Secretaries of Finance and Public Credit, Social Development, Energy, Economy, Health, and Agriculture and Water Resources; it is chaired by the Secretary of Environment and Natural Resources (Water Act, art. 10). This Council is empowered, *inter alia,* to review all policies and programs related to national waters, review the programs and budgets of the Commission, and approve the establishment of basin councils (Water Act, art. 11).

2.10.6.1   River Basin Authorities

The Water Act states, in article 9, that the Commission is responsible for managing water basins. For this purpose, it is required, following a decision of its

---

[168] This responsibility is shared with the PROFEPA.

[169] *See* Water Act, art. 9.

Technical Council, to establish water basin councils (Water Act, art. 13). These basin councils liaise with all applicable authorities and users of water in formulating and implementing programs for the use and management of the water basin (Water Act, Art. 13).

2.10.6.2   Water Users' Associations

The Commission accredits, promotes, and supports organizations of water users.[170] The purpose of these organizations is to improve the development of water resources and the preservation and control of water quality (Water Act, art. 14).[171] They are also involved at the State, regional, and basin level in the management and use of national water resources (Water Act, art. 14 *bis*).

The Federal Government establishes irrigation districts that include all surface and groundwater and related storage facilities and other works in the designated area (Water Act, arts. 71–73).[172] These facilities are managed, operated, and maintained by their users or by persons designated by the users, pursuant to concessions from the Commission (Water Act, art. 65). In addition, each irrigation district has a water committee that proposes regulations for the irrigation district and oversees compliance with the regulations (Water Act, art. 66).

2.10.6.3   Advisory Committees

The Consultative Council of Water is an independent consultative organ comprising people from the private and social sector, academics dealing with issues of water and its management and solutions, and people of altruistic vocation with considerable recognition and respect (Water Act, art. 14 *bis* 1).

The Consultative Council of Water, at the request of the Federal Executive, can advise, recommend, analyze, and evaluate with respect to the national priority or strategic problems related to the exploitation, use, and restoration of the water resources, as well as to conclude international treaties related to these matters. In addition, the Council itself can carry out the recommendations, analysis, and

---

[170] *See* Cecilia M. Gorriz, Ashok Subramanian & José Simas, *Irrigation Management Transfer in Mexico: Process and Progress*, World Bank Technical Paper No. 292 (World Bank 1995). This publication includes, as Annex 1, an English translation of the National Water Act in Mexico of 1992.

[171] For model bylaws and concession agreements in Mexico, see Salman M. A. Salman, *The Legal Framework for Water Users' Associations—A Comparative Study*, World Bank Technical Paper No. 360, 57 & 87 (World Bank 1997).

[172] *See* Sam H. Johnson III, *Irrigation Management Transfer: Decentralizing Public Irrigation in Mexico*, 22 Water Intl. 159 (1997). *See also* Vincente Guerrero Reynoso & Francisco García León, *Proposal for the Decentralization of Water Management in Mexico by Means of Basin Councils*, in Tortajada *et al.* (eds.), *supra* n. 166.

evaluations that are deemed relevant to the integrated management of water resources (Water Act, art. 14 *bis* 1).

Article 12 *bis* 2 establishes a Consulting Committee for each of the basins. The powers of those committees are set forth in article 12 *bis* 3.

2.10.7   Financial Arrangements

The users of water in irrigation districts must pay fees for irrigation services. These fees are approved by the Commission and at a minimum must cover the cost of managing and operating the services and of conserving and maintaining the works associated with the irrigation services (Water Act, art. 68). Other users of water, including groundwater, are required to pay the fees that are set out in the Federal Payments Act and administered by the Commission (Water Act, art. 112).[173] Concession holders and grantees are required to make the payments required under current tax legislation (Water Act, art. 29).

Pursuant to article 109 of the Water Act, the public investment in federal waterworks must be recovered by setting fees that are paid by the persons who directly benefit from the waterworks. These fees should be determined on the basis of the cost of the services provided by these waterworks, "adjusted for economic efficiency" and with due consideration for the financial condition of the service provider (Water Act, art. 110).

The Water Act makes some references to the possible role of the private sector in water services. Article 7 of the Water Act states, for instance, that it is in the public interest to promote private-sector participation in the financing, construction, and operation of federal water infrastructure, as well as in the supply of water and electricity.

2.10.8   Enforcement of Regulations and Dispute Settlement

2.10.8.1   *Enforcement of Regulations*

The Commission has the authority to sanction such infractions as unauthorized or noncompliant discharges of wastewater; unauthorized or noncompliant uses of water; failure to maintain or monitor waterworks in conformity with requirements and standards; obstruction of inspections or examinations by the Commission under the terms of the Water Act and the regulations of the Commission; and failure to comply with the requirements of concessions, grants, or permits (Water Act, art. 119). These infractions, in addition to potentially leading to the

---

[173] *See* Karin E. Kemper & Douglas Olson, *Water Pricing: The Dynamics of Institutional Change in Mexico and Ceará, Brazil*, in Dinar (ed.), *supra* n. 62, at 339.

suspension or termination of concessions and grants, can also lead to fines or the forfeiture of waterworks (Water Act, arts. 120–23).

The Federal Bureau of Environment Protection has the power to formulate complaints and apply sanctions, to embody and to decide the procedures and administrative remedies, and to promote the reparation of environmental damage in the ecosystems associated with water (Water Act, art. 14 *bis* 4).

2.10.8.2   Dispute Settlement

The Commission is empowered to mediate and, if requested by users, to arbitrate disputes related to water (Water Act, art. 9). The Commission has an Internal Auditor, the head of the Internal Audit body, who hears complaints, performs audits, and has other responsibilities designated by the law (Water Act, art. 11 *bis*).[174]

Actions and final decisions of the Commission that cause injury to private persons can be appealed to the head of the Commission (Water Act, art. 124).

2.11   Morocco

2.11.1   Statutory Framework

Water in Morocco is governed by the Water Law of 1995, Law No. 10-95 (Water Law). This law superseded a series of scattered legal instruments that had been updated in stages and at different times.[175]

2.11.2   Underlying Principles and Priorities

The Water Law is based on a number of fundamental principles.[176] Among them are that all water resources belong to the public domain except for "recognized and vested rights"; water use development and water distribution plans are to be based on broad consultation between water users and public authorities; water uses likely to pollute water resources are to be regulated; and agricultural value is to be increased through improvements in harnessing and utilizing water in agriculture.[177] In addition, the preamble to the Water Law states that the authorities will develop new water utilization rules that are "more closely tailored to the

---

[174] For a case study on disputes on groundwater *see* Gro Volkmar Dyrnes & Arild Vatn, *Who Owns the Water? A Study of a Water Conflict in the Valley of Ixtlahuaca, Mexico*, 7 Water Policy 295 (2005).

[175] Water Law, Preamble.

[176] For an overview of water management in Morocco, *see* The Morocco Water Resources Management Project, 1998 (P005521), Staff Appraisal Report (Report No. 15760-MOR), dated January 28, 1998, at 5.

[177] *See supra* n. 175.

economic and social conditions of modern Morocco, and will lay the bases for efficient water management in the future." These rules are discussed in the next section.

Based on these principles, the objectives of the Water Law include, *inter alia,* coherent and flexible planning of water use at both the catchment and national levels; optimum mobilization and rational management of all water resources, taking into account the priorities set by the national water plan; protection and conservation of public water resources; and water administration that involves both public authorities and water users in all water-related decision making. [178]

The Water Law does not establish any particular priority for water uses except, as stated in article 86 of the Water Law, in cases of shortage. Article 86 deals with prioritization of water uses in cases of water shortage due to overutilization or exceptional events. It provides that in such cases the State shall declare a water shortage and enact regulations to deal with it. These regulations must give the highest priority to providing potable water for local population centers and for the watering of livestock. In addition, the administration may declare certain areas to be "domestic water consumption zones," in which all water drawn must be used exclusively to supply population centers and for livestock watering.

2.11.3 Regulation of Water Uses

2.11.3.1 Ownership of Water and Establishment of Water Rights

Water is a public asset (Water Law, art. 1) and cannot be the object of private appropriation unless the rights of ownership or usufruct were properly acquired under previous laws (Water Law, art. 6).[179] These acquired rights cannot be modified except through a process of expropriation for public purposes.[180] However, they will be taken into account and subjected to all provisions related to water uses as defined in the National Water Plan and follow-up Master Plans for integrated water resources development, as defined in Chapter IV of the Water Law.[181]

For purposes of the Water Law (Water Law, art. 2),[182] the public water domain consists of all water tables, whether surface or underground; lakes, ponds, and

---

[178] *See id.*

[179] These laws are the *Dahir* (Royal Decree) of July 1, 1914, related to eminent domain and the *Dahir* (Royal Decree) of August 1, 1925, related to the water regime.

[180] Such purposes are dealt with under Law 7-81 on Expropriation.

[181] Water Law, art. 8, and ch. IV, arts. 13–14.

[182] *See also* Water Law, arts. 3–5.

other surface water resources; wells built for public use; canals built for navigation, irrigation, and drainage; waterworks assigned for public use; permanent or
nonpermanent watercourses and their sources; banks up to the levels attained by
floodwaters; and land parcels that, "although not permanently covered by water,
do not lend themselves to agricultural use in ordinary years" (Water Law,
art. 2(b)).

While landowners have the right to use rainwater falling on their land, article
25 states that the administration will establish regulations to govern the artificial
collection of such rainwater.

2.11.3.2 *Allocation of Right to Use Water*

The Water Law provides that the administration shall draw up an integrated water
resources development master plan for each catchment basin or group of catchment basins. The main purpose of these plans is to manage the basin's water
resources so as to ensure satisfaction in terms of "both quantity and quality of the
present and future water needs of the basin's various water users" (Water Law,
art. 16). Each plan shall deal, *inter alia,* with the following issues: allocating water
to the various uses that are made of the water resources in the basin, the priority
rankings to be applied in sharing the water among these usages, and the conditions
to be attached to the usage in order to optimize use of the water resource and protect its quality (Water Law, art. 16). In addition to the basin-level plan, the administration is required to draw up a national water plan that establishes, *inter alia,*
national priorities with respect to water harnessing and utilization and the support
measures necessary for implementation of the water plan (Water Law, art. 19).

Parties wishing to use water in the public water domain are required to obtain
authorizations or concessions (Water Law, art. 36). Authorizations are applicable
to, *inter alia,* all prospecting projects related to the tapping of both surface and
groundwater, the construction of wells that are deeper than a specified level,
works for utilizing public domain water, and plans for taking water from underground sources or watercourses (Water Law, art. 38). Concessions are required,
inter alia, for the development of mineral and thermal springs, construction of
waterworks on public domain water, water intakes from the water table, and
watercourses or canals for generating hydropower (Water Law, art. 41)[183] and for
irrigation (Water Law, art. 43).

---

[183] Water Law, art. 42, specifies some of the issues that must be addressed in the concession, which are:
- the water volume forming the subject of the concession;
- the method of utilization of the water;
- any special charges and obligations of the concession-holder;
- the fee to be paid by the concession-holder;

Public water domain authorizations and concessions are granted after a public inquiry and the payment of a fee and pursuant to forms of approval established by regulation (Water Law, art. 36.1). The public inquiry is conducted by a special commission that is responsible for gathering the claims of third parties following public notification of the inquiry (Water Law, art. 36.2). The basin authority decides on the application after consulting with the inquiry commission (Water Law, art. 36) and establishes the terms of the permits (Water Law, art. 39).

Chapter IX of the Water Law deals with the allocation of water resources for agricultural use (Water Law, arts. 79–85). These articles provide that any natural or juridical persons wishing to use water for agricultural purposes must obtain an authorization from the relevant Agency basin authority, which will not issue permits for uses that may result in degradation of water resources or arable soils (Water Law, art. 80). Municipalities that plan to construct or modify water systems require an authorization from the national administration (Water Law, art. 61).[184]

2.11.3.3   Transfer of Water Rights

Water permits issued for irrigation purposes are granted for a specific land holding and cannot be used for other holdings without a new permit (Water Law, art. 40). However, the permit shall pass automatically with the transfer of the land to a new landowner (Water Law, art. 40). Concessions can also be transferred to a new owner (Water Law, art. 43). Similarly, article 11 states that agricultural land that uses water for irrigation where the water rights belong to a third party can only be leased or transferred if the acquirer of the land obtains a contract to use the water from the third-party owner of those water rights.

Article 10 provides that the holders of vested rights who do not fully use these rights are required to transfer them to natural or juridical persons that will use them for the benefit of the agricultural lands that they own.

- the duration of the concession, which shall not exceed 50 years;
- the nature of the works comprising the various segments of the planned installations and developments, and the timetable for executing them;
- the measures to be taken by the concession-holder to avoid degradation of the quality of the water;
- where appropriate, the circumstances under which the concessional water intake volume can be altered or reduced, and the compensation to which alteration or reduction of such flow may give rise; and
- where appropriate, the terms of buy-back, withdrawal, or forfeiture of the concession and of return of the works to the government at the end of the concession.

[184] For a general discussion of this issue, *see* R. Maria Saleth & Ariel Dinar, *Water Challenge and Institutional Response—A Cross Country Perspective*, World Bank Policy Research Working Paper 2045, 13 (World Bank 1999).

2.11.3.4 Loss of Right to Use Water

The catchment basin authority may at any time restrict, amend, or revoke permits it has issued for reasons of public interest because the terms of the permit have not been complied with, the permit has not been utilized, or the permit is assigned or transferred without the authority's agreement (Water Law, art. 39). The authority's action is subject to notice to the permit holder and, in the case of actions based on the public interest, requires the payment of compensation for damages suffered by the permit holder as a direct result of the authority's action (Water Law, art. 39).

Water concessions may be forfeited or revised automatically and without compensation if the water is used outside the specified area or for purposes other than those permitted by the law (Water Law, art. 43), or if the concession holder fails to comply with the terms of the concession or to utilize the concession within a stipulated period of time (Water Law, art. 45). Owners of duly recognized vested water rights cannot be deprived of these rights except through expropriation proceedings (Water Law, arts. 8 & 46).

2.11.4 Protection of Water

Pursuant to article 52 of the Water Law, the catchment basin authority can prohibit or regulate the direct or indirect deposit of any materials capable of modifying the physical characteristics of the water resource into any water resource within its jurisdiction. To further ensure the safety of water for human consumption, the producers and distributors of such water are required, under article 66, to permanently monitor its quality and to submit the water periodically to specially approved laboratories for analysis. The Water Law requires them to ensure that water for human consumption is potable and prohibits the sale of nonpotable water for human consumption.[185] In addition, it establishes rules applicable to the use of natural waters for therapeutic purposes.[186]

The Water Law also seeks to conserve water for irrigation. Article 82 provides that the authorities can order the alteration of irrigation systems in order to realize water savings and make fuller use of water resources. They may also prescribe measures to combat pollution. The Water Law provides that the authorities can delineate zones known as "safeguard perimeters" in which the exploitation of groundwater seems likely to endanger existing water resources (Water Law, art. 49). Within these zones, any exploitation of groundwater or construction or modification of wells requires prior authorization and the water can only be used for human consumption and livestock watering (Water Law, arts. 49–50).

---

[185] Water Law, arts. 58, 59, and 60.

[186] Water Law, chapter VIII (arts. 67–78).

Pursuant to article 54, the Water Law prohibits a number of activities that are likely to seriously pollute specified types of water resources. Examples are throwing dead animals into lakes or ponds or burying them near springs or wells; dumping waste water or solid waste into wells, watering points, or washing sites; or burying waste materials capable of polluting groundwater by infiltration or surface water by runoff. Catchment basin authorities are required, under article 56, to carry out periodic investigations of the degree of pollution of the surface and groundwater under their jurisdiction. The scope of the investigation is determined by regulations issued by the authorities.

Any construction or modification of a water system designed to serve the needs of a municipality shall require prior authorization in order to enable the authorities to control the quality of the water (Water Law, art. 61). In addition, article 63 provides that the authorities can establish protection zones that are designed to protect the sources of water used for human consumption.[187]

2.11.5   Regulation of Water Infrastructure

The Water Law prohibits any person or entity from placing within the boundaries of public water resources any obstacles to navigation and free circulation of water, and from placing any objects in the water resource that are likely to clutter up or foster silting of the bed of a watercourse (Water Law, art. 12(a)(2)). In addition, the Water Law forbids any person from removing any plant, crop, or deposit from a hydraulic public domain; making any temporary or permanent changes to a watercourse; or undertaking works on watercourses or public water domain without prior authorization (Water Law, art. 12(b)).

2.11.6   Institutional Arrangements

The Water Law creates a High Council on Water and Climate (*Conseil Supérieur de l'Eau et du Climat*) that is responsible for formulating the guidelines for national water and climate policy (Water Law, art. 13). It is also responsible for advising the government on the acceptability of catchment basin integrated water resources development master plans (Water Law, art. 17). The High Council may also be assigned other responsibilities by the government (Water Law, art. 13). Half the membership of the High Council is composed of central government representatives and catchment basin authority representatives. The other half consists of representatives of water users, local authorities, and professional and scientific bodies (Water Law, art. 14).

---

[187] As will be discussed later, Yemen requires a special permit for use of water in such zones.

Each prefecture or province must establish a Prefecture or Provincial Water Commission (Commission). These Commissions are responsible for assisting the catchment basin authority in preparing the catchment basin integrated water resources development plan, supporting municipalities in designing water protection activities, and educating the public about the need to protect and preserve water resources (Water Law, art. 101). Half the membership of the Commission consists of representatives of the central government and the public establishments responsible for potable water production, hydroelectric power generation, and irrigation. The other half consists of the presidents of the prefecture or provincial assembly, the chamber of agriculture, the chamber of commerce, industry and services representatives, and representatives of municipal councils and ethnic communities (Water Law, art. 101).[188]

2.11.6.1   River Basin Authorities

The Catchment Basin Authorities (CBAs) are public entities with juridical personality and financial autonomy (Water Law, art. 20). A CBA is created for each catchment basin or group of basins. The responsibilities of the CBA include drawing up an integrated water resource development master plan for the basin; monitoring implementation of the plan; issuing public water domain usage authorizations and concessions; providing financial aid and technical assistance to public and private persons who seek to prevent pollution or to use public domain water resources; maintaining a register of recognized water users, water concessions, and authorizations; and building the necessary structures for flood prevention (Water Law, art. 20).

The CBA is administered by a management board that is chaired by the government authority responsible for water resources (Water Law, art. 21). The board has twenty-four to forty-eight members and is composed of one-third government representatives; one-quarter representatives of public bodies responsible for potable water production, hydroelectric power, and irrigation; and the remainder from chambers of agriculture, commerce and industry, local governments, ethnic communities, and associations of water users (Water Law, art. 21). The board is responsible for overseeing the activities of the CBA, drawing up its budget (Water Law, art. 23), and proposing fees for water usage to the governmental water resource authorities. It also approves all concession agreements and authorizations that the CBA enters into (Water Law, art. 21).

---

[188] *See* Mohammed Rachid Doukhali, *Water Institutional Reforms in Morocco*, 7 Water Policy 71 (2005).

2.11.6.2   *Water Users' Associations and Advisory Committees*

The Water Law does not explicitly address the issue of water users' associations. However, such associations do exist because they are represented on the management boards of the CBAs (Water Law, art. 21). The High Council and the provincial Commissions both perform some advisory functions.

2.11.7   Financial Arrangements

Any individual or juridical person who uses public domain water resources is required to pay a water use fee (Water Law, art. 37). The procedures for determining and collecting these fees are set by regulation. In addition, all concession and authorization holders are required to pay a fee for the concession or authorization.[189]

2.11.8   Enforcement of Regulations and Dispute Settlement

2.11.8.1   *Enforcement of Regulations*

The CBAs are authorized to amend, restrict, or revoke permits for reasons of public interest and because the permit holder fails to comply with the terms and conditions of the permit (Water Law, art. 39).

The responsibility for establishing violations of the Water Law and the regulations issued pursuant thereto rests with the officers of the criminal police force and with agents commissioned for this purpose by the administration and CBAs (Water Law, art. 104). These officers and agents have the authority to access waterworks on the terms described in the Code of Criminal Procedure, to require the owner or operator of the work to verify its specifications (Water Law, art. 105), and to take samples of water (Water Law, arts. 106–107). Persons found guilty of violations of the Water Law and its regulations can be fined and/or sentenced to imprisonment by a court of law (Water Law, arts. 110–22).

2.11.8.2   *Dispute Settlement*

The Water Law establishes no specific bodies for resolving disputes arising under it or any actions taken pursuant to it. It is to be assumed that disputes will be dealt with under the Civil Code.

---

[189] *See, for example,* Water Law, art. 39, on permit fees, and arts. 42 and 45, on concession fees.

2.12   Kingdom of Nepal

2.12.1   Statutory Framework

In the Kingdom of Nepal (Nepal) management of water resources is governed by the Water Resource Act, 2049 of September 15, 1992 (WRA).[190]

2.12.2   Underlying Principles and Priorities

The purpose of the WRA is to arrange for the "rational utilization, conservation, management and development" of surface water and groundwater resources in Nepal.[191] The WRA is also intended to establish legal arrangements for determining beneficial uses of water resources, preventing environmental damage, and keeping water resources free from pollution.[192]

The WRA establishes the following priorities for the use of water (in descending order): drinking water and domestic use; irrigation; agricultural uses, such as animal husbandry and fisheries; hydroelectricity; cottage industry, industrial enterprises, and mining; navigation; recreational uses; and other uses (WRA, art. 7).

2.12.3   Regulation of Water Uses

2.12.3.1   Ownership of Water and Establishment of Water Rights

The ownership of the water resources available in Nepal is vested in the Kingdom of Nepal (WRA, art. 1). In general, no person is entitled to use water resources without obtaining a license, which is issued pursuant to the requirements of the WRA (art. 4). However, pursuant to article 4 of the WRA, licenses are not required for the following uses of water resources: drinking and other domestic uses on an individual or collective basis; irrigation of one's own land on an individual or collective basis; running water mills or water grinders as a cottage industry; prescribed uses that are confined to land by the owner of that piece of land; and use of a boat for local transportation.

Any individual or corporate body that wishes to use a water resource must submit an application to the "prescribed officer or authority" along with economic, technical, and environmental studies and other "prescribed particulars" (WRA,

---

[190] Published in the *Nepal Gazette*, December 17, 1992 (2049/9/2).

[191] WRA Preamble.

[192] *See id.*

art. 8). Once the prescribed officer or authority receives the application, it shall conduct the "necessary inquiry" and issue a license to use the water within 120 days (WRA, art. 8). The license shall include the terms on which the applicant can use the water (WRA, art. 8). Any person or corporate body that uses water for beneficial purposes shall do so without causing damage to others (WRA, art. 4).

The WRA does not preclude the government from utilizing and developing water resources on its own (WRA, art. 10). For these purposes, the government is free to acquire water resources and the land, building, equipment, and structures relating thereto from any person, provided the government pays compensation for what it takes (WRA, art. 10).

2.12.3.2   Allocation of Right to Use Water

Notwithstanding the terms of the WRA, the government may enter into a contract with any national or foreign company, corporate body, or person to develop, utilize, and extend the services of any water resource on such terms and conditions as are laid out in the contract (WRA, art. 12).

The license to use water may require that the services generated by the use of the water be made available to any person on the basis of mutually acceptable terms and conditions, including the payment of a charge for the services rendered (WRA, art. 13).[193]

2.12.3.3   Transfer of Water Rights

A license holder can only transfer the license with the approval of the "prescribed officer of authority" (WRA, art. 8). The government may transfer ownership of any water resource projects that it has constructed to water users' associations (WRA, art. 11). The recipient user association will then operate the project as if it had been granted a license under the WRA (WRA, art. 11). Similarly the government can make water services that it generates available to other persons on the payment of a fee (WRA, art. 13).

2.12.3.4   Loss of Right to Use Water

Consumers can lose their access to water services if they fail to pay the charges for these services, if they misuse the services, or if they act in contravention of the terms and conditions on which the services are offered (WRA, art. 14).

---

[193] For discussion of water rights in Nepal, *see* Rajendra Pradhan, Franz von Benda-Beckmann, Keebat von-Benda-Beckmann, H. L. J. Spiertz, Shantam S. Khadga & K. Azharul Haq, *Water Rights, Conflict and Policy* (Intl. Irrigation Mgmt. 1997).

Licensees can lose their licenses if they perform any act that contravenes the WRA or that fails to comply with instructions from the prescribed authority to make improvements to the water resources or to the applicable water infrastructure (WRA, art. 21).

2.12.4   Protection of Water

The government, by notification in the official government gazette, may fix quality standards for water resources (WRA, art. 18). It may also prescribe the "pollution tolerance limit" for water resources (WRA, art. 19). The WRA prohibits the placing of any waste, poison, chemical, or other toxicants in a water resource if this would exceed the pollution tolerance limit for that water resource (WRA, art. 19). Article 20 of the WRA states that water resources must be used in a manner that will ensure that there is no "substantial adverse effect" on the environment by way of soil erosion, flood, landslide, or similar causes.

2.12.5   Regulation of Water Infrastructure

The licensing requirements relating to projects for the generation of hydroelectric power are governed by existing laws, but the utilization of water resources for this purpose requires a license issued pursuant to the provisions of the WRA (art. 9). The government, on the request of a licensee or on its own initiative, may make arrangements for the security of any structure related to the use of water resources (WRA, art. 17). The licensee must pay for any security arrangement that is established at its request (WRA, art. 17).

2.12.6   Institutional Arrangements

The government, pursuant to article 24, can make rules relating to such matters as the use of water, the conservation of water, the conservation of the environment, the fees related to the use of water, the prevention of pollution of water resources, and other matters relating to the development and utilization of water resources.[194] Although not specifically mentioned in the WRA, the Ministry of Water Resources in Nepal has responsibilities over those and other issues related to water resources management.

2.12.6.1   River Basin Authorities and Advisory Committees

There is no information in the Water Resources Act on river basin or catchment management authorities or advisory committees.

---

[194] *See* Sudhindra Sharma, *Foreign Aid and Institutional Plurality: The Domestic Water Sector in Nepal,* 16 Intl. J. Water Resources Dev. 119 (2000).

2.12.6.2   Water Users' Associations

Any persons who wish to use water resources for collective benefits can form a Water Users' Association, provided it is registered in accordance with the requirements of the WRA (WRA, art. 5). Water Users' Associations are autonomous corporate bodies with the power to use, sell, and arrange both movable and immovable property (WRA, art. 6).[195]

2.12.7   Financial Arrangements

The holder of a license to use water is required to pay a charge or annual fee to the government (WRA, art. 8). The government and other license holders who generate services out of their use of water can make these services available to others for a fee (WRA, arts. 13 & 22).

2.12.8   Enforcement of Regulations and Dispute Settlement

2.12.8.1   Enforcement of Regulations

Employees of the government can enter the premises of licensees by giving prior notice to the concerned person, or without notice if there is reasonable ground to suspect that the water resources are being used without authority or are being misused on the premises (WRA, art. 15). The authorities can examine, or cause the examination of, a water resource to determine if the resource has been polluted or if the quality standard has been maintained (WRA, art. 19). The prescribed authority can impose fines or terms of imprisonment on any person who violates the WRA or the rules developed thereunder.

2.12.8.2   Dispute Settlement

If a dispute arises about the utilization of water, "the prescribed committee" shall resolve the dispute on the basis of the statutorily established priorities for water use and the beneficial use made of the water resource and by conducting whatever other inquiries are necessary in order to resolve the dispute (WRA, art. 7). Any person who is dissatisfied with a decision dealing with granting compensation or cancellation of a license or other sanctions can appeal the decision to the applicable appellate court (WRA, art. 23).

---

[195] For an overview of the role and responsibilities of water users' associations in Nepal, *see* Andrew Allan, *The Legal Context of Water User Associations in Nepal—Analysis and Suggestions for Improvement,* 8 U. Denv. Water L. Rev. 547 (2005). *See also* Ohn Myint, *Experience with Groundwater Irrigation in Nepal,* in Salman (ed.), *supra* n. 163, at 125. *See also* Salman, *supra* n. 171.

2.13   Senegal

2.13.1   Statutory Framework

Water in Senegal is regulated by Law No. 81-13 of March 4, 1981 (Law 81-13).[196]

2.13.2   Underlying Principles and Priorities

The preamble to Law 81-13 states that water is owned by the State, which manages it for the public good. In so doing, the State must allocate water equitably among the various needs of society, guided by the public interest. The top priority for the State is providing water for human consumption (Law 81-13, art. 75). The next priority is water for growing food (Law 81-13, art. 76). This is followed by water for agricultural and agro-industrial purposes other than growing food, energy, mining, navigation, and tourism (Law 81-13, art. 76). In case of conflict between various uses, the priority should be determined by the economic needs of the local area (Law 81-13, art. 76), subject to change in case of extraordinary events, such as drought or flood (Law 81-13, art. 77).[197]

2.13.3   Regulation of Water Uses

2.13.3.1   Ownership of Water and Establishment of Water Rights

Water is owned by the State (Law 81-13, preamble).[198] The Minister of Water Affairs (*Ministre chargé de l'Hydraulique et de l'Assainissement*) (the Minister) is responsible for the management of water and water works. The Minister receives all requests to use water and issues all authorizations of water rights (Law 81-13, art. 7).

Any proposed water user requires authorization from the Minister (Law 81-13, arts. 2 & 8). This means that water usage requires a decree issued by the Minister granting rights to individuals or entities to use water according to the terms of the decree. This decree, which can be in the form of a concession, fixes the general rules for water uses. Some water uses require a preliminary authorization, except in the case of uses that utilize less than five cubic meters per hour (Law 81-13, art. 42).

---

[196] The Constitution of the Republic of Senegal, adopted in 2001, states in the Preamble that the people of Senegal shall have equal access to public services. Moreover, art. 8 of the Constitution enumerates a number of rights for the citizens of Senegal, including the right to a healthy environment.

[197] For challenges and emerging strategies in the water sector in Senegal *see* Senegal Water Sector Project, 1995 (P002346), Staff Appraisal Report (Report No. 14008-SE), dated June 12, 1995, at 11.

[198] Law 81-13, Preamble.

2.13.3.2   Allocation of Right to Use Water

Allocation of the right to use water is made by the Minister through decisions on whether or not to authorize the use of water. The authorizations are issued to individuals and public entities.[199] In making these authorizations, the officials must reconcile the interests of the different categories of water users, respect for the law, the rights of prior users, and protection of the nation's water resources (Law 81-13, art. 8). The authorizations stipulate the terms and conditions of the right to use water. These terms and conditions include the volume of water that can be taken on a daily and annual basis from the water resource; the duration of the authorization; the nature and location of any approved water work; the security and health measures that must be taken to guarantee conservation of the quality and quantity of the water; the maximum daily flow allowed during the dry season; and the measures needed to protect the rights of third parties (Law 81-13, art. 12).

2.13.3.3   Transfer of Water Rights

Water authorizations are issued to specific individuals and cannot be transferred to third parties except to the heirs of an authorized individual (Law 81-13, art. 14).

2.13.3.4   Loss of Right to Use Water

Water authorizations can be suspended or the quantity of usage reduced in order to protect the water resource from pollution.[200] They can also be revoked if the public interest requires such a revocation and in cases where the holder of the authorization fails to use, or misuses, such an authorization (Law 81-13, art. 21).

2.13.4   Protection of Water

The measures designed to prevent pollution of water are established by joint decrees of the Minister, the Minister of Health and Public Hygiene, and the Minister of Environment and Protection of Nature (Law 81-13, art. 50). These measures relate to the quality of water for human consumption; the usage of water for agricultural, hydropower, navigational, and recreational purposes; and the protection of specific categories of water resources, such as mangroves, deltas, and groundwater.[201] The Minister also issues decrees that regulate the use

---

[199] Law 81-13, arts. 14, 24, and 27.

[200] Law 81-13, art. 17, and chapter IV, section 1 (arts. 78–81).

[201] Law 81-13, arts. 47, 51, and 52–63.

of water in connection with the exploitation of other natural resources, such as forests (Law 81-13, art. 74).

2.13.5 Regulation of Water Infrastructure

Pursuant to the power to authorize all usages of water, the Minister can also authorize all water works (Law 81-13, art. 7).

2.13.6 Institutional Arrangements

The Minister is responsible for the conservation and management of all water and all water works (Law 81-13, art. 7). He or she is responsible for issuing all regulations, authorizations, and concessions relating to the usage, conservation, and protection of water. In some areas, such as conservation and protection of the quality of water and the use of water for human consumption, the Minister cooperates with the Ministries of Public Health and of the Environment (Law 81-13, art. 50). Similarly, the Minister may cooperate with ministries in charge of specific sectors when formulating regulations or issuing authorizations with regard to activities in a given sector (Law 81-13, art. 69). Law 81-13 does not explicitly establish any local water authorities or water users' associations.

2.13.7 Financial Arrangements

Law 81-13 provides that the regulatory authorities can charge fees for every action that alters the quality of water (Law 81-13, arts. 49 & 61).

2.13.8 Enforcement of Regulations and Dispute Settlement

2.13.8.1 Enforcement of Regulations

Public officials inspect water users to ensure compliance with their authorizations and to protect against unauthorized pollution. These inspectors come from a range of public agencies (Law 81-13, art. 89). The inspectors will report any infractions that they find to the authorities and these reports are provided to the contravening party (Law 81-13, art. 91). The inspectors' findings can result in sanctions that can include revocation of the water authorization (Law 81-13, arts. 21 & 107) and fines (Law 81-13, arts. 97–107).

2.13.8.2 Dispute Settlement

The Minister can initiate proceedings on any disputes or file any claims against any person violating the water Law before a competent judicial authority (Law 81-13, art. 94).

2.14   South Africa

2.14.1   Statutory Framework

The South African Constitution of 1996 (as amended to April 11, 2003) provides in section 27(1)(b) that "Everyone has the right to have access to . . . sufficient . . . water." Section 25(8) recognizes that, notwithstanding the requirements contained in section 25, no provision therein may impede the State from taking legislative measures to achieve water, land, and related reform in order to redress the results of past racial and gender discrimination. This is subject to the condition that any departure from the property rights provisions of section 25 must be in accordance with the Constitution's limitations clause (sec. 36(1)). Furthermore, section 24 of the Constitution enshrines the right to an environment that is not harmful to human health and well being and, *inter alia,* obliges the State to take reasonable legislative and other measures to prevent pollution and ecological degradation and to promote sustainable use and development of the country's natural resources. Pursuant to these requirements, water in South Africa is regulated mainly by

- The National Water Act, No. 36 of 1998 (NWA), as amended by the National Water Amendment Act, No. 45 of 1999;[202] and
- The Water Services Act, No. 108 of 1997 (WSA).

2.14.2   Underlying Principles and Priorities

The NWA's guiding principle is the sustainable and equitable management and use of South Africa's water resources.[203] Based on this principle, the purpose of the NWA is to ensure that the management and use of South Africa's water resources takes into account, *inter alia,* the basic human needs of present and future generations; redress for the results of past racial and gender discrimination; promotion of the efficient, sustainable, and beneficial use of water in the public interest; the need to protect aquatic ecosystems and their biological diversity; the facilitation of social and economic development; and the prevention of pollution and the degradation of water resources (NWA, art. 2).

The National Government, as custodian of the nation's water resources, acting through the Minister of Water Affairs and Forestry (the Minister), is vested with responsibility for implementing these principles and achieving the purposes of the statute (NWA, sec. 3(1)).

---

[202] The drafting of the Act was based on the *White Paper on a National Water Policy for South Africa* (Department of Water Affairs and Forestry 1997), which was prepared and finalized through an extensive consultative process.

[203] *See* Sandford D. Clark, *Reforming South Africa Water Legislation—Australian Examples,* in *Issues in Water Law Reform, supra* n. 160, at 1.

The WSA's main objective is to provide for the right of access to a basic water supply and the right to basic sanitation "necessary to secure sufficient water and an environment not harmful to human health or well-being" (WSA, sec. 2). The WSA stipulates that "everyone has a right of access to basic water supply and sanitation services" (WSA, sec. 3). "Basic water supply" is defined in the WSA as the prescribed minimum amount necessary to provide households, including informal households, with a reliable supply of water, in both quantitative and qualitative terms, to support life and personal hygiene (WSA, sec. 1(iii)). "Basic sanitation," as defined in section 1(iii) of the WSA, means the prescribed minimum standards of services necessary for safe and hygienic collection, removal, disposal, or purification of human excreta, domestic wastewater, and sewerage from households, including informal households.

2.14.3   Regulation of Water Uses

2.14.3.1   Ownership of Water and Establishment of Water Rights

The NWA in section 3 stipulates that the National Government is the "public trustee" of the nation's water.[204] As such, the Government, acting through the Minister, is responsible for ensuring that "water is allocated equitably and used beneficially in the public interest, while promoting environmental values" (NWA, sec. 3(2)). The NWA also gives the Government the power to regulate the use, flow, and control of all water in South Africa (NWA, sec. 3(3)).

Pursuant to part 3 of chapter 3, the NWA establishes a single Reserve that consists of two parts, a Basic Human Needs Reserve and an Ecological Reserve (NWA, secs. 16–18). The Reserve constitutes an amount of water that is set aside for these two purposes. The Basic Human Needs Reserve provides each South African with a minimum amount of water from the appropriate water resource with which to satisfy essential needs for drinking, food preparation, and personal hygiene.[205] The Ecological Reserve is designed to protect the aquatic ecosystems

---

[204] *See* Robyn Stein, *South Africa's New Democratic Water Legislation: National Government's Role as a Public Trustee in Dam Building and Management Activities*, 18 J. Energy & Nat. Resources L. 284 (2000).

[205] As indicated earlier, sec. 27(1)(b) of the South African Constitution states that "Everyone has the right to have access to . . . sufficient . . . water." It is noteworthy that the phrase "has the right to have access" is the same phrase used by the Recommendation of the Mar del Plata Water Conference held in 1977. For discussion of this issue *see supra* nn. 3 and 6. *See also* Anna R. Welch, *Obligations of State and Non-State Actors Regarding the Human Right to Water Under the South African Constitution,* 5 Sust. Dev. L. & Pol. 58 (2004).

of each water resource in the country. The Reserve is a noncompeting water user. The water in these Reserves cannot be allocated for any other purposes (NWA, sec. 16).[206]

Chapter 4 of the NWA deals with water uses.[207] The act defines "water use" for the purpose of the NWA to include, *inter alia,* taking water from a water resource; storing water; impeding, diverting, or reducing its flow; discharging waste into water or disposing of waste in a way that has a detrimental impact on water; removing groundwater; altering the characteristics of a watercourse; and using water for recreational purposes (NWA, sec. 21). The government allocates the right to use any water in excess of the Reserve pursuant to the terms of the NWA (NWA, sec. 16).

The WSA provides that everyone has a right of access to basic water supply and basic sanitation services (WSA, sec. 3(1)) and all water service institutions must take reasonable steps to realize this right (WSA, sec. 3(2)). It further provides that if water services institutions[208] are unable to meet the requirements of all their customers, they must give preference to the provision of basic water supply and basic sanitation to their customers (WSA, sec. 5).[209]

2.14.3.2 Allocation of Right to Use Water

Section 22 of the NWA stipulates that a person may only use water without a license in one of three cases: First, the intended use is included in schedule 1 of the NWA (NWA, sec. 22(1)(a)(i)). Schedule 1 addresses *de minimis* or reasonably insignificant water uses. It states that a person can use water without requiring prior authorization from the relevant authorities if the person is entitled to use water in or from a water resource on land owned or occupied by the person or to which he or she has lawful access for certain stipulated purposes. Permissible uses tend to relate to personal and domestic uses (NWA, sec. 4(1) & sch. 1).

Second, the intended use has already been approved as an existing lawful use (NWA, sec. 22(1)(a)(ii)). Section 32 of the NWA defines an existing lawful use as one that took place at any time during the two years prior to the date of the

---

[206] For further analysis of the concept of the Reserve *see* Falkenmark, *supra* n. 41, at 35.

[207] Chapter 4 of the NWA (secs. 21–55) deals with the regulation of water use. In addition to the issues described in the text, the chapter deals with the treatment of water uses that existed under the prior legislation, the Water Act, No. 54 of 1956: stream flow reduction activities, controlled activities, compulsory licenses, and how contraventions of water use authorizations are handled.

[208] Those water services institutions are described in the WSA as water services authorities and are comprised mainly of local municipalities (WSA, secs. 1(xxi) & (xx)).

[209] *See* David Stephenson & Bruce Randell, *Water Demand Theory and Projections in South Africa,* 28 Water Intl. 512 (2003). *See also* Goldblatt, *et al., supra* n. 11, at 59.

commencement of the NWA and that was authorized by any law in force prior to the NWA. This definition also extends to a water use that was a stream flow reduction activity that reduces the land for afforestation that has been established for commercial purposes or that the Minister has declared to be a stream flow activity (NWA, sec. 32(1)(b)(ii)); or a use that has been declared by the Minister to be a controlled activity, such as irrigation of land with waste water, power generation that alters the flow regime of a watercourse, intentional recharging of an aquifer with waste water, or any activity aimed at modifying atmospheric precipitation (NWA, secs. 32 (1)(b)(iii) & 37).

Third, the use is permissible in terms of a general authorization, which is tantamount to a "blanket license" issued in respect of a particular geographical area. The responsible authority (either the Minister or the catchment management authority to whom the Minister has assigned this responsibility) can issue a general authorization after public consultation and publication in the official Gazette (NWA, sec. 39). In issuing a general authorization, the responsible authority must take into account all relevant factors, including, but not limited to, existing lawful water uses, the socioeconomic impact of the water use, efficient and beneficial use of water in the public interest, the likely effect of the use on the water resource and other water users, and the quality of the water in the water resource that may be required for the Reserve and for meeting international obligations (NWA, sec. 27). This authorization can be restricted to a particular water resource, a particular category of people, or a defined geographic area or period of time. Within the scope of the general authorization, water can be used for any lawful purpose without the need to obtain a license.

Licenses are required for all other water uses. These licenses are issued following a formal application and approval process (NWA, secs. 40–42). This process includes submission of a formal application, publication of the application, and an opportunity for interested persons to file objections to the issuance of the license (NWA, sec. 41), and ends with a reasoned decision by the responsible authority (NWA, sec. 42). In addition, the approval process may include an opportunity for the applicant to make "representations on any aspect of the license application" (NWA, sec. 42(2)(d)). The licenses can be subject to conditions relating to water management and to the protection of the water resource and the rights and interests of other existing and potential water uses.[210] Licenses that are issued for a specified period of time can be renewed (NWA, sec. 52).

Specific licenses are also required for any new stream flow reduction activities or controlled activities as described above (that is, where the new activities in

---

[210] NWA, sec. 29. Sections 27–31 of the NWA enumerate factors that the Government should consider in deciding whether to issue general authorizations and licenses.

both categories have not been recognized as existing lawful water uses under the NWA).

In addition to licenses issued following application and approval, the statute provides for the issuance of compulsory licenses.[211] It is only under the NWA requirements for compulsory licenses that existing lawful water uses may be significantly reduced or extinguished, in which event the NWA makes provision for the payment of compensation under section 22(6). Section 43 of the NWA stipulates that the responsible authority may require people to apply for a license to use one or more water resources if it is desirable that water use in respect of those resources be licensed in order to achieve a fair allocation of water from a water resource that is under stress or when it is necessary to achieve equity in the allocation of water use. The resulting proposed allocation of the water resource among all the applicants must indicate, *inter alia,* the quantity of water to be assigned to the Reserve, to meet the requirement of existing licenses, to each applicant to whom water should be issued to redress the effects of past racial and gender discrimination, and to address other socioeconomic and environmental considerations (NWA, sec. 45). The responsible authority is required to publish the proposed allocation and to invite written comments on it (NWA, sec. 45(4)). The authority must consider the comments it receives before issuing the final allocation schedule (NWA, secs. 46 & 47).

The WSA stipulates that no person can use water from a source other than a water service provider nominated by the water services authority having jurisdiction in the area in question (WSA, secs. 6 & 7). All water service providers must be approved by the municipality, district, or rural council having jurisdiction in the area in question.[212]

2.14.3.3   Transfer of Water Rights

The NWA allows some owners of water rights to change the purpose for which they use the water in limited circumstances. It provides that a water management institution, upon the request of a person authorized to use water for irrigation, may authorize the requester to use the water for another purpose or on another property in the vicinity for the same purpose on a temporary basis (NWA, sec. 25).

---

[211] NWA, chapter 4, secs. 43–48.

[212] WSA, sec. 22. Section 1(xx) defines a "water services authority" as "any municipality, including a district or rural council as defined in the Local Government Transition Act, 1993 (Act No. 209 of 1993), responsible for ensuring access to water services."

The statute refers to "successors-in-title" to licensees, indicating that it is possible for licensees to transfer their rights to use water to a third party (NWA, sec. 25). In fact, the statute does provide that a license holder can formally apply to amend a license in order to change the terms of the license, including changing the identity of the licensee. The responsible authority must ensure that any such amendment shall not have a significant detrimental impact on water resources and the interests of any other person unless such person has consented thereto (NWA, secs. 50 & 52).

2.14.3.4   Loss of Right to Use Water

There are two situations in which rights to use water can be lost. First, a responsible authority may, by notice, suspend or withdraw the entitlement of any person to use water if that person fails to comply with any of the terms of a license or the conditions of an entitlement to use water or with the provisions of the NWA (NWA, sec. 54). Second, a licensee can surrender a license (NWA, sec. 55). The responsible authority must accept the surrender and cancel the license "unless there is a good reason not to do so" (NWA, sec. 55(1)).

The WSA defines a member of a class of "water service intermediaries" as any person who is required to provide water services to another pursuant to obligations in which "the obligation to provide water services is incidental to the main object of the contract" (WSA, sec. 1(xxii)). If these intermediaries fail to provide the services they are required to provide, the water services authority can take over or assign to another entity the functions to be performed by the intermediary (WSA, sec. 26).

2.14.4   Protection of Water

The scheme for protection of water established in the NWA seeks to ensure integrated and comprehensive protection of all water resources (NWA, sec. 26). Consequently, it deals with the use, development, management, and control of water. In pursuance of this objective the NWA requires the Minister to establish a classification system for water resources (NWA, sec. 12).[213] Further, the Minister is required to establish for each class of water resource a procedure for determining the Reserve for the resource.[214] In addition, the Minister must establish objectives for protecting the quality of the water. These should relate to, *inter alia,* instream flow, water level, presence and concentration of particular substances in the water, characteristics of the instream and riparian habitat and

---

[213] This section does not provide any guidance on criteria that the Minister should consider in developing the water classifications.

[214] *See supra* nn. 205 and 206

aquatic biota, and instream and land-based activities that could affect the water resource (NWA, sec. 13(3)).

The NWA also deals with pollution prevention, particularly in the situation where the pollution of a water resource occurs or might occur as a result of activities on land. It stipulates that the person who owns, controls, occupies, or uses the land is responsible for taking measures to prevent pollution of water resources (NWA, sec. 19). In the event that the person fails to do so, the relevant catchment management agency[215] may take the measures it deems necessary to remedy the situation and recover the costs from the persons responsible for the pollution (NWA, sec. 19). The NWA imposes similar responsibilities on persons causing an emergency situation, such as the spillage of substances capable of causing water pollution (NWA, sec. 20). It also gives the catchment management agency similar powers (NWA, sec. 20). In addition, the NWA makes it an offence to negligently or intentionally pollute a water resource (NWA, sec. 151).

2.14.5 Regulation of Water Infrastructure

The NWA gives the government the power to establish and operate waterworks, such as dams, water transfer schemes, and flood attenuation works.[216] It requires the government to satisfy certain procedural requirements before establishing such works. These include preparation of an environmental impact assessment relating to the proposed work, publication of the proposal to construct the water work, and an invitation for written comments on the proposal.[217] In addition, the Minister must consider the comments received and the environmental impact assessment in finally approving the work (NWA, sec. 110).[218] The NWA also authorizes the government to make the water from such waterworks available for allocation in accordance with the terms of Chapter 4 of the NWA, which establishes the rules for use of water.

Section 115 stipulates that the Minister may "transfer, sell or otherwise dispose of any government waterworks to any person." This provision therefore creates the possibility for the State to privatize government waterworks, though this must be in compliance with the requirements of legislation.

---

[215] *See infra,* section 2.14.6.1, for a discussion of composition and responsibilities of catchment management agencies.

[216] NWA, ch. 11, secs. 109–116 , which deal with government water works.

[217] *See Stein, supra* n. 204.

[218] Robyn Stein, *South Africa's Water and Dam Safety Legislation: A Commentary and Analysis on the Impact of the World Commission on Dams' Report, 'Dams and Development,'* 16(6) Am. U. Intl. L. Rev. 1573 (2001).

2.14.6   Institutional Arrangements

The NWA makes the Minister of Water Affairs responsible for the management of the water resources of South Africa.[219] Consequently, the NWA grants the Minister the power to issue and enforce regulations, to establish the necessary institutions—catchment management agencies, water users' associations, internation water bodies, water tribunals—and to expropriate property for any public purpose specified in the NWA (NWA, sec. 64(1)). When making regulations, the Minister is required to follow the procedures stipulated in the NWA, which include inviting public comments on proposed regulations and considering these comments before finalizing the regulation (NWA, sec. 69). The Minister is also responsible for developing a national water resource strategy, which will establish the general parameters for water resource management and utilization in South Africa.

The NWA authorizes the establishment of a number of institutions that participate in the regulation and management of water resources in South Africa. Each of these institutions is discussed below.

The WSA provides that water services must be provided by a water services authority itself or by a water services provider nominated by the water services authority having jurisdiction in the area in question (WSA, sec. 7). The water services authorities are the municipalities and district and local councils responsible for providing water services within their geographic area of authority (WSA, sec. 1(xx)). The water services authority is also responsible for developing a water services development plan for the area (WSA, sec. 12). It must report this plan to the appropriate central government authorities, including the Minister (WSA, sec. 16).

Water services providers that can be nominated by water services authorities to deliver water service in their area include water boards, whose primary activity must be the provision of water services (WSA, secs. 29–34). Water boards have their own independent legal personality and governance structures (WSA, secs. 35–43). Interestingly, however, no court may issue an order against a water board unless the papers on which the order or judgment is based have also been served on the Minister (WSA, sec. 47). The water board is required to submit a report to the Minister annually (WSA, sec. 44).

The WSA also authorizes the Minister to establish water service committees (WSA, secs. 51–61). These committees are intended to perform functions that particular water service authorities are not able to perform (WSA, sec. 51(3)). Thus, they are empowered to provide water services to consumers within their

---

[219] NWA, ch. 6, secs. 63–76, which describe the general powers and duties of the Minister. More specific powers are spelled out in other sections scattered throughout the NWA.

service area and can set tariffs for these services (WSA, secs. 52 & 53(2)). Water service committees have their own independent legal personality (WSA, sec. 53(1)) and their members are appointed by the Minister, taking into account the need for the committee both to have the requisite expertise and to be representative of the inhabitants of its service area (WSA, sec. 55).[220]

2.14.6.1 River Basin Authorities—Catchment Management Agencies

The NWA envisages that the Minister will eventually establish a catchment management agency (CMA) for each water management area in the country.[221] The NWA's objective in creating this requirement is to ensure that the National Government delegates and decentralizes water resource management to the regional or catchment area and to involve local communities in the management of water resources.

Pursuant to the NWA, the CMA is responsible for developing and implementing a catchment management strategy, for coordinating water use in the catchment area subject to its control, and for advising people on appropriate protection and use of the water resources in the area (NWA, sec. 80). It is financed through water use charges, funds appropriated by Parliament, and funds obtained from any other lawful source (NWA, sec. 84).

A CMA can be established either on the initiative of the community or stakeholders in the catchment area or on the Minister's own initiative. The CMA is an independent corporate body (NWA, sec. 79) whose board is either elected by the different water user groups in the area or appointed by the Minister. The composition of the board must reflect the interests of the various stakeholders in the CMA. In addition, the Minister also has the power to disestablish CMAs (NWA, sec. 88).

2.14.6.2 Water Users' Associations

The NWA provides that water users can create Water Users' Associations (WUAs) (NWA, secs. 91–98). These associations function as cooperative associations of local water users who wish to undertake water-related activities for their mutual benefit. They are established by the Minister after receiving a proposal from a person or a group interested in establishing a WUA (NWA, sec. 92).

---

[220] *See* Gerhard R. Backeberg, *Water Institutional Reforms in South Africa*, 7 Water Policy 107 (2005).

[221] NWA, ch. 7, secs. 77–90. River basin authorities are referred to as "catchment management agencies" in the NWA.

The Minister also has the power to disestablish the WUA (NWA, sec. 96) and can order a WUA to take certain actions (NWA, sec. 95). The WUA is an independent corporate body, with its own legal personality, whose membership is determined by the procedures established in its constitution.[222] However, the Minister, after consultations, may order the WUA to admit a person as a member (NWA, sec. 95). The Minister also has the power in certain circumstances, and only after following a formal process that provides opportunity for public comment on the proposed action, to disestablish a WUA. These circumstances include: the WUA is no longer active or effective, disestablishment is in the best interests of the association or its members, and an investigation reveals that disestablishment is an appropriate action (NWA, sec. 96).

The WUA's constitution determines its precise functions. In this regard it is important to note that the WUA's primary purpose is to serve the mutual interests of its members, not to operate as a water management agency.

2.14.6.3 Advisory Committees

The NWA empowers the Minister to establish advisory committees for particular purposes. The function of these committees is to give the Minister advice on specified aspects of water resource management and use. Although these committees are advisory, they can exercise whatever powers have been delegated to them (NWA, secs. 99–101). The WSA, in section 76, provides that the Minister may establish advisory committees to deal with any matters falling within the scope of the WSA.

2.14.7 Financial Arrangements

Chapter 5 of the NWA discusses a number of measures the Minister can use to finance the provision of water management services and the implementation of strategies designed to protect and conserve water and ensure the beneficial use of water (NWA, secs. 56–62).

First, the NWA empowers the Minister, with the concurrence of the Minister of Finance, to establish a pricing strategy for charges for the use of water (NWA, sec. 56).[223] These charges can be used to fund water resources management, the development of waterworks, and achieving an "equitable and efficient allocation of water" (NWA, sec. 56(2)(c)). The pricing strategy developed by the Minister can differentiate "on an equitable basis" between different geographic areas, different categories of water use, and different water users (NWA, secs. 56(3)(a),

---

[222] Schedule 5 of the NWA contains a model WUA constitution. For other model bylaws *see* Salman, *supra* n. 171, appendixes 1 and 3.

[223] The WSA has a similar provision; *see* WSA, sec. 10.

(4) & (5)). In establishing the strategy, the Minister should consider the contributions the pricing strategy can make to achieving social equity in South Africa (NWA, sec. 56) and can also provide that the charges be paid by the appropriate water management institution or by consumers directly (NWA, sec. 56(3)(b)). The Minister, in developing the pricing strategy, must invite public comments on the proposed strategy, make an effort to bring it to the attention of interested persons, and consider the comments in devising the final strategy (NWA, sec. 56(7)).

The NWA also empowers the Minister to direct any water management institution to recover any charges made by the Minister from water users in its water management area (NWA, sec. 58). In this case the water management institution remains jointly and severally liable with the water users for the charges (NWA, sec. 58(3)). In this regard it should be noted that catchment management agencies are empowered to raise the funds required for the purposes of exercising their powers and performing their duties from water use charges (NWA, sec. 84).[224]

In furtherance of its policy of promoting equitable access to water, the NWA provides that the Minister may give financial assistance to any person for the purposes of making license applications or for any other purpose specified in the NWA (NWA, sec. 61(1)). In providing this support the Minister must take into account all relevant considerations, including the need for equity and transparency, the need to redress the results of past racial and gender discrimination, the purpose of the financial assistance, the financial position of the recipient, and the need for water resource protection (NWA, sec. 61(3)). This financial support must be provided out of funds specifically appropriated by Parliament for this purpose or funds which, under the NWA, can lawfully be used for this purpose.

The NWA and WSA include detailed provisions on the role of the private sector in water service delivery. The NWA states in section 116 that the Minister may make regulations providing for the private development of a government waterworks. Section 19 of the WSA states that a water services authority may enter into a contract with a private sector water services provider only after it has considered all known public sector water services providers that are willing and able to perform the relevant functions. Before entering into or renewing a contract with a water services provider[225] or a joint venture with another water services institution other than a public sector water services institution that will provide

---

[224] This section also provides that CMAs can be financed with funds appropriated by Parliament and by funds from any lawful source.

[225] A water services provider is defined as any person who provides water services to consumers or to another water services institution, but does not include a water services intermediary. A water services intermediary means any person who is obliged to provide water services to another in terms of a contract where the obligation to provide water services is incidental to the main object of that contract. *See* WSA, secs. 1(xxiii) and 1(xxii).

services within the joint venture at cost and without profit, the water services authority must publicly disclose its intention to do so.

Section 19 of the WSA provides, furthermore, that any water services provider entering into a contract or joint venture with a water services authority must, before entering into such a contract or joint venture, disclose and provide information on: (i) any other interests it may have that are ancillary to or associated with the relevant water services authority; and (ii) any rate of return on investment it will or may gain by entering into such a contract or joint venture. The Minister may, after consultation with the Minister for Provincial Affairs and Constitutional Development, prescribe: (i) matters that must be regulated by a contract between a water services provider and a water services authority; (ii) compulsory provisions to be included in such a contract; and (iii) requirements for a joint venture between a water services authority and a water services institution, to ensure that water services are provided on an efficient, equitable, cost-effective, and sustainable basis; that the terms of the contract are fair and equitable to the water services authority, the water services provider, and the consumer; and that they are in compliance with the WSA. As soon as such a contract or joint venture agreement has been concluded, the water services authority must supply a copy thereof to the relevant Province and to the Minister. The Minister may provide model contracts to be used as a guide for contracts between water services authorities and water services providers.

2.14.8 Enforcement of Regulations and Dispute Settlement

2.14.8.1 Enforcement of Regulations

Enforcement regulations are spelled out in sections 137 to 145 of the NWA. The NWA requires the Minister to establish a national monitoring system for water resources. This system must provide for the collection of the data necessary to assess, *inter alia*, the quantity and quality of water in water resources, the use of water resources, compliance with resource quality objectives, the rehabilitation of water resources, the health of aquatic ecosystems, and the atmospheric conditions that may influence water resources (NWA, sec. 137). In addition, the Minister is required, after consultation with the relevant state organs, water management institutions, and water users, to establish mechanisms and procedures for coordinating the monitoring of water resources (NWA, sec. 138). The information obtained through this monitoring system must be made publicly available for a fee set by the Minister (NWA, sec. 142).

The NWA creates a set of offenses relating to failure to comply with its requirements. These include using water in ways other than those permitted in the

Act, failure to comply with conditions attached to permissible water use, unlawfully or negligently polluting water or interfering with a waterworks, and committing contempt of the Water Tribunal (NWA, sec. 151). Any person found guilty of any of these offenses is liable to a fine or imprisonment (NWA, sec. 151(2)) and may also be liable to pay damages to any person harmed by the offense (NWA, sec. 153). Cases involving these offenses are heard in a court of law.

The WSA empowers the Minister and provincial authorities to monitor the performance of every water service institution to ensure that all comply with all applicable standards and regulations (WSA, secs. 62 & 63). In pursuance of this obligation, the Minister can authorize a person to enter the property of the water services institution to ascertain compliance with the law and regulations (WSA, sec. 80). Any person who violates the provisions of the WSA is liable for a fine or imprisonment (WSA, sec. 82).

2.14.8.2 Dispute Settlement

The NWA provides for two forms of dispute settlement (NWA, secs. 146–50). First, it establishes a Water Tribunal (the Tribunal) to hear appeals against decisions made by a responsible authority, catchment management agency, or water management institution (NWA, sec. 148). The Tribunal is an independent body with jurisdiction to conduct hearings anywhere in the country. Its members are appointed by the Minister on the recommendation of the Judicial Service Commission and must have knowledge of law, engineering, water resource management, or related fields (NWA, sec. 146). Administrative support for the Tribunal is provided by the Department of Water Affairs of the Ministry of Water and Forestry. The decisions of the Tribunal can be appealed to the High Court (NWA, sec. 149). Nonetheless, the NWA authorizes the Minister to direct people to settle their disputes through a process of negotiation and mediation (NWA, sec. 150).

2.15   Vietnam

2.15.1   Statutory Framework

Articles 17 and 29 of the Constitution of the Socialist Republic of Vietnam (April 14, 1992) set out the framework for water legislation in Vietnam.[226] Water in Vietnam is regulated by the Law on Water Resources, No.8/1998/QH10 of

---

[226] Article 17 of the Constitution of the Socialist Republic of Vietnam states:

> The lands, forests and mountains, rivers and lakes, water sources, underground natural resources, and other resources in the territorial seas, on the continental shelf, and in the air space; capital and assets that the state invests in various enterprises

May 20, 1998 (LWR). The LWR is applicable to all surface water, rainwater, groundwater, and sea water within the territory of the Socialist Republic of Vietnam (LWR, art. 2(1)). It regulates the management, protection, exploitation, and use of these water resources and addresses problems related to water (LWR, art. 2(2)).[227] Water in the exclusive economic zone and mineral and natural thermal waters are regulated by other laws (LWR, art. 2(2)).[228]

Other laws relevant to water resources management include

- Law on Environmental Protection (December 27, 1994) (protection of natural resources, calling for environmental impact statements);
- Land Law (1993) (provisions on water use);[229] and
- People and Health Protection Law (1989).[230]

Additionally, the National Environmental Agency was established in 1993 under the Ministry of Science, Technology and Environment (MOSTE) and handles environmental management. However, the Ministry of Agriculture and Rural Development (MARD) handles implementation of the LWR.[231]

---

and projects falling under different economic, cultural, social, scientific, technical, diplomatic, and national security and national defense programs and other property defined by law as belonging to the state are under the ownership of the entire people.

Article 29 states: "State organs, units of the armed forces, economic and social organizations, and individuals have the duty to implement state regulations on the rational use of natural resources and protection of the environment. All acts of depleting natural resources and destroying the environment are strictly prohibited." *See* Constitution of the Socialist Republic of Vietnam in *Constitutions of the Countries of the World,* Vol. XX (A. Blaustein & G. Flanz, eds., Ocean Publications, Inc. 1992).

[227] *See generally Vietnam—Water Resources Sector Review, Main Report,* A Joint Report by the World Bank, Asian Development Bank, FAO, UNDP, and the NGO Water Resources Group, in cooperation with the Institute of Water Resources Planning, Vietnam (1996).

[228] Mineral water and natural thermal waters are regulated by the Law on Minerals.

[229] Last amended November 26, 2003; became effective July 1, 2004.

[230] Other relevant ordinances include the Dykes Protection Ordinance (1989) and the Ordinance of Aquatic Resource Protection (1989).

[231] A new ministry called the Ministry of Natural Resources and the Environment (MNRE) has been established (by Decree No. 91/2002/ND-CP dated November 11, 2002) and has since taken over all the water management functions of the Ministry of Agriculture and Rural Development (MARD). However, although the MNRE has in fact taken over these functions, the LWR had not been amended as of the completion of this study to incorporate this change.

2.15.2 Underlying Principles and Priorities

The LWR requires the State to adopt a policy for "managing, protecting, and rationally, economically, and efficiently exploiting" Vietnam's water resources and for overcoming any harmful effects caused by their use to the lives of people, the economy, national security, protection of the environment, or the sustainable development of the country (LWR, art. 4(1)). It also has a preferential policy with regard to organizations and individuals who invest in developing water resources (LWR, art. 6(3)).

The regulation and distribution of water resources for "use purposes" must be based on the planning of the river basin and must respect the principles of fairness, reasonableness, and priority in the quantity and quality of water for human lives (LWR, art. 20(1)). Article 25 of the LWR requires the State to give priority to exploitation and use of water resources for "living purposes"[232] by taking specified actions to achieve this objective. These include investing in water projects particularly in areas where water is scarce or that have exceptionally difficult socioeconomic conditions or heavily polluted water sources (LWR, art. 25(1)(a)).

2.15.3 Regulation of Water Uses

2.15.3.1 Ownership of Water and Establishment of Water Rights

Water resources are owned by the "entire people under the unified management of the State" (LWR, art. 1(1)). Organizations and individuals can exploit and use water for life and for production (LWR, art. 1(2)). When doing so, they must protect the water resource and prevent harm (LWR, art. 1(2)).[233]

Organizations and individuals who wish to use water resources must get permission from the competent State agencies unless they intend to use the water on a small scale for their personal or family use or in connection with land already assigned or leased to them (LWR, art. 24). Permission is not required to use water on a small scale for the family in agriculture, forestry, aquaculture, small industry and handicraft production, hydropower, and other purposes (LWR, art. 24(2)). Those who obtain such permission are entitled to compensation in the event permission is withdrawn before the end of its term (LWR, art. 22(3)). Organizations and individuals, that have obtained the necessary permission can use water,

---

[232] Art. 3(4) of the LWR defines water for living purposes to include water for "eating, drinking, and sanitation of humans."

[233] *See* Frederiksen, Berkoff & Barber, *supra* n. 79, at 20.

inter alia, for purposes of living, agriculture, forestry, industrial production, mining, power generation, aquaculture, salt making, sport and recreation, health and medical purposes, and scientific research (LWR, art. 22(1)).

Organizations and individuals lawfully using and exploiting water are entitled to convey water through land that is being managed and used by other organizations and individuals, provided they do so consistent with the applicable law (LWR, art. 33).

2.15.3.2   Allocation of Right to Use Water

The Government is responsible for issuing and revoking permits to use water resources and for protecting the rights of organizations and individuals to legally exploit and use water resources (LWR, art. 61). The MARD carries out this function for the Government, although the Government can assign to other ministries and local authorities certain responsibilities with regard to water resource management (LWR, art. 58).

The regulation and distribution of water must be based on planning for the river basin and the potential of the water source (LWR, art. 20(1)). In cases of shortages, article 20(2) states that the authorities must give priority to using water for human living purposes. Those who obtain the right to use water have an obligation to do so in compliance with the law and to use the water in the manner specified in their permit (LWR, art. 23).

2.15.3.3   Transfer of Water Rights

The Law does not explicitly address the issue of transfer of water rights. It does, however, stipulate, in article 22(2), that organizations and individuals that have permission to exploit water resources have the right to "assign, lease, legate and mortgage their properties" in connection with investments made to exploit the water resource.

2.15.3.4   Loss of Right to Use Water

The LWR makes clear that the State can withdraw permission to use water when this is necessary for national defense and security reasons, provided the permit holder is compensated for the loss (LWR, art. 22(3)). The Government also has the power to revoke any permits it has issued with regard to water resources (LWR, art. 61). The LWR does not state on what grounds the permits can be revoked. The Specialized Inspector of water resources has the power to stop water-related activities that it finds may cause serious harm to water resources and to deal with violations of the Law (LWR, arts. 67 (1)(c) & (d)).

2.15.4 Protection of Water

Chapter II of the LWR (arts. 10–19) deals with the protection of water. It stipulates, in article 10(1), that general responsibility for protecting water resources rests with state agencies, economic organizations, political organizations, social organizations, the armed forces, and individuals. Specific responsibilities are assigned to local administrations to protect the water in their locality and to organizations and individuals to protect the water that they use and exploit (LWR, arts. 10(2) & (3)).

The LWR also stipulates in article 12 that organizations and individuals that use or explore for groundwater have an obligation to comply with rules and norms relating to the protection of groundwater. Similar requirements exist with regard to the use of surface water (LWR, arts. 14–16). Article 13 states that the socioeconomic development plan must include a plan to prevent and combat water pollution and to restore the quality of polluted water. It also prohibits the introduction of waste and unprocessed discharge of water into water resources.[234]

2.15.5 Regulation of Water Infrastructure

The State gives priority to the exploitation of water for living purposes by investing in projects to supply water for this purpose, particularly in areas of water scarcity or difficult socioeconomic conditions (LWR, art. 25). It also encourages individuals and organizations, both in Vietnam and elsewhere, to invest in water projects for this purpose (LWR, art. 25(1)(b)). In addition, the State invests in and supports the exploitation and use of water for agricultural purposes (LWR, art. 26) and hydropower (LWR, art. 29).

Water conservancy works are defined in article 3(17) as works for the "exploitation of the benefits of the water, preventing and fighting against harmful effects caused by water and protecting the environment and the ecological balance." Such works must be under the direct management of an organization or individual selected by the State (LWR, art. 47(1)). This organization or individual is responsible for protecting the water conservancy work (LWR, art. 48) and must have a plan for doing so that is approved by the Government (LWR, art. 49). The LWR also prohibits certain acts, such as conducting unsafe activity in the area around water conservancy work and building supplementary water conservancy works without the prior approval of the competent State agency (LWR, art. 52).

---

[234] *See also* LWR, arts. 17–19.

2.15.6   Institutional Arrangements

Chapter VII of the LWR (arts. 57–65) deals with institutional arrangements. Article 57 stipulates that state management of water resources includes the following elements: developing and directing a plan for using and protecting water resources and overcoming their harmful effects; developing the rules, criteria, and procedures pertaining to the management and use of water resources; issuing and revoking permits relating to water use; inspecting implementation of water use permits and plans; and dealing with violations of water use laws, regulations, and permits.[235]

Article 58 of the LWR stipulates that the Government exercises unified management of the water resource. Within the Government, the MARD is responsible for carrying out the State management function with respect to both water resources (LWR, art. 58(2)) and flood prevention (LWR, art. 65). Its responsibilities include ratifying general plans for river basins, water conservation, and synthesizing and managing the results of water surveys and studies and directing flood and storm prevention.[236]

Other ministries, ministerial level agencies, and State agencies can participate in this function (LWR, art. 58(3)). Their responsibilities can include ratifying draft projects on water resources and participating in surveys and studies (LWR, arts. 59(4) & 60(2)).

The People's Committees are responsible for managing water resources at the provincial and local levels (LWR, art. 58(4)). In particular, pursuant to article 60(4), they conduct studies and surveys relating to water resources in their jurisdiction. Decisions on waterworks are usually taken by the Government, but decisions on waterworks of national importance are made by the National Assembly (LWR, art. 59(1)). The Government is responsible for issuing and revoking permits dealing with water use (LWR, art. 61).

The LWR also establishes a Specialized Inspector to oversee compliance with water resource regulation (LWR, arts. 66–69). The Specialized Inspector conducts its inspections of water resources under the supervision of the MARD (LWR, art. 66(2)).

Article 63 of the LWR establishes a National Water Resource Council. This Council provides the Government with consulting services with regard to "important decisions on water resource that come under the tasks and powers of the Government" (LWR, art. 63(1)). The Council is chaired by a Deputy Prime Minister, and the Minister of Agriculture and Rural Development is a permanent member

---

[235] *See* Hector Malano, Michael Bryant & Hugh Turral, *Management of Water Resources: Can Australian Experiences Be Transferred to Vietnam?* 24 Water Intl. 307 (1999).

[236] LWR, arts. 59(2), 60(3), and 65(2).

(LWR, art. 63(2)). The other members represent other Ministries, branches, and localities, and scientists and water resources specialists (LWR, art. 63(2)).

2.15.6.1   River Basin Authorities

The LWR has established a regulatory framework for river basins, which it defines (LWR, art. 3(15)) as the "geographical area in which surface and groundwater naturally flows" into a specific river. The agency responsible for managing each river basin is a "nonbusiness" agency of the MARD (LWR, art. 64(2)). The management of a river basin includes elaborating and implementing plans for the unified management of the river basin (LWR, art. 64(1)(a)); coordinating with other regulatory bodies involved in monitoring the implementation of the plan (LWR, art. 64(1)(b)); and helping to resolve disputes relating to the water resources of the river basin (LWR, art. 64(1)(c)). The LWR does not contain any provisions dealing with water users' associations or advisory committees.

2.15.7   Financial Arrangements

Organizations and individuals who use water resources are required under article 7(1) to contribute both financially and in terms of manpower to the building of waterworks for the protection and use of the water resources and to the prevention of harm to the water.

2.15.8   Enforcement of Regulations and Dispute Settlement

2.15.8.1   Enforcement of Regulations

The Specialized Inspector is empowered to inspect the development and implementation of the general water plan; issue and revoke permits to use water resources; and enforce compliance with the process, rules, and norms for the protection and use of water resources (LWR, arts. 66(1)(a), (b), (c)). In carrying out inspections, the Inspection Team and Inspector have the power to ask concerned organizations and individuals to provide documents and information and to answer questions, conduct on-site inspections, and stop activities they are investigating (LWR, art. 67).

Persons who are found to have engaged in acts that cause serious deterioration and depletion of a water source, or who engage in acts that otherwise fail to comply with their obligations with regard to a water source, are subject to sanctions. Such sanctions can include fines, jail terms, and other forms of discipline (LWR, art. 71). On the other hand, people who have good records in the protection and use of water or in the prevention of harm to water can be rewarded for their actions (LWR, art. 70).

2.15.8.2 Dispute Settlement

As stated in section 2.15.3.4, the Specialized Inspector of water resources has the power to stop water-related activities that it finds may cause serious harm to water resources and to deal with violations of the LWR. Organizations or individuals that object to the Specialized Inspector's investigations can file a complaint with a "competent State agency" (LWR, art. 69) against the decisions of the Inspector.[237] The agency has the responsibility under article 69(3) to settle the dispute.

2.16   Yemen

2.16.1   Statutory Framework

The Constitution of the Republic of Yemen establishes the general principles applicable to water regulation in Yemen. Article 8 of the Constitution provides that "all types of natural resources and sources of energy, whether above ground, underground . . . are owned by the state, which assures their exploitation for the common good of the people." Article 18 stipulates that any contracts granting concessions related to natural resources must be undertaken pursuant to law, while article 135 mandates that the Council of Ministers be responsible for preparing drafts of laws and resolutions to present to the House of Representatives and the President.

Pursuant to these constitutional provisions, the State has adopted the Environmental Protection Law, No. 26 of 1995. This, Yemen's main environmental law, requires environmental impact assessments for all projects that may affect the environment. In 2002, the Parliament adopted, and the President approved, the Water Law (Law No. 33 of 2002). However, at the time this study was completed, a number of amendments were being proposed to the Law, particularly with regard to the institutional arrangements. Because those amendments had not been approved by Parliament at the time this study was completed, this section does not incorporate them.

2.16.2   Underlying Principles and Priorities

The goals of the Water Law, as stated in article 3, are developing and rationing the exploitation of water resources; protecting water resources from depletion and pollution; improving the allocation of water and the operation and maintenance of water installations; and promoting the participation of beneficiaries in

---

[237] Furthermore, art. 67(2) of the LWR states that the Inspection Team and the Inspector must take responsibility before the law for their decisions.

the management, development, and conservation of the water resources from which they benefit.[238]

The Water Law provides in article 6 that all potential beneficiaries of any water resources shall enjoy the right to benefit from the relevant water resource, provided they do so in a way that does not harm the interests of other beneficiaries and they carry out all duties relating to the conservation and safeguarding of the water resources. The Government regulates the rights and responsibilities of those benefiting from these resources.

The law establishes a priority for the use of water. The highest priority is accorded to water for drinking and domestic purposes (Water Law, art. 20). Thereafter water may be allocated to any of the following purposes: watering livestock, use in public facilities, industrial purposes, and meeting environmental needs (Water Law, art. 21).

2.16.3 Regulation of Water Uses

2.16.3.1   Ownership of Water and Establishment of Water Rights

The Water Law does not address the issue of water ownership explicitly. Instead, article 4 stipulates that "water is a right that is accessible to all"[239] and cannot become privately owned except through transportation, acquisition, or other similar means. Although this may be interpreted to mean that water is publicly owned, the law does allow private ownership of water under certain conditions. The water in *wadis* is held in common by all beneficiaries and all the water installations and water wells set up by the government are considered public property that is subject to a registration and licensing regime (Water Law, art. 5).

Article 15 of the Water Law requires all government agencies and private and public legal entities to submit their water projects to the National Water Resources Authority (NWRA) for review and approval no later than sixty days from the day of submission. If NWRA does not provide its opinion within this period, the project will be deemed to have been approved. Under article 41 of the Water Law, the Government has the authority to construct projects for water

---

[238] For discussion and analysis of the challenges faced in the water sector in Yemen, *see Yemen Water Strategy Report,* World Bank Report No. 15718-YEM (August 1997).

[239] *See* Dante A. Caponera, *Water Law in Moslem Countries*, Irrigation and Drainage Paper 20/1 & 20/2 (FAO 1973); and *Water Management in Islam* (Naser I. Faruqui, Asit Biswas & Murad Bino, eds., United Nations Univ. Press 2001). *See also* Hussein A. Amery, *Islamic Water Management,* 26 Water Intl. 481 (2001); and Walid A. Abderrahman, *Application of Islamic Legal Principles for Advanced Water Management,* 25 Water Intl. 513 (2000).

development and harvesting. However, the NWRA can, when necessary, review and revise the amount of water licensed for such a project to conform to overall water availability and use.[240]

The right to use water entitles the holder of the right to use water in a way that does not conflict with the public interest or with the prevailing customs and traditions in each water zone or basin (Water Law, art. 27). The authorities concerned, in coordination with NWRA, issue permits to those interested in disposing of wastewater and of constructing installations needed to treat waste water or desalinate water (Water Law, art. 47).

A permit is required to exploit groundwater (Water Law, art. 6). No individual, group, or entity of the government may dig water wells or build water installations designed to hold back water without the appropriate permit issued by the NWRA (Water Law, arts. 35 & 36). Article 73 states that the regulations shall specify the rules and procedures relating to permits, their validity period, and the fees to be charged by NWRA. However, one-time deepening of wells with a depth not exceeding 20m is allowed without a permit (Water Law, art. 35(b)). Moreover, in connection with traditional and customary water rights that existed prior to the adoption of this law, digging of wells with a depth not exceeding 60m is allowed without a permit from NWRA, subject to the following: (a) complying with the specification for water resources and the rules regarding protected zones and not causing harm to another party; and (b) complying with the customs and traditions relating to the use of water resources in the area (Water Law, art. 45, read with art. 29).[241] All users of groundwater from wells that existed prior to the issuance of the Water Law are required to register such use rights with the NWRA within three years from the date of issuance of the law (Water Law, art. 33).

Accordingly, the Water Law recognizes all existing and acquired water rights. These rights must be maintained and cannot be altered except in case of necessity and with payment of fair compensation (Water Law, art. 27). In this regard, proper recognition should be given to the traditional rights to rainwater harvesting and natural runoff flow to be used in irrigation when they are linked to the agricultural land that benefits from the water (Water Law, art. 28). Similarly, the traditional or customary rights to benefit from natural springs, stream brooks, creeks, and wells not exceeding sixty meters, and the common rights associated

---

[240] *See* Rafik A. Al-Sakaf, Yangxiao Zhou & Michael J. Hall, *A Strategy for Controlling Groundwater Depletion in the Sa'dah Plain, Yemen,* Intl. J. Water Resources Dev. 349 (1999).

[241] For a critical overview of those issues, as well as other issues related to the Water Law, *see* Yemen, Sana'a Basin Water Management Project, 2003 (P064981), Project Appraisal Document (Report No. 25460-YEM), dated April 23, 2003, at 8.

with them that existed prior to this law, remain as rights (Water Law, art. 29).[242] However, these rights may be transferred and the new owner acquires the full rights (Water Law, art. 29). If the land using such water is subdivided, the water rights would be subdivided in proportion to the land (Water Law, art. 29). All the holders of these traditional rights are required to register their rights with the NWRA within three years from the date of the law (Water Law, art. 32). NWRA shall maintain a register of these rights (Water Law, art. 34).

2.16.3.2   Allocation of Right to Use Water

Yemen is divided into water zones and water basins (Water Law, art. 8). A water plan that becomes part of the National Water Plan is developed for each water basin and zone. This plan must be consistent with the water policy and general foundations for water policy in Yemen (Water Law, art. 16).

The NWRA formulates the foundations for water planning in Yemen based on assessments of the water basins and water zones, general indicators of the water situation in the country, the trends in long-term demand for all types of water use, and the water budget (Water Law, art. 17). The NWRA is also responsible for developing a classification scheme for water basins and water zones in light of the water situation therein to ensure that basins and zones having similar water situations are handled under similar procedures (Water Law, art. 14). These plans inform NWRA decisions relating to permits establishing the right to use water.

The NWRA, after undertaking the relevant studies and considering the possible options, can, with the approval of the Council of Ministers, permit specified volumes of groundwater or surface water to be pumped from one water basin or zone to another, provided the conveyance of the water will not have any future adverse effect on the water in the basin or zone from which it is conveyed; the water will only be used for drinking or domestic purposes; there is a shortage of water in the recipient water zone or basin; and there is coordination and consultation with all stakeholders—local authorities, water basin committees, and beneficiaries—of the water basin from which the water is conveyed (Water Law, art. 50).

2.16.3.3   Transfer of Water Rights

Permits to use water can only be assigned to another person with the permission of the NWRA (Water Law, art. 38).

---

[242] *See* Awadh Bahamish, *Legal Survey of Existing Traditional Rights in the Spate Irrigation Systems in Wadi Zabid and Wadi Tuban in Yemen* (Report to the National Water Resources Authority, Sana'a, Yemen, August 2004).

2.16.3.4   Loss of Right to Use Water

Permits issued pursuant to the Water Law are deemed cancelled if the permit holder does not commence the proposed water use within one year of the date of issuance of the permit; if the permit holder uses the permit for purposes other than those for which the permit was issued; if the permit holder violates the conditions in the permit; or if there is an unauthorized transfer of the permit (Water Law, art. 38).

The NWRA can cancel or amend the right to benefit from water for certain periods of time if the water in the well or the water installation is found to be polluted or harmful to public health and if treatment of the water to remove the threat is not possible (Water Law, art. 40). The NWRA can also modify any permit or license if it determines that the circumstances under which the license was issued have changed and the continuation of the permitted activity will cause damage (Water Law, art. 58).

2.16.4   Protection of Water

The NWRA has the power to protect water resources against pollution; to maintain water quality; to prevent activities that may lead to pollution or degradation of the quality of the water; and to prepare procedures for regulating potentially polluting activities (Water Law, art. 54). Entities that are engaging in activities that may lead to the pollution of water are required to comply with the standards and specifications related to the disposal of waste and to refrain from specified activities (Water Law, art. 54). These standards may include undertaking a study of the environmental impacts of the proposed activity (Water Law, art. 56).[243]

Water used for the following purposes should conform to the standards established by the NWRA, except in cases of necessity: water used for domestic purposes; water used in the manufacture and processing of medicinal materials; water used for livestock, irrigation, and tourism and in hospitals; treated wastewater used for irrigation and other purposes; and desalinated water (Water Law, art. 23). In case of necessity, the permit specifies the minimum standards to be complied with. A permit is needed to perform any treatment on water that will lead to a change in the physical and chemical characteristics of the water (Water Law, art. 24). The Ministry of Agriculture and Irrigation is responsible for flood control activities and policies (Water Law, arts. 61 & 62).

2.16.5   Regulation of Water Infrastructure

The Government shall undertake projects that develop water resources and water harvesting projects (Water Law, art. 41). The following activities cannot be

---

[243] *See also* Environmental Protection Law, No. 26 (1995).

undertaken without prior permission from the NWRA: drilling water wells, exploring for groundwater, and distribution of the water drawn from water wells through private supply networks or by bottling (Water Law, art. 42). However, as stated earlier, one-time deepening of wells for no more than 20m and drilling of wells for up to 60m, subject to the circumstances specified in article 45, are both allowed without a permit from NWRA. Persons who undertake construction activities must meet certain technical qualifications (Water Law, arts. 42 & 43).

In some circumstances the Council of Ministers, based on a proposal from the NWRA, can prohibit the construction of any structure or the development of any industrial, agricultural, or other activities that could increase the burden on the water reserves in a specific region (Water Law, art. 49).

2.16.6 Institutional Arrangements

The Ministry of Agriculture and Irrigation and authorities and corporations affiliated with it operate installations and regulate and ration water allocated for irrigation and drinking use in rural areas in accordance with the Water Plan developed by the NWRA. They also carry out all necessary activities in this regard, including preparing and executing policies, undertaking studies, and installing, maintaining, and operating water works (Water Law, art. 25).

The Ministry of Electricity and Water and its affiliated authorities and corporations regulate, manage, and ration the water allocated to it in the Water Plan.[244] They also carry out all necessary activities in this regard, including preparing and executing policies related to the water and sanitation sector, undertaking studies, protecting the quality of the water used for domestic purposes, supplying water for all public and private sector activities, and undertaking all activities related to the treatment and management of waste water (Water Law, art. 26).

The NWRA is responsible for formulating the National Water Plan (Water Law, arts. 13–17) and issuing all permits for water use. The National Water Plan, which should include consideration of efforts designed to promote public participation, must ultimately be approved by the Council of Ministers (Water Law, art. 18). The National Water Plan, after final approval, is binding on everyone (Water Law, art. 19).

The NWRA is also responsible for developing water basin and water zone plans (Water Law, art. 16). All water plans should include qualitative and quantitative assessments of the water in the relevant water basin or zone; estimates of current and future water demand; planned projects, activities, and measures related to the management and development of water resources; equitable

---

[244] The proposed amendments to the Water Law referred to earlier include establishment of a Ministry of Water and Environment, which would be responsible for water resources in Yemen. NWRA would continue to exist but within this Ministry.

allocation of water; treatment and use of waste water; plans for the protection of rainwater runoff and for the management and development of both surface and groundwater; and economic and technical justification for the plans and their implementation (Water Law, art. 17). The Government, acting through the NWRA, undertakes the following tasks: providing support and facilities to farmers; seeking to encourage them to adopt modern irrigation methods that are aimed at using water more efficiently in irrigation; building dams, dikes, and reservoirs to make optimum use of rainwater; providing such services as soil conservation and vegetative cover that are designed to conserve water; and supporting and encouraging community participation in the management and conservation of water resources (Water Law, art. 48).

2.16.6.1   River Basin Authorities

The NWRA, in collaboration with the relevant authorities, is responsible for establishing Water Basin and Water Zone Committees. These committees operate under the supervision of the NWRA (Water Law, art. 11). The responsibilities of these committees and their composition are determined by regulations issued pursuant to the mandate under the Water Law (Water Law, art. 11).[245]

2.16.6.2   Water Users' Associations and Advisory Committees

Water users' and beneficiary associations may be formed for the purpose of involving users in managing water resources or in the operation and maintenance of water installations (Water Law, art. 10). More detailed rules to govern these associations are to be included in regulations issued pursuant to the Water Law (Water Law, art. 10). There is no specific information on advisory committees in the Water Law.

2.16.7   Financial Arrangements

The NWRA can collect fees, charges, and deposits for the permits it issues and for the technical services it renders (Water Law, art. 77). The fees that the NWRA collects can be used to support the development of water resources and also the operations of the NWRA (Water Law, art. 77). Similarly fees and revenues collected by other entities must be used to support their operations (Water Law, art. 77).[246] The amount of the fees, charges, and deposits that the NWRA can collect should be set out in regulations issued pursuant to the Water Law (Water Law, arts. 73 & 76).

---

[245] *See also* Local Government Law (Law No. 4 of 2000).

[246] *See* Christopher Ward, *The Political Economy of Irrigation Water Pricing in Yemen,* in Dinar (ed.), *supra* n. 62, at 381.

2.16.8   Enforcement of Regulations and Dispute Settlement

2.16.8.1   Enforcement of Regulations

Staff members of the NWRA have the status of judicial enforcement officers (Water Law, art. 63). They are responsible for enforcing the Water Law and regulations and for reporting violations thereof (Water Law, art. 64). Sanctions for violating the Law and regulations include both jail terms and fines (Water Law, arts. 67–71). Employees assigned by NWRA to undertake studies and to take water measurements have the right to enter any privately owned lands, farms, and any commercial, industrial, or water installations that are subject to the Water Law (Water Law, arts. 51 & 53).

2.16.8.2   Dispute Settlement

There are no provisions on dispute settlement in the Water Law. However, the Water Law does state that when it is silent on an issue, the civil law and the principles of Islamic jurisprudence apply (Water Law, art. 80).

CHAPTER 3

Comparative Analysis of the Regulatory Frameworks for Water Resources Management

The survey and analysis of the regulatory frameworks for water resources management in sixteen jurisdictions in chapter 2 were based on certain key elements: the statutory framework, underlying principles and priorities, regulation of water use, protection of water, regulation of water infrastructure, institutional and financial arrangements, enforcement of regulations, and dispute resolution.

The purpose of this chapter is to provide a comparative analysis of the approaches of those jurisdictions to these elements, with the view to identifying similarities and differences and to understand the underlying reasons for them.

3.1 Statutory Framework

3.1.1 Constitutions and Statutes

The constitutions of half of the national jurisdictions included in this study—Brazil, China, Costa Rica, Kazakhstan, Mexico, South Africa, Vietnam, and Yemen—address, directly or indirectly, the issue of water resources. In some of those jurisdictions the constitution gives the state the authority to regulate water. The Brazilian, Mexican, and Vietnamese constitutions specifically assign to the government the responsibility to regulate water. The Chinese constitution stipulates that the State is responsible for ensuring the "rational use" of all natural resources, including water.

A number of the constitutions address the issue of ownership of water resources. The constitutions of Brazil, Kazakhstan, and Yemen all indicate that the State owns the water resources in those countries. The Chinese and Vietnamese constitutions stipulate that the State holds the water resources in the name of the people. According to the South African Constitution, the Government acts as a custodian of the country's water resources.

The South African constitution is the only constitution to grant its citizens the right of access to water; the Constitution of Brazil is the only constitution to include a requirement for implementing a national water resources management system.[247] It is worth noting, however, that the water statutes in Armenia, Kazakhstan, and Yemen establish in a general way the right of their citizens to water: In Kazakhstan the law states that all citizens have the right to water for their personal use, provided they can take it without using any technical means or devises. The law in Yemen gives all potential human beneficiaries the right to benefit from water, provided they can do so in ways that do not cause any harm.

The statutes in the remaining jurisdictions establish as a general rule ownership of water by the State or by the whole community, with some exceptions allowed, such as for existing and traditional rights (Morocco and Yemen) and for rainwater captured on private land (Costa Rica, Morocco, and Yemen).

3.2   Underlying Principles and Priorities

A number of principles can be identified as underlying the water statutes studied in chapter 2. First, most of those statutes require the efficient management and use of water resources,[248] though they vary in precisely how they state this principle. For example, Brazil stresses that water management should ensure that water is put to multiple uses and that there is appropriate coordination of water use at all levels of governance. The Chinese statute indicates that the state must promote multipurpose and sustainable use of water in furtherance of the economic and social development of the Chinese people. The French statute stipulates that water must be managed so as to ensure an appropriate balance between the needs of all water users and the environment. Kazakhstan establishes principles of public administration that underlie the management of water resources; the principles include the creation of optimal and sustainable conditions for water use. The statutes of Nepal and Vietnam also require the rational use of water.

Second, most jurisdictions include conservation and protection of water as one of the underlying principles of their statutes. This principle is stated with varying degrees of detail. The more detailed statutes include:

- *Brazil*: The statute contains six guiding principles for water management, three of which relate to conservation and protection of water. The three are: showing equal regard for the quality and quantity of water, adjusting water management to the specific social and environmental conditions of each region, and coordinating water and land use management.

---

[247] *See supra* n. 1.

[248] For a general discussion of this issue, *see* Peter Rogers, *Comprehensive Water Resources Management—A Concept Paper*, World Bank Policy Research Working Papers: WPS 879 (World Bank 1992).

- *China*: The statute requires comprehensive planning that takes into account all factors, including avoiding floods and other disasters, and the unified treatment of surface and groundwater.
- *European Union*: The Water Framework Directive states that it creates a framework for the protection of water and that water policy must be integrated with energy, transport, agricultural, forestry, and tourism policies. The Directive is also linked to environmental directives that aim at preserving, protecting, and improving the quality of the environment and that seek to apply precautionary and polluter-pays principles to environmental matters.[249]
- *Germany*: The statute stipulates that water must be protected, efforts must be made to ensure that there is no ecological damage done to water, and all due caution must be taken to avoid pollution of water.
- *South Africa*: The statute requires the protection of aquatic ecosystems and biological diversity, as well as the prevention of pollution.

Third, the majority of the statutes have sustainability as one of their underlying principles; most of those statutes clarify that sustainability means balancing the needs of present and future generations.[250] The water statute in Mexico, for instance, specifies that national water plans must be based on natural replenishment of water levels.

Fourth, a few jurisdictions include either equity or fairness as one of the principles underlying their water statutes. The statutes of South Africa and Kazakhstan refer to equity; Vietnam's law states that fairness is one of its underlying principles.

Fifth, the statutes in a number of jurisdictions stipulate priorities for water use. In all cases the highest priority is given to drinking water for human beings. Thereafter the priorities vary depending on the specific situation in each country. However, usually greater priority is given to using water for other domestic human purposes, livestock, and agriculture than to industrial use. Transportation and recreational uses are usually given lower priorities.

Costa Rica has an unusual list of priorities. It gives highest priority to drinking water and then to public services, drinking troughs for animals, milk

---

[249] *See* in this connection the Convention on Environmental Impact Assessment in Transboundary Context (signed in Espoo, Finland, on February 25, 1991), which entered into force on September 10, 1997, 30 ILM 800 (1991). *See also* Bosnjaovic, *supra* n. 122.

[250] A number of international and regional conventions and treaties now incorporate the principle of sustainability. For example, the United Nations Convention on the Law of the Non-Navigational Uses of International Watercourses (36 ILM 700, 1997) refers in the preamble to the need for "the promotion of the optimal and sustainable utilization thereof for present and future generations."

production, transportation, and finally small-scale irrigation, industrial use, and large-scale irrigation. In China, France, Nepal, Vietnam, and Yemen the priorities are of general applicability, while in the cases of Brazil, Costa Rica, and Morocco the priorities are only explicitly applicable to situations of water shortage.

Sixth, three jurisdictions—Armenia, Kazakhstan, and South Africa—establish some form of water reserve that is set aside exclusively to provide people with certain minimum quantities of water for their personal use. In Armenia and South Africa, part of this reserve is also set aside for ecological purposes.[251]

Seventh, the water statutes of Armenia and Brazil explicitly recognize the economic value of water as one of their underlying principles. Furthermore, Armenia defines economic value.[252]

Finally, a number of jurisdictions (Armenia, Brazil, China, the European Union, Kazakhstan, Mexico, Morocco, South Africa, and Yemen) specify that one of the objectives of their statutes is to establish a national plan for the water under their authority.

3.3 Regulation of Water Uses

3.3.1 Ownership and Establishment of Water Rights

As specified earlier, ownership of water resources in all the jurisdictions is vested as a general rule in the state, the people, or the state acting as a custodian. Nevertheless, in a number of jurisdictions, a certain amount of private ownership is permitted. In Armenia, Costa Rica, Morocco, and Yemen the water statutes explicitly provide that people have ownership rights over the rainwater that falls on or is found exclusively on their land.[253] In Brazil, France, and Germany individuals can secure, subject to certain restrictions, some rights in a water body through riparian land ownership. Costa Rica, Morocco, Senegal, South Africa, and Yemen recognize certain traditional or acquired rights in water that predate the water statute.[254]

---

[251] *See* Stein, *supra* n. 204.

[252] The "economic value" of water, according to the Water Law of Armenia, consists of the sum of the "drinking, environmental, energy potential and agricultural value of water." *See* Water Law of Armenia, art. 5(ll).

[253] For an analysis of methods of harvesting rain water and the importance of such water for the livelihoods of the rural population in India, *see Dying Wisdom—Rise, Fall and Potential of India's Traditional Water Harvesting Systems* (Anil Agarwal & Sunita Narain, eds., Centre for Science and Environment 1997).

[254] *See* Stefano Burchi, *The Interface Between Customary and Statutory Water Rights—A Statutory Perspective*, FAO Legal Papers online #45, March 2005, available at http://www.fao.org/Legal/prs-ol/lpo45.pdf.

In all the jurisdictions studied, individuals and entities have to obtain a license, permit, or concession (collectively referred to hereinafter as "license") in order to use water, to establish water systems, or to dig a well. However, most jurisdictions make an express exception to the licensing requirement for domestic or small uses.

3.3.2 Allocation of Water Rights

In most of the jurisdictions, a license granted by an agency of the State is required to use water for any purpose other than domestic or in any quantity above specified amounts. In Brazil and Cameroon, the statutes set out criteria that the State authority should consider in making its licensing decision. In some jurisdictions the statute explicitly requires public participation in the permitting process. It is noteworthy that the South African statute authorizes the authorities to issue compulsory licenses as well as licenses on application. The purpose of these compulsory licenses is to enable the authorities to ensure that water is in fact used appropriately and in ways that advance all the principles underlying the statute.[255]

Brazil, Kazakhstan, South Africa, and Yemen either establish or require the pertinent state authority to establish a system for classifying water resources. Different rules may apply to the use of water in different categories.

In half the jurisdictions (Armenia, Cameroon, Costa Rica, France, Germany, Mexico, Morocco, and Yemen), the statute explicitly treats groundwater as a separate category: In Costa Rica and Mexico groundwater can be used freely by those who have access to it or who own the land above the water. In Armenia, Cameroon, France, Germany, Morocco, and Yemen groundwater use requires a permit or license, which is obtained pursuant to the same procedures used to obtain a license to use surface water. Yemen provides an exception for existing traditional or customary uses, as well as for deepening wells up to a certain specified limit.

3.3.3 Transfer of Water Rights

A number of jurisdictions allow license or permit holders to transfer their license or permit, although in most of them prior approval or notification to the authorities is required before the transfer can take place. In Senegal, transfers can only be made to the licensee's heirs. Kazakhstan allows transfer of any permit to use water except for the general right to use water. The reason is that a general right

---

[255] *See,* by way of comparison, Ma. Concepcion J. Cruz, Luzvimnda B. Cornista & Diogenes C. Dayan, *Legal and Institutional Issues of Irrigation Water Rights in the Philippines* (Agrarian Reform Institute 1987).

is a personal right, which each natural individual has by virtue of birth. This is comparable to the right of each South African to a minimum amount of water to meet basic human needs. This right is based on a personal constitutional right, which also cannot be transferred.

Mexico and South Africa explicitly allow licensees or permit holders to change the use to which they put the water they have been allocated under the terms of their license or permit. Other jurisdictions require prior approval of the authorities, and a few do not allow such a change.

3.3.4 Loss of Right to Use Water

The water statutes of most jurisdictions state that the authorities can suspend or revoke licenses or permits to use water because the permit or license holder has misused the water or has failed to comply with the law or the terms of the license, or in the public interest. In Germany and Vietnam the holder of a permit or license may be entitled to compensation if the license or permit is revoked or suspended in the public interest.[256] The statutes in Brazil and Germany allow for partial suspension and revocation of licenses.

The laws in some jurisdictions allow the authorities to amend the terms of the license. In Kazakhstan and Morocco the statutes stipulate that the amendment must be in the public interest.

In most jurisdictions licenses will be lost if the license holder fails to use the license within a specified period of time or stops using it for a specified period. The purpose of these provisions is to ensure that the water resources of the jurisdiction are actually used in ways that are consistent with the principles underlying the statutes.

In almost all cases, licenses are issued for set periods of time and can be renewed. Usually, however, the statute does not explicitly address renewal, the exceptions being Armenia, Brazil, and Costa Rica, where the statutes authorize such renewals.

3.4 Protection of Water

The statutes in all the jurisdictions examined in this study include provisions dealing with protection of water against pollution. However, they do so with varying degrees of specificity and scope of protection. Some statutes address specific aspects that must be protected. The Armenian statute stresses protecting water for

---

[256] It is possible that other jurisdictions also offer compensation in these circumstances. Their water laws, however, do not explicitly address this issue, though it might be addressed under other laws.

human needs and for the ecosystem.[257] The Brazilian statute requires protection of the quality, quantity, and flow of water. China, in addition to including provisions dealing with protection of water in its basic water law, has a separate statute that deals exclusively with water pollution. Germany and South Africa take a comprehensive and detailed approach to protection of water.

Armenia, Germany, South Africa, and Yemen establish specially protected water resource zones or areas. Armenia and South Africa establish legally defined water reserves that are protected to meet both present and future human and ecological needs. Germany and Yemen require the authorities to designate certain water resources as protected areas in which the use of water is substantially restricted and requires special approval.

In most jurisdictions, the statutes specify the parties that are responsible for protecting water. In some of these jurisdictions responsibility is shared between state authorities, subnational authorities, and users. In three of these jurisdictions, responsibility is shared between state authorities and users.

The statutes take different approaches to the issues of setting standards for water quality, quantity, and flow and determining acceptable levels of pollutants in water. Some establish basic standards, while others delegate responsibility for developing such standards to a specific regulatory body. In the case of the European Union, while the Water Framework Directive contains extensive annexes that spell out specific standards, it also delegates to the Member States responsibility to protect water and to develop standards for water within their jurisdictions.

3.5 Regulation of Water Infrastructure

In most jurisdictions, the water statute stipulates that licenses are required not only for water use but also to construct water installations or infrastructure for water use. Some jurisdictions stipulate that the State is responsible for either constructing or overseeing the construction and operation of water infrastructure. In Armenia and Kazakhstan, the owner or operator of the infrastructure is responsible for the safety of the infrastructure. In France, Kazakhstan, Mexico, South Africa, and Vietnam private individuals and entities are allowed to own or operate water infrastructure; in China, only agricultural collectives may do so. The

---

[257] For definition of the term "ecosystem," *see* Malin Falkenmark, *supra* n. 41. *See also* the definition in the Convention on Biological Diversity and the World Bank Water Policy, both *supra* n. 41. As discussed earlier the concept of the ecosystem is broad and includes flora, fauna, and land contiguous to the water source. For further analysis of the concept of "ecosystem," *see* David Hunter, James Salzman & Durwood Zaelke, *International Environmental Law and Policy* 842 (Foundation Press 1998).

water statutes in Brazil and Cameroon have no provisions dealing with water infrastructure, which is regulated under other laws.[258]

3.6 Institutional Arrangements

In most of the jurisdictions, the main water statute assigns to the national government or a designated agency in the national government explicit responsibility for regulation and management of water. It is interesting to note the wide variation in the agencies responsible for water in the countries covered in this study, as well as in other countries. While China, Nepal, and Senegal have each created a ministry dedicated exclusively to water (the Ministry of Water Resources, or Water Affairs), other countries have placed responsibility for water and one or more other responsibilities in a single ministry. In Morocco, it is the Ministry of Land Management, Water and Environment, in Yemen, the Ministry of Electricity and Water.[259] In South Africa, water is under the Ministry of Water Affairs and Forestry, in Vietnam, the Ministry of Agriculture and Rural Development. In Armenia, water is under the Ministry of Nature Protection, in Brazil, the Ministry of Environment. In Cameroon, water was under the Ministry of Mines, Water and Energy until recently, when the Ministry of Energy and Water was created.[260]

The picture outside the countries studied is equally diverse. India has established the Ministry of Water Resources, exclusively dedicated to water matters,[261] while other countries have placed responsibility for water with other sectors in a single ministry. In Namibia and Uzbekistan it is the Ministry of Agriculture and Water. In Egypt, Jordan, and Sudan, it is the Ministry of Irrigation and Water. In Zambia, it is the Ministry of Energy and Water, and in Saudi Arabia the Ministry of Electricity and Water.

Some of the countries studied have established a national water council and assigned it responsibilities over water (Armenia, France, and Morocco). Others

---

[258] For an analysis of the regulatory frameworks for dam safety in Brazil, China, Mexico, and South Africa, among other countries, *see* Daniel Bradlow, Alessandro Palmieri & Salman M. A. Salman, *Regulatory Frameworks for Dam Safety—A Comparative Study* (World Bank 2002).

[259] As indicated earlier, proposed amendments to the Water Law in Yemen have established the Ministry of Water and Environment, replacing the Ministry of Electricity and Water.

[260] *See* Decree of the Cameroon Government No. 2004/322 of December 8, 2004.

[261] In addition to the Ministry of Water Resources, India has also established the Central Water Commission (CWC), which is presently functioning as an attached office of the Ministry of Water Resources. The CWC is charged with the general responsibilities of initiating, coordinating, and furthering, in consultation of the State Governments concerned, schemes for control, conservation, and utilization of water resources throughout India. *See* Saleth, *supra* n. 2.

have created a special agency for this purpose, such as the National Water Agency (ANA) in Brazil, the National Water Resources Authority (NWRA) in Yemen, or the National Water Commission (NCA) in Mexico. This is a clear indication of the multidisciplinary nature of water and a testimony to its close connection to other sectors.

In some jurisdictions, subnational governmental authorities or a designated agency within them are assigned some responsibility for the regulation and management of water. The designated subnational authorities can be a combination of state or provincial governments and local municipalities, prefectures, or districts.[262]

3.6.1   River Basin Authorities

In Brazil, the European Union, Kazakhstan, Morocco, South Africa, Vietnam, and Yemen the water statute stipulates that the river basin must be the unit for water management. In Germany, the unit is the water district, which often coincides with the river basin. In most of those jurisdictions the government appoints a river basin authority that has responsibility for managing water affairs in a particular basin. Armenia, Brazil, France, Morocco, and South Africa explicitly provide for nongovernmental participation in the basin authority.

3.6.2   Water Users' Associations

Most jurisdictions provide for water users' associations to represent the interests of users and to play some role in the management of water and the operation and maintenance of water facilities. Some of the jurisdictions provide that the associations are to be established at the initiative of users, while others stipulate that the government will establish the associations.[263] The South African statute allows water users' associations to be established at the initiative of either the users or the government. Some statutes include details on the establishment and responsibilities of water users' associations, while others have left those details to subsidiary legislation.[264] Thus, the extent of decentralization and public participation in water management varies considerably from one jurisdiction to another.[265]

---

[262] *See* Harald Frederiksen, *Water Resources Institutions: Some Principles and Practices*, World Bank Technical Paper 191 (World Bank 1992).

[263] *See* Gorriz, Subramanian & Simas, *supra* n. 170.

[264] *See* Vishal Narain, *Brackets and Black Boxes: Research on Water Users' Associations*, 6 Water Policy 185 (2004).

[265] *See* Krchnak, *supra* n. 31.

3.6.3   Advisory Committees

Armenia, France, Morocco, and Vietnam have created specific advisory bodies. The South African statutes give the government the authority to establish advisory bodies if it wishes to do so. The rest of the statutes are silent on this issue.

3.7   Financial Arrangements

The majority of the jurisdictions provide for fees or charges to be levied for water use, and most of them allow for specific user fees, including licensing fees. Those jurisdictions also state principles on which the fees or charges should be based. The principle of cost recovery is specifically stipulated in Armenia, Brazil, China, the European Union, Mexico, and South Africa. Brazil, South Africa, and Yemen also stipulate that the fees should help finance the cost of investments in water infrastructure and of developing water resources. The statutes in Brazil, Mexico, and South Africa provide that the authorities should consider all relevant factors in setting fees or charges.[266]

The Chinese statute, in addition to mentioning cost recovery, requires regulators to base fees on an equitable sharing of costs and on higher prices for higher-quality water. The Moroccan statute does not state any particular criteria or principles that should be applied in setting fees; instead it requires the authorities to establish, through regulations, procedures that must be followed in setting fees and charges. Vietnam stipulates that users can be required to provide both fees and manpower in return for the water they use.[267] The Senegalese statute stipulates that fees must be charged for any use that alters the quality of water.[268] Armenia, Kazakhstan, and South Africa state that the authorities can provide direct or indirect financial support to specific categories of water users based on their income.

A few of the regulatory frameworks examined in chapter 2 deal with the role of the private sector in water resources management. As the country studies indicate, only the water statutes of South Africa refer in detail to the role of the private sector, though those of Armenia and Mexico provide general references to this role. Such general references are intended to provide the enabling

---

[266] *See* Dinar & Subramanian (eds.), *supra* n. 62. Twenty-two countries are surveyed in this Technical Paper, including Brazil and France.

[267] *See* art. 7 (1) of the Law on Water Resources in Vietnam. Manpower can also be mobilized under art. 41 to combat floods.

[268] In this connection *see* Jean G. Chatila, *Water Tariffs in Lebanon: A Review and Perspective*, 7 Water Policy 215 (2005). *See also* Warren Musgrave, *The Political Economy of Water Price Reform in Australia*, in Dinar (ed.), *supra* n. 62, at 299.

framework for participation of the private sector, leaving the details for agreement between government water agency or authority and private entity. As discussed above in section 2.1.7, the Armenia Water Code provides in article 48 that State-owned water systems can be under State and/or private management. The article further provides that preference be given to private entities with more extensive professional experience and knowledge, and that the transfer of rights for the use of a water system shall not exceed the term specified in the water system use permit.

Similarly, as stated in section 2.10.7, the Water Act in Mexico refers to the possible role of the private sector in water services. Article 7 of that act states that it is in the public interest to promote private sector participation in the financing, construction, and operation of federal water infrastructure, as well as in the supply of water and electricity.[269]

The South African NWA and WSA provide more details about the role of the private sector than any other statutes examined in this study. As discussed in section 2.14.7, the NWA authorizes the Minister, with regard to a government waterworks, to make regulations providing for the private development of government waterworks. Article 19 of the WSA states that a water services authority may enter into a contract with a private sector water services provider, but only after it has considered all known public sector water services providers that are willing and able to perform the necessary functions. The water service authority is required to disclose to the public its intention of entering into or renewing a contract with a water services provider other than a public water services institution, as well as the rate of return on the investment. The law gives the Minister of Water Affairs and Forestry wide authority in regulating the role of the private sector.

Thus, only the South African water codes provide relatively detailed provisions on the role of the private sector in water service delivery. The references in the Armenia and Mexico statutes to the role of the private sector are general, leaving the details for the contract with the private entity.

The South African constitution and statutes, as discussed earlier, also include explicit provisions regarding the right of all citizens to access to sufficient quantities of water. There are similar provisions in the water statutes of Armenia, France, and Kazakhstan. The underlying purpose of those provisions is to protect the poorest and most vulnerable segments of society. This is particularly important in those countries, given the role that their statutes provide for private sector participation in water service delivery.

---

[269] For an example of the roles of the public and private sector in water resources management, *see* Carlos Salazar, *Water Resources Management in Chile*, in Tortajada *et al.* (eds.), *supra* n. 166, at 113.

3.8 Enforcement of Regulations and Dispute Resolution

3.8.1 Enforcement of Regulation

The statutes in all jurisdictions provide for inspections as part of the regime for enforcing water law and regulations. In Armenia, Nepal, South Africa, and Yemen the enforcement regime includes monitoring and studies in addition to inspections. Armenia is the only jurisdiction that explicitly requires periodic reporting by users and lower-level regulators as part of the enforcement and monitoring regime. Similarly, all the jurisdictions stipulate that acts and omissions that amount to noncompliance with the laws and regulations and with the terms of licenses, as well as unauthorized uses of water, can lead to sanctions.

There is some variation in the sanctions that can be applied in the case of violations of laws, regulations, and the terms of permits and licenses. All jurisdictions levy fines for violations, and many provide for jail terms. Other sanctions include injunctions (Brazil), censures (Brazil), and damages to those harmed by the violation (South Africa).[270] Interestingly, the water statutes in China and Vietnam, besides providing sanctions against violators, provide for rewards for those who perform particularly well in executing their responsibilities.

3.8.2 Dispute Settlement

The jurisdictions studied take a number of approaches to resolving disputes between water users and between water users and the authorities. Armenia, Costa Rica, Mexico, and South Africa have created special bodies to resolve such disputes—Armenia has a Dispute Resolution Commission, Costa Rica Inspectors of the National Electricity Service, and Mexico the National Water Commission. South Africa has established a Water Tribunal to hear appeals on decisions rendered by the management authority. In Brazil, river basin authorities are assigned specific responsibility for resolving disputes between water users subject to their authority. Armenia assigns this responsibility to the local water users' association.[271]

Furthermore, the water statutes in Brazil, China, France, Kazakhstan, South Africa, and Vietnam do assign some responsibility for dispute resolution to the

---

[270] In some jurisdictions, such as British Columbia, Canada, other sanctions include community service, and contributions to the state conservation fund.

[271] For discussion of the role of nongovernmental entities in dispute resolution, *see* J. Delli Priscoli, *Collaboration, Participation and Alternative Dispute Resolution: Process Concepts for the World Bank's Role in Water Resources,* Agriculture and Rural Development Department (World Bank 1992).

regulatory authorities. In China, the regulators act as mediators in disputes between individuals and between lower levels of government.

Courts are assigned a role by most jurisdictions in resolving disputes between individuals and between individuals and the water agency. In China, the courts will hear disputes between individuals or organizations. The courts' role in civil disputes in Armenia, Nepal, and South Africa is limited to hearing appeals from other water dispute settlement bodies. In France and South Africa, the courts will hear cases involving violations that can lead to jail sentences. The state authority in Senegal can prosecute any disputes or file a claim against any person alleged to have violated the law before any competent judicial authority. In Kazakhstan, disputes can be brought to court by the interested parties at any time. In most jurisdictions, cases against the government can only be instituted in the court system.

CHAPTER 4

Regulatory Frameworks for Water Resources Management: Essential Elements and Emerging Trends

Chapter 2 of this study describes the regulatory frameworks for water resources management in sixteen jurisdictions. It specifies certain key elements and examines how the legislation in each jurisdiction has addressed those elements. Chapter 3 provides a comparative analysis of the approaches of those jurisdictions to the elements discussed in the first part of the study, with the view to identifying similarities and differences. This chapter will now set forth the elements that any country needs to consider when debating, designing, and preparing a regulatory framework for water resources management.[272] The goal is to lay out essential elements, together with explanations for the choices. The chapter also analyzes emerging trends in water legislation. It should be emphasized that this chapter is not intended as a rigid prescription or as an endorsement of one particular approach over others.

The detailed road map for water legislation that was set forth in the recommendations and resolutions of the Mar del Plata Water Conference is, in our view, still valid, relevant, and useful.[273] Most of the substantive and procedural elements laid down in that road map have been reflected in water legislation worldwide. The Dublin Principles underscored those recommendations and have sharpened and focused them. However, it should be emphasized that water legislation of necessity must keep evolving to accommodate emerging trends in water resources management, development, and protection.

4.1 Process for Preparing Water Legislation

The process of preparing a new water law or revising an existing one should be transparent, participatory, and inclusive. All entities and individuals involved with water—government ministries and agencies, academic institutions, civil society organizations, representatives of different sectors of users, and the private

---

[272] *See also* Stefano Burchi, *Preparing National Regulations for Water Resources Management—Principles and Practice,* FAO Legislative Studies 52, 44 (FAO 1994).

[273] *See supra* n. 3.

sector—need to be involved in the process. One of the four Dublin Principles discussed earlier calls for water development and management to be based on a participatory approach involving users, planners, and policy makers at all levels.[274]

This process needs to start, as the Mar del Plata Water Conference recommended, with a review of existing rules and regulations. The purpose of such a review would be to ascertain areas of weaknesses and strengths and examine, based on the implementation experience, where the rules worked and where they did not. This would facilitate the process of identifying both issues that need to be addressed in the proposed statute and gaps that need to be filled.

The process should lead to the preparation of a background policy paper—a white paper, as South Africa called it.[275] Such a paper would outline the main policies, principles, and procedures to be included in the draft law and agree on institutions that will manage and develop water. The more transparent, participatory, and inclusive this process is, the better the chances that the regulatory framework will be widely accepted, supported, and owned.[276] Such ownership and acceptance will remove considerable obstacles that would otherwise be faced in implementation. Indeed, Principle 10 of the Rio Declaration calls for participation of all concerned citizens at all relevant levels on environmental issues. Such participation would include access to information and the opportunity to participate in the decision-making processes.[277]

Because water is a multidisciplinary subject, provisions governing its use, management, development, and protection may be incorporated into a number of laws and regulations. It is important that the basic elements for the regulatory

---

[274] *See* Principle 2 of the Dublin Statement, *infra* appendix I. *See also supra* n. 14.

[275] Department of Water Affairs and Forestry of South Africa, *supra* n. 202, at 4. Namibia also adopted the National Water Policy White Paper in 2001 as a basis for the preparation of its water law. Similarly, Bangladesh issued its National Water Policy in 1999. One of the main objectives of this policy is to develop a legal and regulatory environment. Bangladesh has not yet adopted a water law.

[276] *See* Erik Mostert, *The Challenge of Public Participation,* 5 Water Policy 179 (2003). *See also* Jerome Delli Priscoli, *What Is Public Participation in Water Resources Management and Why Is it Important?* 29 Water Intl. 221 (2004).

[277] Principle 10 of the Rio Declaration states that

Environmental issues are best handled with the participation of all concerned citizens, at the relevant level. At the national level, each individual shall have appropriate access to information concerning the environment that is held by public authorities, including information on hazardous materials and activities in their communities, and the opportunity to participate in decision-making processes. States shall facilitate and encourage public awareness and participation by making information widely available. Effective access to judicial and administrative proceedings, including redress and remedy, shall be provided.

For the Rio Declaration *see* U.N. Doc.A/CONF. 151/26, 31 ILM 874 (1992).

framework for water resources management, to the extent possible, be included in one legal instrument, the basic water law. This way, policymakers, managers, users, and other concerned entities and citizens have a single specific legal instrument on which they can rely for guidance.[278] This approach decreases the possibility of having inconsistent, or even conflicting, provisions dealing with water resources management scattered in a number of laws. It also decreases the possibility of gaps or overlapping provisions in legislation.

Obviously, subsidiary legislation, such as bylaws, regulations, and decrees, would still be needed to address in detail some of the basic provisions in the water law. The advantage of subsidiary legislation is that it provides flexibility for meeting evolving and changing circumstances without the need for amendment of the legislation, where the usual cumbersome legislative process would have to be followed. However, as with any subsidiary legislation, this flexibility should be used only where necessary because overuse could result in loss of predictability in water legislation.

As we have seen in the previous chapters, major water resources issues like ownership, protection, and accessibility are increasingly finding a place in the constitutions of countries. Such constitutional provisions provide guiding principles for water legislation and underscore basic principles therefor.

4.2   Ownership of Water Resources

One main issue that any water legislation needs to address is ownership of the resource. The various historical theories that prevailed in the last two centuries have gradually given way to a considerable state role in ownership and allocation of water resources. One of those theories, the doctrine of riparian rights that gave land owners rights over waters bordering their land, is losing its grip in most parts of the world. So is the doctrine of prior appropriation, which is based on the rule "first in time, first in right"—meaning that whoever used the water first has a superior right over other users or claimants.[279] The current thinking is that water resources, both surface and groundwater, should be owned, controlled, regulated,

---

[278] It should be noted, however, that some countries have dealt with water resources issues in two separate laws. Armenia has a Water Law and a Water Users' Associations Law. China has a Water Law and a Water Pollution Law. South Africa has a Water Law and a Water Services Law.

[279] For a detailed discussion of those theories, *see* Ludwick Teclaff, *Water Law in Historical Perspective* 6 (William S. Hein & Co. 1985); and Ludwick Teclaff, *What You Always Wanted to KnowAabout Riparian Rights but Were Afraid to Ask,* 12 Natural Resources J. 30 (1972). *See also* Dante A. Caponera, *Principles of Water Law and Administration—National and International* 65 (A. A. Balkema 1992); David Getches, *Water Law in a Nutshell* (West Publishing 1997); and Joshua Getzler, *A History of Water Rights at Common Law* (Oxford Univ. Press 2004).

and allocated by the State. This is based on the public property status of water and the superior user right of the government. It is also based on vesting in the State a public trust over water on behalf of the entire population, whereby the government becomes the public custodian of water resources.[280]

Some countries, like South Africa, have effectively and explicitly abolished the riparian system of allocation of water and replaced it with the public trust doctrine.[281] In other countries, like the United States, states have gradually started to subject the principle of prior appropriation of water to the public trust doctrine.[282] The basic principles of Islamic water law prescribe that water is the entitlement of the whole community, thus proclaiming as a general rule communal ownership.[283]

Accordingly, public ownership of water has gradually emerged as the rule worldwide.[284] As discussed earlier, the Bonn Declaration emphasized that the primary responsibility for ensuring sustainable and equitable management of water resources rests with governments.[285] The Declaration went even further, stating

---

[280] For a discussion of how Chile developed its approach, *see* Carl J. Bauer, *Siren Song—Chilean Water Law as a Model for International Reform* 31 (Resources for the Future 2004).

[281] *See* Department of Water Affairs and Forestry of South Africa, *supra* n. 202. *See also* the discussion of the South Africa Water Law in section 2.14 above.

[282] *See* Eric L. Garner, *How States in the United States Have Handled the Transition from Common Law Riparianism to Permitting Regulation,* in *Issues in Water Law Reform, supra* n. 160, at 135. *See also* Jan Stevens, *Current Developments in the Public Trust Doctrine and Other Instream Protection Measures,* in *Water Law, Trends, Policies and Practice* 141 (Kathleen Marion Carr & James D. Crammond, eds., American Bar Association 1995). Stevens reviewed and analyzed in this article the decision of the California Supreme Court in *National Audubon v. Superior Court* (33 Cal. 3d 419, 189 Cal. Rptr. 346, 658 p.2d 709 (1983)), in which the Supreme Court discussed the diversion by the City of Los Angeles of water from four streams that feed Lake Mono. That diversion resulted in a sharp decrease in the level of the lake. It also resulted in extreme adverse effects to aquatic life in and the ecological situation of the lake. The Court ruled that there is an affirmative duty to take the public trust into account in the planning and allocation of water resources. *See* Stevens, *id.* at 142. Other authors argued further that the case represents the demise of the principle of prior appropriation. *See* Stevens, *id.* at 149. The latter view is based on the statement by the Court that the public trust doctrine presents an "integrated system of preserving the continuing sovereign power of the state to protect public uses, a power which precludes any one from acquiring a vested right to harm the public trust, and imposes a continuing duty on the state to take such uses into account in allocating water resources."

[283] For a discussion of the concept of water ownership in Islamic law, *see* Caponera, *supra* n. 239. *See also* Faruqui, Biswas & Bino (eds.), *supra* n. 239.

[284] *See also* Food and Agriculture Organization of the United Nations, *Law and Sustainable Development Since Rio—Legal Trends in Agriculture and Natural Resources Management,* FAO Legislative Studies 73, 145 (FAO 2002).

[285] *See* Declaration of the Ministerial Session of the International Conference on Freshwater, held in Bonn, Germany, December 2001. *See also supra* n. 30.

that "Privately managed service delivery should not imply private ownership of water resources."[286] Ownership includes surface water and atmospheric water as well as groundwater. It should be noted in this regard that a number of statutes do exempt from public ownership rainwater falling on and stored in privately owned land, considering such waters the private dominion of the owner of the land.[287]

For groundwater, there are still challenges in some parts of the world to the concept of state ownership or custodianship, based on the belief that whoever owns the land owns the water beneath it.[288] Although this belief stems from custom and tradition, it is gradually losing its strength.[289] Under the doctrine of the public property status of water, the owner of the overlying land has only the right to use of the water under the land, subject to certain restrictions and limitations imposed by the state as a custodian of the country's water resources.[290] However, enforcement of this doctrine is facing challenges in many parts of the world.[291]

4.3   Underlying Principles and Priorities

Water legislation would usually specify principles and priorities that are expected to guide decisions concerning water. Such principles can include conservation and protection of the state's water resources, equitable division of

---

[286] *See id.,* sec. 2 of the Declaration under "G.—Governance."

[287] *See* the discussions in chapter 2 under Armenia, Costa Rica, Morocco, and Yemen.

[288] *See* Food and Agriculture Organization of the United Nations, *Groundwater Legislation in Europe,* Legislative Series No. 5 (FAO 1964). *See also* Ludwick Teclaff, *Water Law in Historical Perspective, supra* n. 279, Ch. III—Groundwater, the Elusive Resource: A Search for Pattern, at 145.

[289] *See* Jacob Burke & Marcus Moench, *Groundwater and Society: Resources, Tensions and Opportunities—Themes in Groundwater Management for the Twenty-First Century,* United Nations Department of Economic and Social Affairs (United Nations 2000).

[290] One question that has often been raised is whether the owners of the land are entitled to compensation from the government for what might be considered the taking away of private property, that is, ownership of water in such land. Court decisions in a number of countries have consistently rejected this argument and upheld the superior common good doctrine, as well as the public trust doctrine presented by governments for taking over ownership of groundwater, allowing the owner only a limited right of use. For an analysis of the issues related to land ownership and groundwater, *see* Stefano Burchi, *National Regulations for Groundwater: Options, Issues and Best Practices,* in Salman (ed.), *supra* n. 163, at 55.

[291] It is worth noting that some countries, like Jordan, have issued a specific policy on groundwater. *See* Hashemite Kingdom of Jordan, Ministry of Water & Irrigation, *Groundwater Management Policy* (1998). This is a detailed document addressing such issues as exploration, resource protection, sustainability and quality control, priority allocation, regulation and control, institutional arrangements, research, development and technology, shared groundwater resources, public awareness, and private sector participation. However, it should be added that this is a policy statement intending to influence legislation, not a groundwater law, and as such is not a binding legal instrument.

the resource among all potential users, sustainable use of water resources, use of water to promote economic development, and efficient management of water resources. The concept of integrated water resources management (IWRM) is increasingly being stated as one of the principles.[292]

The United Nations Conference on Environment and Development (UNCED) has addressed the concept, stating that

> the holistic management of freshwater as a finite and vulnerable resource, and the integration of sectoral water plans and programs within the framework of national economic and social policy, are of paramount importance. . . . Integrated water resources management is based on the perception of water as an integral part of the ecosystem, a natural resource and social and economic good.[293]

As discussed earlier, IWRM aims to ensure the coordinated development and management of water, land, and related resources by maximizing economic and social welfare without compromising the sustainability of vital environmental systems.[294]

Sustainable and efficient water management requires good planning. This suggests that each jurisdiction needs to develop plans for how it will manage and regulate its water resources. Consequently, water legislation could stipulate the types of plans—national, regional, basin plans—the authorities are required to

---

[292] *See* Torkil Jonch-Clausen & Jens Fugl, *Firming up the Conceptual Basis of Integrated Water Resources Management,* 17 Intl. J. of Water Resources Dev. 501 (2001). *See also* B. P. F. Braga, *Integrated Urban Water Resources Management: A Challenge into the 21st Century*, 17 Int'l J. Water Resources Mgmt. 581 (2001).

[293] *See* Earth Summit, Agenda 21, *supra* n. 18. This approach has been adopted by the African Development Bank, which defines IWRM as "A comprehensive approach to water resources management that views water as a single resource with competing uses and interlinkages with the ecological, social and economic systems." *See* African Development Bank & African Development Fund, *supra* n. 5, at iii.

[294] *See* Global Water Partnership, *supra* n. 17. The Asian Development Bank definition of IWRM is in line with this approach. It defines IWRM as

> a process to improve the planning, conservation, development, and management of water, forest, land, and aquatic resources in the river basin context, to maximize economic benefits and social welfare in an equitable manner without compromising the sustainability of vital environmental systems. IWRM addresses quantity and quality concerns of surface and groundwater, and opportunities for their conjunctive use.

See Asian Development Bank, *supra* n. 6, at 19. The policy goes on to link decentralization and IWRM when it suggests "It is typical for the IWRM to be undertaken in a river basin context because river basins, or in some cases groundwater basins, form the natural unit to manage water resources." *See* Asian Development Bank, *id.* at 19.

develop, and the issues that they should address. The legislation could also stipulate how the information needed to develop these plans should be collected.

The list of guiding principles is usually supplemented by a specific set of priorities in water uses. The highest priority is usually given to personal and domestic uses. This is generally followed by water for livestock. Agriculture and industry uses follow thereafter, with the order depending on the priorities of the country. In this connection, one of the issues that the legislation may want to address is how to guarantee the right of the poor and vulnerable groups in the society to adequate water for personal and domestic use. This issue, now articulated as the larger concept of the human right to water, is discussed in section 4.10 below.

It is worth noting, too, that the South Africa NWA specifies that one of its purposes is to ensure that its water resources are protected, used, developed, conserved, managed, and controlled in ways that take into account, among other factors, "meeting international obligations." It is generally argued that protection of the ecosystems of water resources is indeed a domestic legislative step to give effect to a State's international obligations.[295] However, not all water resources are shared with other States. Thus, the South African requirement is perhaps the first time that national water legislation has referred to a State's international obligations.[296]

4.4 Regulation of Water Uses

As a public trustee of the nation's water, the State is entrusted with responsibility for ensuring that water is allocated equitably and beneficially, as well as with authority for regulating the use, flow, and control of all types of water in the State. A general rule in most statutes relates to the requirement for a permit or license to be issued by the government in accordance with clear and transparent criteria and procedures before a person can use water or construct water infrastructure. In essence, the permit grants a water right to this person.

Such a permit would describe the types of water uses allowed, the quantity of water that can be used, the water standards with which the permit holder must comply, the duration of the permit,[297] the process for its renewal, and the water permit fees. In relation to groundwater, well spacing and the current amount of

---

[295] *See* Philippe Sands, 1 *Principles of International Environmental Law* 9 (Manchester Univ. Press 1994).

[296] *See* Stein, *supra* n. 204, at 294. As discussed earlier, art. 78 of the China Water Law subjects China's domestic law to its international treaties and agreements dealing with international rivers and lakes.

[297] In most legislation the duration of the permit extends between ten to thirty years and is renewable.

water being drawn from the aquifer in question can be other factors to be considered in deciding whether to award a permit. However, in some countries permits are not required if the depth of the well does not exceed a specified limit. In addition, most legislation exempts domestic uses, up to a specified amount per day, from the requirement for a permit.[298] Other issues to be addressed include procedures for challenging unfavorable decisions on water rights.

One issue facing most countries preparing water legislation is how to verify and regularize water uses that existed before the legislation is adopted. Some of those existing rights may be traditional or customary water rights acquired by local communities long before the water law was adopted. Others may simply be claimed through use over time. Detailed procedures are needed to ensure equity, fairness, efficiency, and transparency when confirming, all or in part, or rejecting existing uses.[299]

Other matters that need to be addressed by water legislation include transfer of water rights to a third party and the conditions under which transfer can take place. They also include the circumstances under which the right to use water is lost, suspended, amended, or revoked. It is worth mentioning that in all cases studied the transfer requires prior authorization from the government, which has the discretion to refuse it. However, not all water statutes allow transferring the right of use to a third party and transfer could be a reason for revocation of a permit. Other reasons for the loss or suspension of a permit include failure to use the water over which the right is granted for a specified uninterrupted period of time; failure to comply with the terms of the permit, as a result of a court ruling to that effect; and failure to start using the right within a certain period of time.[300]

Some water statutes authorize the government to amend the permit if the person is using considerably less water than the permit allows. However, if amendment of the permit to decrease the amount of water granted is not the result of the person using less water or is not due to an emergency situation, compensation

---

[298] As discussed earlier, art. 22 of the Armenia Water Code lists six uses for which a permit is not required. Those uses are termed "free water use" and justified by the fact that they do not have a profit-making purpose. They are recreation, swimming and water sports, nonentrepreneurial fishing and hunting, the use of precipitation on privately held lands, water use for fire prevention, and water flows to maintain ecological balance for sanitary purposes.

[299] *See* in this regard arts. 32–35 of the South Africa National Water Act on "Existing Lawful Water Uses." Art. 32 states that such uses should have taken place any time during a period of two years immediately before the date of commencement of the NWA. Art. 35 lays down detailed procedures for verification of such uses.

[300] *See Negotiating Water Rights* (Bryan Randolph Bruns & Ruth Meinzen-Dick, eds., Intl. Food Policy Research Inst. 2000). *See also* Chhatrapati Singh, *Water Rights in India,* in *Water Law in India* 8 (Chhatrapati Singh, ed., Indian Law Institute & Sweet & Maxwell, Ltd. 1992).

may be payable to the holder of the permit.[301] In addition, the legislation would need to address the fact that the government, as a public trustee, should be vested with authority in case of an emergency, such as drought, to suspend or amend the right and reprioritize water uses, with no provision for compensation.

4.5 Protection of Water Resources

Protection of water resources is another element that proposed legislation needs to address. Protection includes

- prevention and abatement of both point source pollution and diffuse pollution;[302]
- regulation of the discharge of wastewater and other wastes;
- regulation of land use, particularly land cultivation practices; and
- adoption of detailed procedures for enforcement of water quality standards, particularly for water for domestic uses.

Those issues may be addressed under the umbrella of environmental management of water resources.[303] The legislation would need to specify the party or parties at each level of the government (national, regional, and local) that are responsible for ensuring protection of water quality.

Some water statutes, like that of Armenia, have expanded the concept of protection to require protection of the water ecosystem, which is a wider concept. Such an ecosystem would go beyond water to cover fauna and flora as well as the land contiguous to the water resource, which should be used in a manner that does not harm the water resource.[304] It should be noted that the concept of protection of the entire ecosystem can be traced to the Mar del Plata Conference, where it was suggested that the legislation should aim at the "protection of water and water-related ecosystem."[305] As we have seen, the EC Directive and other European legislation, such as the Protocol on Water and Health, have laid down more stringent requirements regarding water quality.

---

[301] For an analysis of some of the problem areas in water rights, *see* Chris Perry and Geoff Kite, *Water Rights—Importance, Difficulties, and New Approaches to Data Collection and Analysis,* 24 Water Intl. 341 (1999).

[302] The most widely accepted definition of the term "pollution" is that used by the U.N. Convention on the Law of the Non-Navigational Uses of International Watercourses (36 ILM 700, 1997). Art. 21 of the Convention defines "pollution" to mean any detrimental alteration in the composition or quality of the water that results directly or indirectly from human conduct.

[303] *See* Yahia Abdel Mageed, *Environmentally Sound Water Management and Development,* 9 Intl. J. Water Resources Dev. 155 (1993).

[304] For detailed analyses of the concept of "ecosystem," *see* Malin Falkenmark, *supra* n. 41, and David Hunter, James Salzman & Durwood Zaelke, *supra* n. 257.

[305] *See supra* n. 3, at 11.

Groundwater needs stricter and more detailed rules for its protection because it is more vulnerable than surface water to pollution and other forms of contamination. This is due to the fact that groundwater "flows at much slower rates than surface water, which causes contamination and other problems to manifest at slower rates and reduces aquifers' natural reclamation abilities."[306] Moreover, pollution of groundwater is usually irreversible.[307] It is further argued that non-replenishable groundwater (fossil aquifers) requires more stringent protection rules.[308] Some legislation addresses the environmental sustainability of the water source, requiring that part of the water be left as a "reserve" to maintain the ecosystem of the river.[309] These developments indicate clearly that the standards for protecting water resources are evolving; therefore the legislation should be flexible enough to accommodate such evolving standards.

Two concepts that have been evolving and are now receiving increasing attention in water legislation are the precautionary principle and the polluter-pays principle. The precautionary principle has been given wide recognition by the Rio Declaration, where it is included as principle 15. That principle states: "In order to protect the environment, the precautionary approach shall be widely applied by States according to their capabilities. Where there are threats of serious or irreversible damage, lack of full scientific certainty shall not be used as a reason for postponing cost-effective measures to prevent environmental degradation."[310] The main rationale for the precautionary principle is the often irreversible character of damage to the environment and the limitations inherent in

---

[306] *See* Gabriel Eckstein, *Protecting a Hidden Treasure: The U.N. International Law Commission and the International Law of Transboundary Ground Water Resources,* 5 Sust. Dev. L. & Policy 5 (2004).

[307] *See* Stephen Foster, *Essential Concepts for Groundwater Regulators,* in Salman (ed.), *supra* n. 163, at 15. *See also* Stephen Foster, Adrian Lawrence & Brian Morris, *Groundwater in Urban Development—Assessing Management Needs and Formulating Policy Strategies,* World Bank Technical Paper No. 390, 11 (World Bank 1998); and Stephen Foster, John Chilton, Marcus Moench, Franklin Cardy & Manuel Schiffler, *Groundwater in Rural Development—Facing the Challenges of Supply and Resources Sustainability,* World Bank Technical Paper No. 463 (World Bank 2000).

[308] *See Guidelines for Development and Management of Groundwater Resources in Arid and Semi-Arid Regions,* 8 Intl. J. Water Resources Dev. 145 (1992).

[309] *See supra,* section 2.14.3.1, on the concept of the Reserve in South Africa.

[310] For the Rio Declaration *see supra* n. 277. The precautionary principle is now recognized as a general principle of international environmental law; *see The Precautionary Principle in International Law—The Challenge of Implementation* (David Freestone & Ellen Hey, eds., Kluwer Law Intl. 1996). *See, for example,* Preamble to the Convention on Biodiversity, 31 ILM 818 (1992) (entered into force December 29, 1993); article 3.3 of the United Nations Framework Convention on Climate Change, 31 ILM 818 (1992) (entered into force December 29, 1993); and the Convention on the Protection and Use of Transboundary Watercourses and International Lakes, *supra* n. 122.

the very mechanisms for reparation of this type of damage.[311] As discussed earlier, the EC Directive calls for using the precautionary principle as one of the bases for protection of the environment.[312] It is generally argued that achieving sustainable water resources management will be difficult if the precautionary principle is overlooked.

The polluter-pays principle is based on the simple premise that responsibility to pay for the costs of pollution prevention, control, reduction, and cleaning measures rests with those who cause it. This principle is in fact traceable to the Mar del Plata Water Conference, whose recommendations called on States to "adopt the general principle that, as far as possible, direct or indirect costs attributable to pollution should be borne by the polluter."[313] Similarly, the Rio Declaration urged that the polluter should, in principle, bear the cost of pollution.[314] The water policies of the World Bank and the African Development Bank called for the principle to form part of the water resources management system.[315] The principle is being increasingly incorporated into both international agreements[316] and national instruments. However, in the latter case it is often limited to waste water discharge fees, as in China.

4.6 Regulation of Water Infrastructure

Regulation of the works that are needed to provide adequate water services is not purely an issue of water law. The construction and operation of such works raises legal issues related to construction, land acquisition, environmental, and zoning law, and, in the case of public works, government procurement law. The water statute needs to address this because these works affect the quality, quantity, and flow of water. Consequently, it is important that water legislation stipulate who

---

[311] *See* International Court of Justice, Case Concerning the Gabcikovo-Nagymaros Project (Hungary/Slovakia), General List No. 92, 25 September 1997, para. 140.

[312] For a detailed discussion of the evolution and context of the precautionary principle *see* Freestone & Hey (eds.), *supra* n. 310.

[313] *See supra* n. 3, at 27.

[314] *See* Rio Declaration, *supra* n. 310, para. 16. That paragraph reads "National authorities should endeavour to promote the internalization of environmental costs and the use of economic instruments, taking into account the approach that the polluter should, in principle, bear the cost of pollution, with due regard to the public interest and without distorting international trade and investment."

[315] *See* World Bank, *supra* n. 4, at 59, and African Development Bank, *supra* n. 5, at 22.

[316] *See, for example,* Convention on the Protection and Use of Transboundary Watercourses and International Lakes, *supra* n. 122, art. 2(5)(b). *See also* Protocol for the Sustainable Development of Lake Victoria Basin (concluded in November 29, 2003), available at: http://www.eac.int/lvdp/Protocol_LV_Basin.pdf.

can operate such works and the procedures for getting permission to undertake them. This issue may be addressed, *inter alia,* through a requirement for a permit from the relevant government authority if the works are to be carried out by a private party. Both public and private entities would need to adhere to laws and regulations in this regard.

The legislation would endow the government with responsibility for the use, protection, capital investment, and safety of all state-owned water infrastructures, while making private owners responsible for their infrastructure. Private owners include water users' associations, which are allowed in some countries to build and operate their own water infrastructure. Some statutes require that water infrastructures that have special strategic importance be owned only by the state. The government has the authority to inspect privately owned water infrastructure and ensure its compliance with standards, permits, and registration requirements, including any requirements for an environmental impact assessment, as well as its proper functioning and safety.[317]

It is worth noting that the issues related to water infrastructure are quite complex and are usually covered in a large number of legal instruments. The World Bank Policy Paper on Water Resources Management refers to the World Bank policies that are related to water resources. They include the policies on environmental assessment, environmental action plans, involuntary resettlement, projects on international waterways, indigenous peoples, physical and cultural resources, safety of dams, how to involve nongovernmental organizations, poverty reduction, and disclosure of information.[318]

4.7 Institutional Arrangements

Institutional arrangements for dealing with water resources are covered widely in water legislation. Such arrangements designate one or more government agencies with ultimate responsibility over water resources, including allocation and supervision of water rights and the preparation of plans, programs, and policies, as well as enforcement provisions. The previous part of this study noted the

---

[317] On the need for carrying out an environmental impact assessment, *see* Cecilia Tortajada, *Environmental Impact Assessment of Water Projects in Mexico*, 16 Intl. J. Water Resources Dev. 73 (2000). *See also* Bradlow, Palmieri & Salman, *supra* n. 258. *See also* John D. Pisaniello & Jennifer M. McKay, *A Farmer-Friendly Dam Safety Evaluation Procedure as a Key Part of Modern Australian Water Laws*, 28 Water Intl. 90 (2003).

[318] *See* World Bank, *supra* n. 4, app. D at 116, and Operational Policy (OP) 4.07, *supra* n. 22. The World Commission on Dams has identified a wider group of issues emanating from dam construction. *See* World Commission on Dams, *Dams and Development—A New Framework for Decision-making (the Report of the World Commission on Dams)* 206 (Earthscan Publications Ltd. 2000).

variety of those agencies: ministries, national councils, agencies, and commissions. Whatever choice is made, the line of responsibility should be made clear to avoid duplication and overlapping of responsibilities, and the entity should be provided with financial and administrative autonomy. As noted in the World Bank Water Policy: "The lessons of experience suggest that an important principle in restructuring public service agencies is their conversion into financially autonomous entities, with effective authority to charge and collect fees, and with freedom to manage without political interference."[319]

The institutional arrangements should also reflect decentralization of decision making and public participation. Decentralization is based on the principle that "nothing should be done at a higher level of government that can be done satisfactorily at a lower level."[320] This is reflected in the establishment of basin management authorities that are responsible for developing water management plans for a specific basin.[321] The legislation should clearly define the watershed limits, composition, and responsibilities of the basin authority. Public representation in such agencies would strengthen their role and provide a base for support of their decisions. The responsibilities of such entities could extend to both management and protection of the basin. This approach of decentralization and public participation in water management would incorporate two of the Dublin Principles.

Water users' associations are established under most legislation as legal entities with responsibility over the operation and maintenance of the irrigation facilities in their district and for collection of water charges.[322] Furthermore the authority of those associations is extended in some countries to water supply as well. It is widely argued that participation of users "increases the likelihood that the system under their responsibility will be well maintained and contributes to community cohesion and empowerment in ways that can spread to other

---

[319] *See* World Bank, *supra* n. 4, at 55.

[320] *See id.* at 15.

[321] *See* Frank G. W. Jaspers, *Institutional Arrangements for Integrated River Basin Management,* 5 Water Policy 77 (2003).

[322] For a discussion of the role and responsibilities of water users' associations, *see User Organizations for Sustainable Development,* World Bank Technical Paper No. 354 (Ashok Subramanian, N. Vijay Jagannathan & Ruth Meinzen-Dick, eds., World Bank 1997); and Salman, *supra* n. 171. *See also* the Dublin Statement on Water and Sustainable Development, *supra* n. 14. The process of transferring parts of the irrigation system to water users' associations for operation and management is generally known as "participatory irrigation management." For an overview of the concept, *see* David Groenfeldt & Mark Svendsen, *Case Studies in Participatory Irrigation Management* (World Bank Institute 2000).

development activities."[323] Moreover, because association-managed systems have a consumer orientation, they are likely to provide better service and improve willingness to pay for such service.[324]

Detailed procedures for the functioning of water users' associations and their relationship with the government authority are usually laid down in separate subsidiary regulation.[325] The bylaws of the water users' association would detail the responsibilities of the association and the relationship of the members with their executive committee, as well as the members among themselves. Concession or transfer agreements would clarify the relationship between the water users' association and the irrigation or water agency. Such agreements also specify the level of the irrigation system being transferred to each water users' association.[326] However, in some countries, ownership of the system itself may be transferred to the water users' association, rather than transferring only operation and maintenance.[327] Moreover, a number of water statutes provide for establishment of a federation of water users' associations. In addition to the advantages of economy of scale, federations could be entrusted with operation and maintenance responsibilities over the next level of the irrigation system, as well as over resolution of disputes between different water users' associations.[328]

In addition to those entities, some legislation provides for the establishment of advisory boards, where all the entities and organizations concerned with water would be represented, including civil society organizations and academic institutions. Such advisory bodies would assist the government in preparing water policies, programs, and plans, and in coordinating their implementation. Indeed, public participation in the design and implementation of water policy and legislation is now considered an important element in ensuring the success of the policies and the legislation.[329]

---

[323] *See* World Bank, *supra* n. 4, at 44.

[324] *See id.* at 55.

[325] *See* Salman, *supra* n. 171.

[326] *See* Gorriz, Subramanian & Simas, *supra* n. 170. *See also* Keith Oblitas & J. Raymond Peter, *Transferring Irrigation Management to Farmers in Andhra Pradesh, India,* World Bank Technical Paper No. 449 (World Bank 1999).

[327] In Chile, for example, ownership of the irrigation and drainage system itself, including dams, can be transferred to water users' associations. *See* Renato Gazmuri, *Chilean Water Policy,* Short Paper Series, No.3, 8 (Intl. Irr. Mgmt. Inst. 1994). *See also* Peter J. Farley, *Privatization of Irrigation Schemes in New Zealand,* Short Paper Series, No. 2 (Intl. Irr. Mgmt. Inst. 1994).

[328] *See* Salman, *supra* n. 171, at 23. *See also* Garcia-Betancourt, *supra* n. 47.

[329] *See* Delli Priscoli, *supra* n. 276. *See also* Anna Barreira, *The Participatory Regime of Water Governance in the Iberian Peninsula,* 28 Water Intl. 350 (2003).

4.8   Financial Arrangements

One of the complex issues, and a major challenge in water resources management, is water charges.[330] Charging fees is intended to recognize water as an economic good,[331] manage demand, encourage rationalization of water use, and raise revenues for operation and maintenance of the system.[332] Most of the statutes state that charges for water must be set at a level that is adequate to cover the costs associated with operation and maintenance of the water infrastructure.[333] Because some cultures perceive water as a God-given gift for which no charges should be imposed, such charges can be presented as fees for delivery of the service, not necessarily for the water itself.[334]

One of the elements taken into account in setting charges for water is the volume of water used, sometimes with progressive increases in prices for water usage exceeding certain amounts. This approach is being applied for domestic, industrial, and irrigation uses, though for irrigation uses approaches other than volume of water delivered have been used. Such approaches include the size of the area irrigated, the kind of crop irrigated, and the season for irrigation (the wet or the dry season, with higher charges during the dry season).[335] Some laws use the source of water as a factor, charging more for groundwater than for surface water. Other laws include location of the area of delivery, the furthest points paying the highest fees. In many countries water charges are set out in a separate regulation rather than in the water law itself, since updating a regulation is less cumbersome than amending a law.

Water pricing has been one of the most difficult issues faced in the water sector, particularly charges for irrigation.[336] Irrigation is the largest single user of water, accounting for about 73 percent of global water use, with the figure exceeding 80 percent for developing countries.[337] Irrigation water in most

---

[330] In addition to water charges, many countries charge for the issuance of water permits, for transfer or renewal of a permit, and for permits for discharge of waste water.

[331] *See* the Dublin Statement on Water and Sustainable Development, *supra* n. 14.

[332] *See* Hubert H. G. Savenije & Pieter van der Zaag, *Water as an Economic Good and Demand Management—Paradigms and Pitfalls,* 27 Water Intl. 98 (2002).

[333] For a discussion of water charges approaches worldwide, *see* Dinar & Subramanian (eds.), *supra* n. 62.

[334] *See* Faruqui, Biswas & Bino (eds.), *supra* n. 239.

[335] *See* Yacov Tsur, Terry Roe, Rachid Doukkali & Ariel Dinar, *Pricing Irrigation Water— Principles and Cases from Developing Countries* (Resources for the Future 2004).

[336] *See, for example,* Philip Gyau-Boakye & Ben Y. Ampomah, *Water Pricing and Water Sector Reforms Information Study in Ghana,* 28 Water Intl. 11 (2003).

[337] *See* World Bank, *World Development Report 1992, Development and the Environment* 100 (World Bank 1992).

countries is heavily subsidized,[338] with no more than 10 percent of operating costs being paid by the users.[339] This is notwithstanding water law in many of those countries that would call for full cost recovery for water services.[340] The vicious cycle of farmers not paying because water is not being delivered, and water not being delivered because the system is in disrepair and cannot be fixed because of lack of funds, is often quoted as one reason for this state of affairs.

Partly because of this reasoning, some countries have followed the approach of charging a flat rate for water, whether for irrigation or domestic use, with all users or consumers paying the same rate regardless of the amount used. This approach does not create any incentives for managing demand or using water efficiently. Indeed, it creates perverse incentives for exactly the opposite, thus exacerbating an already difficult situation. The vicious cycle applies more vividly to water utilities where supply, demand, and pricing keep hopelessly chasing each other because of the flat rate approach. The problem of unaccounted-for water exacerbates this situation.[341] One reason for promoting the use of water users' associations in both irrigation and rural water supply is the expectation that they can play a major role in water management, including operation and maintenance and collection of water charges.[342]

---

[338] Sandra Postel gives the example of India, where

> Government spending to operate and maintain medium and large canal projects exceeds the total revenue collected from farmers by 23.5 billion rupees ($816 million). Adding in capital cost subsidies would lift this figure even higher. Irrigation officials set the water charges according to the size of farmers' plots and the crops they are growing, so payments bear no relation to the amount actually used in the fields. Moreover, charges are so low—typically amounting to 2–5 percent of the harvest's value—that they have no influence on farmers' management decisions.

See Sandra Postel, *Last Oasis—Facing Water Scarcity,* Worldwatch Environmental Alert Series, 167 (Worldwatch Inst. 1992).

[339] *See* World Bank, *supra* n. 337, at 100. One justification frequently given for water subsidies is that such subsidies are "a means for offsetting low farm prices controlled to keep down food prices in the cities." *See* Jeremy Berkoff, *A Strategy for Managing Water in the Middle East and North Africa* 36 (World Bank 1994).

[340] *See* Suren Kulshreshtha, *Water Pricing Under Joint Benefits—A Case Study of Accounting for Positive Externalities,* 27 Water Intl. 195 (2002).

[341] Unaccounted-for water is defined as "The difference between the volume of water delivered to a supply system and the volume of water accounted for by legitimate consumption, whether metered or not (or the measured volume of supplied water that is produced or treated less the water that is consumed legitimately, the difference being what is stolen or lost)." *See* World Bank, *supra* n. 4, at 7.

[342] For a thorough discussion of the problems and challenges faced in the irrigation sector, *see* Sandra Postel, *Pillar of Sand—Can the Irrigation Miracle Last?* (Worldwatch Institute 1999). *See also Institutional Reform for Irrigation and Drainage,* World Bank Technical Paper No. 524 (Fernando Gonzalez & Salman M. A. Salman, eds., World Bank 2002).

4.9 Private Sector Participation

As discussed in chapter 3, water legislation in Armenia, Mexico, and South Africa provides for participation of the private sector in water service delivery. This can be justified by the large financial needs of the water sector, which the public sector may not be able to provide.[343] Another justification relates to the efficiency gains the private sector may bring. In the few countries where the private sector has been contracted to provide water services, it has been confined by and large to urban water supply.[344] Because ownership of water resources usually remains with the public authority and the role of the private sector is limited to providing service, this process is often referred to as a public-private partnership.[345] However, as noted by one expert:

> There are no guarantees that privatization will actually yield the desired performance improvements. Simply converting a public sector monopoly into a private one provides no competitive incentives for the utility to operate efficiently, make appropriate investments or respond to consumer demands. Likewise, privatization per se need do little to improve sector performance if governments are unwilling or unable to tackle such underlying problems as over-manning, uneconomic water pricing policies, financing the provision of public and merit goods, and restricting over-intrusive political intervention.[346]

For this and other reasons, a number of countries have approached water service delivery through public utilities that are legally and financially fully autonomous and accountable.

The World Bank "Toolkits for Private Participation in Water and Sanitation" provide basic guidelines.[347] Toolkit 1 deals with "Selecting an Option for Private

---

[343] The Report of the World Panel on Financing Water Infrastructure estimates the cost of meeting the Millennium Development Goal of reducing by half the proportion of people without sustainable access to adequate quantities of affordable safe water and sanitation as $180 billion, from the current figure of $75 billion. *See* World Water Council, *Report of the Panel on Financing Water Infrastructure, Financing Water for All* 3 (World Water Council 2003).

[344] For samples of urban water supply projects involving the private sector, *see* World Bank, *supra* n. 4, at 110.

[345] *See, for example,* Brazil Federal Law 11,097 of 2004, on Public-Private Partnership, referred to in section 2.2.5.

[346] Judith Rees, *Regulation and Private Participation in the Water and Sanitation Sector,* Global Water Partnership, Technical Advisory Committee, TAC Background Papers, No. 1, 4 (GWP, Swedish Intl. Dev. Coop. Agency 1998).

[347] The Toolkits were published by the World Bank in 1997. Toolkit 2 deals with "Designing and Implementing an Option for Private Sector Participation" and Toolkit 3 with "What a Private Sector Participation Arrangement Should Cover."

Sector Participation." The options it lists include service contracts, management contracts, leases, concessions, build-operate-transfer contracts, and full or partial divestiture.[348] The framework for regulating private sector participation needs to be comprehensive, addressing, *inter alia,* price, service standards, the decision-making process, independent review, competition, and the social and cultural contexts.[349]

Because the issue of private sector participation is complex, it has to be dealt with carefully. Factors to be considered include which option is best for the country and the ability to regulate such participation effectively, including the country's institutional capacity.[350]

4.10   The Right to Water

One of the emerging issues related to financial arrangements and water charges is protecting poor and vulnerable segments of the society by guaranteeing them a specified amount of water, despite their inability to pay for it. As discussed earlier, this issue, which can be traced to the Mar del Plata United Nations Water Conference,[351] has since been developed into the concept of the human right to water. The concept is now being widely debated and there is a large regime of international legal instruments supporting the argument that there is a human right to water under international law.[352] The debate has been energized by General Comment No. 15, issued by the United Nations Committee on Economic, Social and Cultural Rights in November 2002, which recognizes a human right to water.[353] The crux of General Comment No. 15 is paragraph 2, which states that

> the human right to water entitles everyone to sufficient, safe, acceptable, physically accessible and affordable water for personal and domestic uses.

---

[348] For a detailed discussion and analysis of those options, *see* Jeffrey Delmon, *Water Projects—Commercial and Contractual Guide* (Kluwer Law Intl. 2001).

[349] *See* Delmon, *id.* at ch. 4; and Rees, *supra* n. 346, at 26. *See also* World Bank, *supra* n. 4, at 57.

[350] *See* Daniel Rivera, *Private Sector Participation in the Water Supply and Wastewater Sector—Lessons from Six Developing Countries,* Directions in Development (World Bank, 1996). *See also* Dimosthenis Voivontas *et al., Public-Private Partnership in the Water Sector—A Case Study in the Cyclades Islands, Greece,* 27 Water Intl. 330 (2002).

[351] *See supra* n. 3.

[352] This regime of international legal instruments includes a number of conventions and treaties, United Nations General Assembly Resolutions, and declarations of some of the international water conferences and forums. For analysis of those instruments, *see* Salman & McInerney Lankford, *supra* n. 10.

[353] For a detailed discussion of the role of the committee, General Comment No. 15, and the text of the comment itself, as well as other conventions and treaties dealing with the human right to water, *see* Salman & McInerney Lankford, *supra* n. 10, at 8. *See also* McCaffrey, *supra* n. 10, and Gleick, *supra* n. 10.

An adequate amount of water is necessary to prevent death from dehydration, to reduce the risk of water-related diseases and to provide for consumption, cooking, personal and hygienic requirements.

The argument that there is a human right to water is further strengthened by the Millennium Declaration, which established as one of the Millennium Development Goals reducing by half, by 2015, the proportion of people without sustainable access to safe drinking water and sanitation.[354]

A number of countries now have provisions in their constitutions or water statutes that guarantee such a right. As mentioned earlier, South Africa has such provisions in both its constitution and its Water Services Act,[355] and those in the latter have been the subject of court review.[356] Armenia has similar

---

[354] *See* United Nations General Assembly Resolution 55/2 of 8 September 2000, para. 19. *See also supra* n. 29.

[355] *See supra* sections 2.14.1 and 2.14.2. South Africa provides a certain amount of water free of charge to people who are below a certain income, for which the water utility bills the provincial authorities.

[356] *See* the case of *Manquele v. Durban Transitional Metropolitan* Council, Case No. 2036/2000, at http://www.communitylawcentre.org.za/localgov/bulletin2001/2001_1_manquele.php#manquele. The case deals with arts. 3 and 4(3) of the Water Services Act. Art. 3 states that:

(1) Everyone has a right of access to basic water supply and basic sanitation.
(2) Every water services institution must take reasonable measures to realize these rights.
(3) Every water services authority must, in its water services development plan, provide for measures to realize these rights.
(4) The rights mentioned in this section are subject to the limitations contained in this Act.

Furthermore, art. 4(3) states that:

(3) Procedures for the limitation or discontinuation of water services must-
(a) be fair and equitable;
(b) provide for reasonable notice of intention to limit or discontinue water services and for an opportunity to make representations, unless-
  (i) other consumers would be prejudiced;
  (ii) there is an emergency situation; or
  (iii) the consumer has interfered with a limited or discontinued service; and
(c) not result in a person being denied access to basic water services for non-payment, where that person proves, to the satisfaction of the relevant water services authority, that he or she is unable to pay for basic services.

In the cited case, the applicant had failed to pay for water in excess of the free six kilolitres per month provided by the Durban Transitional Metropolitan Council (DTMC). The DTMC, invoking its bylaws, gave the applicant written notice and allowed for representations to be made before disconnecting her water supply. The applicant argued that the bylaws were inconsistent with the Water Services Act because the disconnection resulted in her being denied access to basic water services while she was unable to pay for basic

provisions in its water law.[357] Chile has implemented a water stamps system for the needy in its population who live below a certain level of income.[358] Consequently, there is increasing pressure on governments from international and civil society organizations to guarantee such a right to the poor and vulnerable segments of society through incorporation of this right into water statutes, as well as through specific action and procedures to implement the provisions of the statutes.

4.11 Enforcement of the Regulations

The credibility of any legislation, including water legislation, depends on its enforcement provisions and how to get the different parties to comply with them. Such provisions need to enumerate acts that are considered violations of the law and specify sanctions. The tools that authorities can use in enforcing the requirements of the statute and identifying violations are limited to monitoring and inspections. To facilitate enforcement, most water law statutes give employees of the water agency the authority necessary to monitor compliance with the law, and some even create a special category of employees for that purpose.

Violations would include diverting or using water for any purpose without having been awarded the right to use water for that purpose; in contravention of the permit, actions that alter the flow rate, quality, or quantity of water without

---

services. The Court noted that in sec. 4(3) of the Water Services Act, "basic water supply" is "the prescribed minimum standard of water supply services necessary for the reliable supply of a sufficient quantity and quality" and that the term "prescribed" indicates that regulations made under the Act must give further content to the term "basic water supply." Because no such regulations existed, the court indicated that the issue would concern policy matters that were outside the purview of the court. Furthermore, the court was satisfied that the procedures for disconnection under the bylaws were not inconsistent with the Water Services Act. Another factor cited by the court as a reason for its judgment was an earlier tampering of the applicant with the service during a previous disconnection. One of the questions asked in connection with this case is whether the decision of the court would have been different had the applicant based her arguments on the constitutional provisions on the right to water, rather than on the Water Services Act.

[357] The Armenian water law provides for tax breaks and subsidies for the water utility in return for providing a certain amount of water free of charge. *See supra* section 2.1.7. *See also* Salman & McInerney Lankford, *supra* n. 10, at 71–72.

[358] In Chile, water stamps are provided to certain segments of the population whose income is below a certain limit. Such water stamps would be used to pay the water bills. For discussion of the Chilean approach *see* World Water Council, World Water Vision (Commission Report) *A Water Secure World: Vision for Water, Life and the Environment* 36 (2000).

prior authorization; construction of unauthorized works; or committing fraud in measuring the volume of water used. Such violations can result in sanctions that include temporary or permanent revocations of the permit, fines, or even jail sentences for acts that involve criminal activity,[359] though such sanctions are subject to appeal. Violators may even be liable to pay damages to any person harmed by their acts, as prescribed by the statutes of Armenia and South Africa. On the other hand, the statutes of China and Vietnam, as discussed earlier, provide incentives for compliance.

4.12   Dispute Settlement

Given the increasing scarcity of water resources and the rising quality problems, disputes between different users, or between a user and the government, are bound to arise. Water legislation therefore needs to address the issue of how to deal with those disputes. Furthermore, the legislation may also need to address situations where the dispute is between two government agencies.

Water disputes can be dealt with in widely varying ways. Initial authority to resolve disputes between users may be granted to the water agency established and operating under the water law. Special commissions are established in some jurisdictions to mediate or arbitrate water disputes between users that do not involve the government. Water users' associations are also given powers in some countries to resolve disputes among members. A special water tribunal is established in some jurisdictions to deal with water disputes.[360] The rationale for those less formal mechanisms is to avoid cost and delays. However, in most cases, appeals are allowed to the court system. Cases against the government, in most jurisdictions, can only be dealt with by the court system.

Disputes between different government agencies or basin authorities may be referred to the regulatory authority. Disputes between different water users' associations are referred, as mentioned earlier, to the federation of water users' associations, if such a federation exists.[361]

Clearly, a wide array of key and emerging issues has to be addressed in water legislation. Those issues include ownership of the water resources, underlying

---

[359] *See* Burchi, *supra* n. 254.

[360] In this connection *see* arts. 146–48 of the South Africa National Water Act, 1998, discussed in chapter 2 of this study, establishing a special water tribunal to hear appeals against decisions made by a responsible authority, catchment management agency, or water management institution.

[361] For the responsibilities of such a federation of water users' associations in general, and in relation to dispute resolution in particular, *see* Garcia-Betancourt, *supra* n. 47.

principles and priorities, regulation of water uses and water infrastructure, protection of water resources, institutional and financial arrangements, enforcement of regulations, and dispute settlement. Some of the components of those issues are still evolving. Decentralization and participation, including broad participation in the preparation of water legislation, are gaining wide recognition and are becoming overarching principles for the regulatory framework for water resources management.[362]

---

[362] For the role of decentralization and participation in irrigation reform, *see* Djibril Aw & Geert Diemer, *Making a Large Irrigation Scheme Work—A Case Study from Mali*, Directions in Development (World Bank 2005).

CHAPTER 5

Conclusion

Water resources globally are facing tremendous and ever-increasing pressures. The population of the world has more than tripled in the last century, presenting a major challenge, particularly in the water sector, to governments around the world. Environmental degradation and hydrological variability, urbanization and industrialization, have compounded the challenges. Disputes resulting from competing demands between different uses and users at the local, district, provincial, national, and international levels keep multiplying. Issues related to international waters are now becoming increasingly apparent, and indeed are intertwined with domestic uses. Utilization of shared waters by one country is, more than ever before, having direct effects on other countries sharing the same watercourse.

All those challenges have pushed the need to rethink water resources management to the top of national as well as regional and global agendas.[363] The search for solutions has extended across various paths, including the managerial, technological, financial, social, economic, political, institutional, and legal, confirming the multidisciplinary, or transdisciplinary, nature of water. The Marrakech Declaration recognized the urgent need for a better understanding of all those complex issues, including the legal ones, as a prerequisite for shaping a water policy for this millennium.

The relevance and importance of water legislation to the proper management and protection of water resources was recognized a long time ago. This recognition has been underscored by more recent international conferences on water, starting with the Mar del Plata United Nations Water Conference in 1977. Indeed, that conference went beyond urging States to adopt water legislation and issued a detailed road map highlighting the basic elements to be included in water legislation, as well as in the national water plan, policy, or strategy. The road map also included the process for preparing water legislation.

That road map is still valid and relevant, almost thirty years after its adoption. Moreover, the road map undoubtedly paved the way for the Dublin Statement,

---

[363] For a detailed discussion of those challenges, *see* World Water Assessment Programme, *Water for People, Water for Life,* United Nations World Water Development Report (UNESCO Publishing 2003). *See also* William J. Cosgrove & Frank R. Rijsberman, *World Water Vision—Making Water Everybody's Business* (World Water Council 2000).

which we termed the *magna carta* for water resources management and development. The four Dublin Principles continue to guide policies, strategies, and legislation around the globe and without a doubt have had major influence on our thinking about how water should be used, managed, and developed. Chapter 18 of the United Nations Conference on Environment and Development on Freshwater Resources and the declarations of the three world water forums, as well as other international water conferences, have incorporated and emphasized those principles and underscored the importance of water legislation. Indeed, the only effective way for recognizing and giving effect to the Dublin Principles is through their incorporation in water legislation.

Some thirty years after Mar del Plata, the overall picture around the world with regard to water legislation is quite mixed. While a number of countries have adopted comprehensive water statutes, others are still struggling to agree on one. Countries in a third group have addressed water issues in scattered provisions in a number of laws and regulations. Some of the countries with a federal system of government have assigned authority over water to their states or provinces, with little responsibility left for the central government.

As stated earlier, the purpose of this study is to provide policy makers and technical experts with a toolkit of issues to be considered in water legislation. Based on the survey and analysis of the regulatory frameworks for water resources management in sixteen jurisdictions, the study has identified key elements that for the most part have been addressed, in varying ways, by the countries surveyed. The study has also identified what we have referred to as emerging trends in water legislation.

However, as the previous chapters indicate, the jurisdictions whose regulatory frameworks for water resources management are examined in this study have addressed the various basic issues in ways that are influenced largely by their legal history and their socioeconomic, political, and cultural milieu. State ownership or custodianship of water resources is gradually emerging as the rule. Yet exceptions are allowed in some countries for some form of private ownership; and traditional and customary rights are still gaining recognition. Private ownership of rainwater harvested in private lands for domestic use is explicitly allowed in a number of countries. Groundwater continues to present special challenges because a number of countries still allow the ownership of land to carry with it ownership of the water beneath it. Moreover, even in countries that have claimed custodianship over such groundwater, effective measures for exercising such custodianship responsibilities are still lacking. The fact that groundwater is highly susceptible to externalities[364] poses additional

---

[364] For discussion of such externalities, *see* World Bank, *supra* n. 4, at 83.

problems, particularly when the aquifer in question is a fossil, nonreplenishable one.[365]

Variations in the incorporation of the four Dublin Principles in water legislation are quite evident. Financial arrangements are given wide coverage in some legal frameworks, underscoring the belief that treating water as a socioeconomic good will assist in demand management as well as in rationalizing water use. Yet a few countries have missed or ignored this principle, thereby compounding the challenges to the sustainability of their water resources. However, even in some countries that have adopted provisions for cost recovery, enforcement of those provisions has proven quite difficult.

Decentralization of decision making at the basin level and participation of users in the planning and management of water resources are the rule in some countries, the exception in a second group, and absent in others. Indeed, some countries have gone a long way towards incorporating public participation, not just users' participation, into decision making over water resources management issues. As discussed in the previous chapters, such participation includes public notice of water use permits, inviting public comments on proposed regulations to be issued by the executive authority, the establishing or disestablishing of a water institution, and water pricing strategies. As the discussion in the previous chapters indicates, decentralization and users' participation are the pillars of any water legislation.

Similarly, variations in institutional arrangements for the water resources sector in the countries surveyed are quite apparent. They include oversight by one or more ministries, councils, commissions, or simply administrative agencies or water utilities. However, it is the authority and independence of such entities that should actually matter, not whether they are ministries with multiple responsibilities or separate water agencies. Legal and financial autonomy is particularly important for public water utilities.[366] Where there are multiple entities, the need for coordination and avoidance of overlapping responsibilities is necessary. But in a number of countries this need may not be that clear, in theory, in practice, or in both.

With the challenges to the quality of water resources multiplying by the day, compounded by environmental degradation and industrialization, the need for an elaborate protective framework is evident. Yet a number of countries still fail this test. Decisions on water rights—how to allocate them, using what criteria, and

---

[365] For a case study on issues of ownership and use of groundwater, and the ensuing disputes, *see* Volkmar Dyrnes & Vatn, *supra* n. 174.

[366] As discussed in section 4.9, public utilities with full legal and financial autonomy are being presented in a number of countries as a viable option to private entities.

how to verify existing ones—and how to administer them will only be accepted as legitimate when they are made in a transparent, equitable, and fair manner, accompanied by mechanisms to redress grievances. Some legislation does provide for public participation in such decisions. Yet those elements, and the details elaborating them, are missed in a number of water laws.

As the previous chapters indicate, water resources management is clearly a dynamic and evolving concept and should be dealt with accordingly.[367] Our understanding of the elements that need to be addressed in water legislation is constantly evolving. It is also noteworthy that "water legislation is rapidly evolving towards integrated water planning to satisfy environmental objectives, economic requirements and social concerns."[368] This fact is further buttressed by some emerging trends in water legislation. The underlying purposes for legislation now include new elements, such as the sustainable utilization of water resources to protect future generations. Such sustainable utilization is also needed to enable states to meet their international obligations with regard to shared water resources.

Integrated water resources management is increasingly finding a place in water legislation and policies. As discussed earlier, IWRM aims to ensure the coordinated development and management of water, land, and related resources by maximizing economic and social welfare without compromising the sustainability of vital environmental systems.

Closely related to the concept of IWRM is the need for protection of the water source ecosystem, which is broad and includes the flora, fauna, and land contiguous to the water source.[369] Similarly, the notion of the "reserve" is becoming increasingly relevant for water legislation. Furthermore, concepts that have been reserved to international environmental law, such as the precautionary and polluter-pays principles, are gradually being incorporated as rules in domestic water legislation.

The human right to water for the needy and vulnerable groups of the society is being debated, and as discussed earlier, it is widely agued that such a right does indeed exist under international law, buttressing the emerging calls to recognize this right. The argument for the existence of such a right has been strengthened by the Millennium Development Goal with regard to water. Indeed, the 2005

---

[367] For an overview of emerging approaches to water management, *see* Peter H. Gleick, *The Changing Water Paradigm—A Look at Twenty-first Century Water Resources Development,* 25 Water Intl. 127 (2000); and Slobodan P. Simonovic, *Tools for Water Management—One View of the Future,* 25 Water Intl. 76 (2000).

[368] *See* Solanes & Gonzalez-Villarreal, *supra* n. 16, at 14.

[369] *See supra* nn. 41 and 257. *See also* Millennium Ecosystem Assessment, *Ecosystems and Human Well-Being: Synthesis* (World Resources Institute 2005).

World Summit Outcome, as discussed earlier, establishes linkages between the need for preparation of IWRM and water efficiency plans and the achievement of the Millennium Development Goal with regard to water.[370] As noted before, some countries have already started incorporating the concept of the human right to water in their legislation. To give effect to this right, innovative approaches are being pursued, such as water stamps or direct targeted subsidies for the poorest and most vulnerable segments of the society.

Nonetheless, the manner in which the detailed provisions of water legislation in each country are drafted should cater to the special circumstances of that country, taking into account socioeconomic, cultural, and historical considerations, as well as the country's implementation capacity. The effective participation of users in all aspects of water planning and management is undoubtedly a *sine qua non* for successful implementation of the legislation. Equally important is the political will of the authorities to implement and enforce the legislation in a transparent, fair, and consistent manner, as well as the capacity of the institutional framework entrusted with implementation and enforcement of such legislation.

As such, the regulatory framework for water resources management will not by itself resolve existing and emerging challenges and problems of the water sector. Nonetheless, it is equally important to emphasize that such problems and challenges will not be resolved without a comprehensive, flexible, and implementable regulatory framework for water resources development, management, and protection.

---

[370] *See supra* n. 32.

The Dublin Statement on Water and Sustainable Development

International Conference on Water and the Environment— Development Issues for the 21st Century 26–31 January 1992, Dublin, Ireland

Scarcity and misuse of freshwater pose a serious and growing threat to sustainable development and protection of the environment. Human health and welfare, food security, industrial development and the ecosystems on which they depend, are all at risk, unless water and land resources are managed more effectively in the present decade and beyond than they have been in the past.

Five hundred participants, including government-designated experts from a hundred countries and representatives of 80 international, intergovernmental and non-governmental organizations attended the International Conference on Water and the Environment (ICWE) in Dublin, Ireland, on 26–31 January 1992. The experts saw the emerging global water resources picture as critical. At its closing session, the Conference adopted this Dublin Statement and the Conference Report. The problems highlighted are not speculative in nature; nor are they likely to affect our planet only in the distant future. They are here and they affect humanity now. The future survival of many millions of people demands immediate and effective action.

The Conference participants call for fundamental new approaches to the assessment, development and management of freshwater resources, which can only be brought about through political commitment and involvement from the highest levels of government to the smallest communities. Commitment will need to be backed by substantial and immediate investments, public awareness campaigns, legislative and institutional changes, technology development, and capacity building programmes. Underlying all these must be a greater recognition of the interdependence of all peoples, and of their place in the natural world.

In commending this Dublin Statement to the world leaders assembled at the United Nations Conference on Environment and Development (UNCED) in Rio de Janeiro in June 1992, the Conference participants urge all governments to study carefully the specific activities and means of implementation recommended in the Conference Report, and to translate those recommendations into urgent action programmes for Water and Sustainable Development.

Guiding Principles

Concerted action is needed to reverse the present trends of overconsumption, pollution, and rising threats from drought and floods. The Conference Report sets out recommendations for action at local, national and international levels, based on four guiding principles.

Principle No. 1—Freshwater is a finite and vulnerable resource, essential to sustain life, development and the environment

Because water sustains life, effective management of water resources demands a holistic approach, linking social and economic development with protection of natural ecosystems. Effective management links land and water uses across the whole of a catchment area or groundwater aquifer.

Principle No. 2—Water development and management should be based on a participatory approach, involving users, planners and policy-makers at all levels

The participatory approach involves raising awareness of the importance of water among policy-makers and the general public. It means that decisions are taken at the lowest appropriate level, with full public consultation and involvement of users in the planning and implementation of water projects.

Principle No. 3—Women play a central part in the provision, management and safeguarding of water

This pivotal role of women as providers and users of water and guardians of the living environment has seldom been reflected in institutional arrangements for the development and management of water resources. Acceptance and implementation of this principle requires positive policies to address women's specific needs and to equip and empower women to participate at all levels in water resources programmes, including decision-making and implementation, in ways defined by them.

Principle No. 4—Water has an economic value in all its competing uses and should be recognized as an economic good

Within this principle, it is vital to recognize first the basic right of all human beings to have access to clean water and sanitation at an affordable price. Past failure to recognize the economic value of water has led to wasteful and environmentally damaging uses of the resource. Managing water as an economic good is an important way of achieving efficient and equitable use, and of encouraging conservation and protection of water resources.

The Action Agenda

Based on these four guiding principles, the Conference participants developed recommendations which enable countries to tackle their water resources problems on a wide range of fronts. The major benefits to come from implementation of the Dublin recommendations will be:

Alleviation of poverty and disease

At the start of the 1990s, more than a quarter of the world's population still lack the basic human needs of enough food to eat, a clean water supply and hygienic means of sanitation. The Conference recommends that priority be given in water resources development and management to the accelerated provision of food, water and sanitation to these unserved millions.

Protection against natural disasters

Lack of preparedness, often aggravated by lack of data, means that droughts and floods take a huge toll in deaths, misery and economic loss. Economic losses from natural disasters, including floods and droughts, increased three-fold between the 1960s and the 1980s. Development is being set back for years in some developing countries, because investments have not been made in basic data collection and disaster preparedness. Projected climate change and rising sea levels will intensify the risk for some, while also threatening the apparent security of existing water resources.

Damages and loss of life from floods and droughts can be drastically reduced by the disaster preparedness actions recommended in the Dublin Conference Report.

Water conservation and reuse

Current patterns of water use involve excessive waste. There is great scope for water savings in agriculture, in industry and in domestic water supplies.

Irrigated agriculture accounts for about 80% of water withdrawals in the world. In many irrigation schemes, up to 60% of this water is lost on its way from the source to the plant. More efficient irrigation practices will lead to substantial freshwater savings.

Recycling could reduce the consumption of many industrial consumers by 50% or more, with the additional benefit of reduced pollution. Application of the 'polluter pays' principle and realistic water pricing will encourage conservation and reuse. On average, 36% of the water produced by urban water utilities in developing countries is 'unaccounted for'. Better management could reduce these costly losses.

Combined savings in agriculture, industry and domestic water supplies could significantly defer investment in costly new water resource development and have enormous impact on the sustainability of future supplies. More savings will come from multiple use of water. Compliance with effective discharge standards, based on new water protection objectives, will enable successive downstream consumers to reuse water which presently is too contaminated after the first use.

Sustainable urban development

The sustainability of urban growth is threatened by curtailment of the copious supplies of cheap water, as a result of the depletion and degradation caused by past profligacy. After a generation or more of excessive water use and reckless discharge of municipal and industrial wastes, the situation in the majority of the world's major cities is appalling and getting worse. As water scarcity and pollution force development of ever more distant sources, marginal costs of meeting fresh demands are growing rapidly. Future guaranteed supplies must be based on appropriate water charges and discharge controls. Residual contamination of land and water can no longer be seen as a reasonable trade-off for the jobs and prosperity brought by industrial growth.

Agricultural production and rural water supply

Achieving food security is a high priority in many countries, and agriculture must not only provide food for rising populations, but also save water for other uses. The challenge is to develop and apply water-saving technology and management methods, and, through capacity building, enable communities to introduce institutions and incentives for the rural population to adopt new approaches, for both rainfed and irrigated agriculture. The rural population must also have better access to a potable water supply and to sanitation services. It is an immense task, but not an impossible one, provided appropriate policies and programmes are adopted at all levels—local, national and international.

Protecting aquatic ecosystems

Water is a vital part of the environment and a home for many forms of life on which the well-being of humans ultimately depends. Disruption of flows has reduced the productivity of many such ecosystems, devastated fisheries, agriculture and grazing, and marginalized the rural communities which rely on these. Various kinds of pollution, including transboundary pollution, exacerbate these problems, degrade water supplies, require more expensive water treatment, destroy aquatic fauna, and deny recreation opportunities.

Integrated management of river basins provides the opportunity to safeguard aquatic ecosystems, and make their benefits available to society on a sustainable basis.

Resolving water conflicts

The most appropriate geographical entity for the planning and management of water resources is the river basin, including surface and groundwater. Ideally, the effective integrated planning and development of transboundary river or lake basins has similar institutional requirements to a basin entirely within one country. The essential function of existing international basin organizations is one of reconciling and harmonizing the interests of riparian countries, monitoring water quantity and quality, development of concerted action programmes, exchange of information and enforcing agreements.

In the coming decades, management of international watersheds will greatly increase in importance. A high priority should therefore be given to the preparation and implementation of integrated management plans, endorsed by all affected governments and backed by international agreements.

The Enabling Environment

Implementation of action programmes for Water and Sustainable Development will require a substantial investment, not only in the capital projects concerned, but, crucially, in building the capacity of people and institutions to plan and implement those projects.

The knowledge base

Measurement of components of the water cycle, in quantity and quality, and of other characteristics of the environment affecting water are an essential basis for undertaking effective water management. Research and analysis techniques, applied on an interdisciplinary basis, permit the understanding of these data and their application to many uses.

With the threat of global warming due to increasing greenhouse gas concentrations in the atmosphere, the need for measurements and data exchange on the hydrological cycle on a global scale is evident. The data are required to understand both the world's climate system and the potential impacts on water resources of climate change and sea-level rise. All countries must participate and, where necessary, be assisted to take part in the global monitoring, the study of the effects and the development of appropriate response strategies.

Capacity building

All actions identified in the Dublin Conference Report require well-trained and qualified personnel. Countries should identify, as part of national development plans, training needs for water-resources assessment and management, and take steps internally and, if necessary, with technical co-operation agencies, to provide the required training, and working conditions which help to retain the trained personnel.

Governments must also assess their capacity to equip their water and other specialists to implement the full range of activities for integrated water-resources management. This requires provision of an enabling environment in terms of institutional and legal arrangements, including those for effective water demand management.

Awareness raising is a vital part of a participatory approach to water resources management. Information, education and communication support programmes must be an integral part of the development process.

Follow-Up

Experience has shown that progress towards implementing the actions and achieving the goals of water programmes requires follow-up mechanisms for periodic assessments at national and international levels.

In the framework of the follow-up procedures developed by UNCED for Agenda 21, all Governments should initiate periodic assessments of progress. At the international level, United Nations institutions concerned with water should be strengthened to undertake the assessment and follow-up process. In addition, to involve private institutions, regional and non-governmental organizations along with all interested governments in the assessment and follow-up, the Conference proposes, for consideration by UNCED, a world water forum or council to which all such groups could adhere.

It is proposed that the first full assessment on implementation of the recommended programme should be undertaken by the year 2000.

UNCED is urged to consider the financial requirements for water-related programmes, in accordance with the above principles, in the funding for implementation of Agenda 21. Such considerations must include realistic targets for the timeframe for implementation of the programmes, the internal and external resources needed, and the means of mobilizing these.

The World Bank Operational Policy (OP) 4.07— Water Resources Management

These policies were prepared for use by World Bank staff and are not necessarily a complete treatment of the subject.

February 2000

> *Note:* This document, which replaces the version dated July 1993, is based on *Water Resources Management: A World Bank Policy Paper* (Washington, D.C.: World Bank, 1993) and is consistent with *Rural Development from Vision to Action, a Sector Strategy* (1997). It complements OP/BP 4.01, *Environmental Assessment*; OP/BP 4.02, *Environmental Action Plans*; OP/BP 4.10, *Indigenous Peoples*; OP/BP 4.12, *Involuntary Resettlement*; OP/BP 7.50, *Projects on International Waterways*; and GP 14.70, *Involving Nongovernmental Organizations in Bank-Supported Activities.* Questions may be addressed to the Director, Rural Development (RDV).

1. Bank[1] involvement in water resources management entails support for providing potable water, sanitation facilities, flood control, and water for productive activities in a manner that is economically viable, environmentally sustainable, and socially equitable.

2. The Bank assists borrowers in the following priority areas:

(a) Developing a comprehensive framework for designing water resource investments, policies, and institutions. Within this framework, when the borrower develops and allocates water resources, it considers cross-sectoral impacts in a regional setting (e.g., a river basin).

(b) Adopting pricing and incentive policies that achieve cost recovery, water conservation, and better allocation of water resources.

(c) Decentralizing water service delivery, involving users in planning and managing water projects, and encouraging stakeholders to contribute to policy formulation. The Bank recognizes that a variety of organizations—private firms, financially autonomous entities, and community organizations—may contribute to decentralizing water delivery functions. Thus it supports

---

[1] "Bank" includes IBRD and IDA, and "loans" includes IDA credits and grants.

projects that introduce different forms of decentralized management, focusing on the division of responsibilities among the public and private entities involved.

(d) Restoring and preserving aquatic ecosystems and guarding against over-exploitation of groundwater resources, giving priority to the provision of adequate water and sanitation services for the poor.

(e) Avoiding the waterlogging and salinity problems associated with irrigation investments by (i) monitoring water tables and implementing drainage networks where necessary, and (ii) adopting best management practices to control water pollution.

(f) Establishing strong legal and regulatory frameworks to ensure that social concerns are met, environmental resources are protected, and monopoly pricing is prevented. The Bank requires legislation or other appropriate arrangements to establish effective coordination and allocation procedures for interstate water resources.

These issues are discussed in the project documents.

3. Individual water lending operations are explicitly linked to the country's priorities for reform and investment and to the Bank's program of support.

4. If inadequate progress by borrowers in these priority areas leads to serious resource misuse and hampers the viability of water-related investments, Bank lending is limited to operations that provide potable water for poor households or conserve water and protect its quality without additionally drawing on a country's water resources.

Bibliography

Abdel Mageed, Yahia, *Environmentally Sound Water Management and Development,* 9 *Intl. J. Water Resources Dev.* 155 (1993).

Abderrahman, Walid A., *Application of Islamic Legal Principles for Advanced Water Management,* 25 Water Intl. 513 (2000).

African Development Bank & African Development Fund, *Policy for Integrated Water Resources Management* (April 2000).

Agarwal, Anil, & Sunita Narain, eds., *Dying Wisdom—Rise, Fall and Potential of India's Traditional Water Harvesting Systems* (Centre for Science and Environment 1997).

Aït-Kadi, Mohamed, Aly Shady, & Andras Szöllösi-Nagy (eds.) *Water, the World's Common Heritage,* Proceedings of the First World Water Forum, Marrakech, Morocco (Elsevier 1997).

Allan, Andrew, *The Legal Context of Water User Associations in Nepal—Analysis and Suggestions for Improvement,* 8 U. Denv. Water L. Rev. 547 (2005).

Al-Sakaf, Rafik A., Yangxiao Zhou & Michael J. Hall, *A Strategy for Controlling Groundwater Depletion in the Sa'dah Plain, Yemen,* Intl. J. Water Resources Dev. 349 (1999).

Amery, Hussein A., *Islamic Water Management,* 26 Water Intl. 481 (2001).

Asian Development Bank, *Water for All: The Water Policy of the Asian Development Bank* (2001).

Aw, Djibril & Geert Diemer, *Making a Large Irrigation Scheme Work—A Case Study from Mali,* Directions in Development (World Bank 2005).

Backeberg, Gerhard R., *Water Institutional Reforms in South Africa,* 7 Water Policy 107 (2005).

Bahamish, Awadh, *Legal Survey of Existing Traditional Rights in the Spate Irrigation Systems in Wadi Zabid and Wadi Tuban in Yemen* (Report to the National Water Resources Authority, Sana'a, Yemen, August 2004).

Baltar, Alexander M., Luiz Gabriel T. de Azevedo, Manuel Rego & Rubem La Laina Porto, *Decision Support Systems for Water Rights in Brazil,* Brazil, Water Series No. 3 (World Bank 2003).

Barreira, Anna, *The Participatory Regime of Water Governance in the Iberian Peninsula* 28 Water Intl. 350 (2003).

Bauer, Carl J., *Siren Song—Chilean Water Law as a Model for International Reform* (Resources for the Future 2004).

Berkoff, Jeremy, *A Strategy for Managing Water in the Middle East and North Africa* (World Bank 1994).

Biswas, Asit K., Cesar Herrera Toledo, Héctor Garduño Velasco & Cecilia Trotajada Quiroz, eds., *National Water Master Plans for Developing Countries* (Oxford Univ. Press 1997).

Blöch, H., *The European Community Water Framework Directive,* in *Management of Transboundary Water in Europe* 25 (Malgorzata Landsberg-Uczciwek, Martin Adriaanse & Rainer Enderlein, eds., Ministry of Environment Protection, Natural Resources and Forestry, Poland 1998).

Boisson de Chazournes, Laurence, & Salman M. A. Salman, eds., *Water Resources and International Law* (Martinus Nijhoff Publishers 2005).

Bosnjaovic, Branko, *UN/ECE Strategies for Protecting the Environment with Respect to International Watercourses: The Helsinki and Espoo Convention,* in *International Watercourses—Enhancing Cooperation and Managing Conflict,* World Bank Technical Paper No. 414 (Salman M. A. Salman & Laurence Boisson de Chazournes, eds., World Bank 1998).

Bradlow, Daniel, Alessandro Palmieri & Salman M. A. Salman, *Regulatory Frameworks for Dam Safety—A Comparative Study* (World Bank 2002).

Braga, B. P. F., *Integrated Urban Water Resources Management: A Challenge into the 21st Century,* 17 Intl. J. Water Resources Mgmt. 4 (2001).

Braga, Benedito P. F., Claire Strauss & Fatima Paiva, *Water Charges: Paying for the Commons in Brazil,* 21 Intl. J. Water Resources Dev. 119 (2005).

Branscheid, Volker, *Irrigation Development in Eastern Europe and the Former Soviet Union,* ECSRE Rural Development and Environment Sector Working Paper No. 3 (World Bank 1998).

Bruns, Bryan Randolph & Ruth Meinzen-Dick (eds.) *Negotiating Water Rights* (Intl. Food Policy Research Inst. 2000).

Burchi, Stefano, *The Interface between Customary and Statutory Water Rights—A Statutory Perspective,* FAO Legal Papers online #45, March 2005.

———, *National Regulations for Groundwater: Options, Issues and Best Practices,* in *Groundwater—Legal and Policy Perspectives,* World Bank Technical Paper No. 456 (Salman M. A. Salman, ed., World Bank 1999).

———, *Preparing National Regulations for Water Resources Management— Principles and Practice,* FAO Legislative Studies 52 (FAO 1994).

Burke, Jacob, & Marcus Moench, *Groundwater and Society: Resources, Tensions and Opportunities—Themes in Groundwater Management for the Twenty-First*

Century, United Nations Department of Economic and Social Affairs (United Nations 2000).

Caponera, Dante A., *National and International Water Law and Administration* (Kluwer Law Intl. 2003).

———, *Principles of Water Law and Administration—National and International* (A. A. Balkema 1992).

———, *Water Law in Moslem Countries,* Irrigation and Drainage Paper 20/1 & 20/2 (FAO 1973).

Carr, Kathleen Marion, & James D. Crammond, eds., *Water Law, Trends, Policies and Practice* 141 (Am. Bar Assoc. 1995).

Cassese, Antonio, *International Law* (Oxford Univ. Press 2005).

Chatila, Jean G., *Water Tariffs in Lebanon: A Review and Perspective,* 7 Water Policy 215 (2005).

Chauhan, B. R., *Settlement of International and Inter-State Water Disputes in India* (Indian Law Institute 1992).

Clark, Sandford D., *Reforming South Africa Water Legislation—Australian Examples,* in *Issues in Water Law Reform,* FAO Legislative Study 67 (FAO 1999).

Cosgrove, William J., & Frank R. Rijsberman, *World Water Vision—Making Water Everybody's Business* (World Water Council 2000).

Coskun, Aynur Aydin, *Water Law—The Current State of Regulation in Turkey,* 28 Water Intl. 70 (2003).

Cruz, Ma. Concepcion J., Luzvimnda B. Cornista & Diogenes C. Dayan, *Legal and Institutional Issues of Irrigation Water Rights in the Philippines* (Agrarian Reform Inst. 1987).

de Azevedo, Luiz Gabriel T., & Musa Asad, *The Political Process Behind the Implementation of Bulk Water Pricing in Brazil,* in *The Political Economy of Water Pricing Reforms* (Ariel Dinar, ed., Oxford Univ. Press 2000).

Delli Priscoli, Jerome, *What Is Public Participation in Water Resources Management and Why Is it Important?* 29 Water Intl. 221 (2004).

———, *Collaboration, Participation and Alternative Dispute Resolution: Process Concepts for the World Bank's Role in Water Resources,* Agriculture and Rural Dev. Dept. (World Bank 1992).

Delmon, Jeffrey, *Water Projects—Commercial and Contractual Guide* (Kluwer Law Intl. 2001).

Dinar, Ariel, ed., *The Political Economy of Water Pricing Reforms* (Oxford Univ. Press 2000).

Dinar, Ariel, & Ashok Subramanian, eds., *Water Pricing Experiences—An International Perspective,* World Bank Technical Paper No. 386 (World Bank 1977).

Doukhali, Mohammed Rachid, *Water Institutional Reforms in Morocco,* 7 Water Policy 71 (2005).

Dyrnes, Gro Volkmar, & Arild Vatn, *Who Owns the Water? A Study of a Water Conflict in the Valley of Ixtlahuaca, Mexico,* 7 Water Policy 295 (2005).

Dziegielewski, Ben, *Message from the Executive Editor,* 30 Water Intl. 269 (2005).

Eckstein, Gabriel, & Yoram Eckstein, *A Hydrogeological Approach to Trans-boundary Ground Water Resources and International Law,* 19 Am. U. Intl. Law Rev. 201 (2003).

Eckstein, Gabriel, *Protecting a Hidden Treasure: The U.N. International Law Commission and the International Law of Transboundary Ground Water Resources,* 5 Sust. Dev. L. & Policy 5 (2004).

Embid Irujo, Antonio, *Water Law in Spain after 1985,* 28 Water Intl. 290 (2003).

European Community Environment Legislation (Office of Official Publications of the European Communities 1992).

Falkenmark, Malin, *Water Management and Ecosystems: Living with Change,* Global Water Partnership, Technical Committee, TEC Background Papers, No. 9 (GWP 2003).

Farley, Peter J., *Privatization of Irrigation Schemes in New Zealand,* Short Paper Series, No. 2 (Intl. Irr. Mgmt. Inst. 1994).

Faruqui, Naser, Asit Biswas & Murad Bino, eds., *Water Management in Islam* (U.N. Univ. Press 2001).

Food and Agriculture Organization of the United Nations, *Law and Sustainable Development Since Rio—Legal Trends in Agriculture and Natural Resources Management,* FAO Legislative Studies 73 (FAO 2002).

———, *Groundwater Legislation in Europe,* Legislative Series No. 5 (FAO 1964).

Foster, Stephen, *Essential Concepts for Groundwater Regulators,* in *Groundwater—Legal and Policy Perspectives,* World Bank Technical Paper No. 456 (Salman M. A. Salman, ed., World Bank 1999).

Foster, Stephen, John Chilton, Marcus Moench, Franklin Cardy & Manuel Schiffler, *Groundwater in Rural Development—Facing the Challenges of Supply and Resources Sustainability,* World Bank Technical Paper No. 463 (World Bank 2000).

Foster, Stephen, Adrian Lawrence & Brian Morris, *Groundwater in Urban Development—Assessing Management Needs and Formulating Policy Strategies,* World Bank Technical Paper No. 390 (World Bank 1998).

Frederiksen, Harald, *Water Resources Institutions: Some Principles and Practices,* World Bank Technical Paper 191 (World Bank 1992).

Frederiksen, Harald D., Jeremy Berkoff & William Barber, *Water Resources Management in Asia,* Vol. 1, World Bank Technical Paper No. 212 (World Bank 1993).

Freestone, David, & Ellen Hey, eds., *The Precautionary Principle in International Law—The Challenge of Implementation* (Kluwer Law Intl. 1996).

Ganesan, C. T., *Water Resources Development and Management—A Challenging Task for Botswana,* 26 Water Intl. 80 (2001).

Garcia-Betancourt, Gilberto, *The Emergence of FEDERRIEGO: The Colombian Federation of Irrigation Districts,* Intl. Irr. Mgmt. Inst., Short Report No. 8 (1994).

Garduño Velasco, Héctor, *Modernization of Water Legislation: The Mexican Experience,* in *Issues in Water Law Reform,* FAO Legislative Studies 67 (FAO 1999).

Garner, Eric L., *How States in the United States Have Handled the Transition from Common Law Riparianism to Permitting Regulation,* in *Issues in Water Law Reform* FAO Legislative Study 67 (FAO 1999).

Gazmuri, Renato, *Chilean Water Policy,* Short Paper Series, No. 3 (Intl. Irr. Mgmt. Inst.).

Getches, David, *Water Law in a Nutshell* (West Publishing 1997).

Getzler, Joshua, *A History of Water Rights at Common Law* (Oxford Univ. Press 2004).

Gleick, Peter, & Jon Lane, *Large International Water Meetings: Time for a Reappraisal,* 30 Water Intl. 410 (2005).

Gleick, Peter H., *The Changing Water Paradigm—A Look at Twenty-first Century Water Resources Development,* 25 Water Intl. 127 (2000).

Gleick, Peter, *The Human Right to Water,* 1 Water Policy 492 (1998).

Global Water Partnership, Technical Advisory Committee (TAC), *Integrated Water Resources Management,* TAC Background Papers, No. 4 (GWP 2000).

Goldblatt, M., J. Ndamba, B. van der Merwe, F. Gomes, B. Haasbroek & J. Arntzen, eds., *Water Demand Management: Towards Developing Effective Strategies for Southern Africa* (IUCN 2000).

Gonzalez, Fernando, & Salman M. A. Salman, eds., *Institutional Reform for Irrigation and Drainage,* World Bank Technical Paper No. 524 (World Bank 2002).

Gonzalez-Villareal, Fernando, & Héctor Garduño Velasco, *Water Resources Management and Planning in Mexico,* 10 Intl. J. Water Resources Dev. 239 (1994).

Gorriz, Cecilia M., Ashok Subramanian & Jose Simas, *Irrigation Management Transfer in Mexico, Progress and Process,* World Bank Technical Paper No. 292 (World Bank 1995).

Groenfeldt, David, & Mark Svendsen, *Case Studies in Participatory Irrigation Management* (World Bank Inst. 2000).

Guerrero Reynoso, Vincente, & Francisco García León, *Proposal for the Decentralization of Water Management in Mexico by Means of Basin Councils,* in *Water Policies and Institutions in Latin America,* Water Resources Management Series (Cecilia Tortajada, Benedito P. F. Braga, Asit K. Biswas & Luis E. Garcia, eds., Oxford Univ. Press 2003).

Guidelines for Development and Management of Groundwater Resources in Arid and Semi-Arid Regions, 8 Intl. J. Water Resources Dev. 145 (1992).

Gyau-Boakye, Philip, & Ben Y. Ampomah, *Water Pricing and Water Sector Reforms Information Study in Ghana,* 28 Water Intl. 11 (2003).

Horinkova, Vilma, & Iskandar Abdullaev, *Institutional Aspects of Water Management in Central Asia: Water Users' Associations,* 28 Water Intl. 237 (2003).

Hu, Xindeng, *Integrated Catchment Management in China: An Application of the Australian Experience,* 24 Water Intl. 323 (1999).

Hunter, David, James Salzman & Durwood Zaelke, *International Environmental Law and Policy* (Fdtn. Press 1998).

Jaspers, Frank G. W., *Institutional Arrangements for Integrated River Basin Management,* 5 Water Policy 77 (2003).

Johnson III, Sam H., *Irrigation Management Transfer: Decentralizing Public Irrigation in Mexico,* 22 Water Intl. 159 (1997).

Jonch-Clausen, Torkil, & Jens Fugl, *Firming up the Conceptual Basis of Integrated Water Resources Management,* 17 Intl. J. Water Resources Dev. 501 (2001).

41 Journal of Water SRT Aqua, No. 3 (1992).

Kemper, Karin, *Groundwater Management in Mexico: Legal and Institutional Issues,* in *Groundwater: Legal and Policy Perspectives,* World Bank Technical Paper No. 456 (Salman M. A. Salman, ed., World Bank 1999).

Kemper, Karin E., & Douglas Olson, *Water Pricing: The Dynamics of Institutional Change in Mexico and Ceará, Brazil,* in *The Political Economy of Water Pricing Reforms* (Ariel Dinar, ed., Oxford Univ. Press 2000).

Krchnak, Karin M., *Improving Water Governance Through increased Public access to Information and Participation,* 5 Sust. Dev. L. & Policy 34 (2004).

Kulshreshtha, Suren, *Water Pricing Under Joint Benefits—A Case Study of Accounting for Positive Externalities,* 27 Water Intl. 195 (2002).

Lanz, Klaus & Stefan Scheuer, *EEB Handbook on EU Water Policy under the Water Framework Directive* (Eur. Env. Bur. 2001).

Le Moigne, Guy, Ashok Subramanian, Mei Xie & Sandra Giltner, *A Guide to the Formulation of Water Resources Strategy,* World Bank Technical Paper No. 263 (World Bank 1994).

Malano, Hector, Michael Bryant & Hugh Turral, *Management of Water Resources: Can Australian Experiences Be Transferred to Vietnam?* 24 Water Intl. 307 (1999).

Margulis, Segio, Gordon Hughes, Martin Gambrill & Luiz Gabriel T. de Azevedo, *Brazil: Managing Water Quality—Mainstreaming the Environment in the Water Sector,* World Bank Technical Paper No. 532 (World Bank 2002).

McCaffrey, Stephen, *A Human Right to Water: Domestic and International Implications* 5 Geo. Intl. Envtl. L. Rev. 13 (1992).

Mejia, Abel, Luiz Gabriel T. de Azevedo, Martin P. Gambrill, Alexander M. Baltar & Thelma Triche, *Water, Poverty Reduction and Sustainable Development,* Brazil, Water Series No. 4 (World Bank 2003).

Merrett, Stephen, & Nick Walton, *Nitrate Pollution on the Island of Jersey— Managing Water Quality Within European Union Community Directives,* 30 Water Intl. 155 (2005).

Milaszewski, R., *Economic Instruments Used in Water Management,* in *Management of Transboundary Water in Europe* (Malgorzata Landsberg-Uczciwek, Martin Adriaanse & Rainer Enderlein, eds., Ministry of Environment Protection, Natural Resources and Forestry, Poland 1998).

Millennium Ecosystem Assessment, *Ecosystems and Human Well-Being: Opportunities and Challenges for Business and Industry* (World Resources Institute 2005).

Millennium Ecosystem Assessment, *Ecosystems and Human Well-Being: Synthesis* (World Resources Inst. 2005).

Mostert, Erik, *The Challenge of Public Participation,* 5 Water Policy 179 (2003).

Myint, Ohn, *Experience with Groundwater Irrigation in Nepal,* in *Groundwater: Legal and Policy Perspectives,* World Bank Technical Paper No. 456 (Salman M. A. Salman, ed., World Bank 1999).

Narain, Vishal, *Brackets and Black Boxes: Research on Water Users' Associations,* 6 Water Policy 185 (2004).

Nilson, José, B. Campos & Ticiana M. C. Studart, *An Historical Perspective on the Administration of Water in Brazil,* 25 Water Intl. 148 (2000).

Ongley, Edwin D., *Non-Point Source Water Pollution in China: Current Status and Future Prospects,* 29 Water Intl. 299 (2004).

Ongley, Edwin D., & Xuejun Wang, *Transjurisdictional Water Pollution Management in China: The Legal and Institutional Framework,* 29 Water Intl. 270 (2004).

Oblitas, Keith, & J. Raymond Peter, *Transferring Irrigation Management to Farmers in Andhra Pradesh, India,* World Bank Technical Paper No. 449 (World Bank 1999).

Perry, Chris, & Geoff Kite, *Water Rights—Importance, Difficulties, and New Approaches to Data Collection and Analysis,* 24 Water Intl. 341 (1999).

Pisaniello, John D., & Jennifer M. McKay, *A Farmer-Friendly Dam Safety Evaluation Procedure as a Key Part of Modern Australian Water Laws,* 28 Water Intl. 90 (2003).

Porto La Laina, Rubem, & Monica F. A. Porto, *Planning as a Tool to Deal with Extreme Events: The New Brazilian Water Resources Management System,* 27 Water Intl. 14 (2002).

Postel, Sandra, *Pillar of Sand—Can the Irrigation Miracle Last?* (Worldwatch Inst. 1999).

———, *Last Oasis—Facing Water Scarcity,* Worldwatch Environmental Alert Series, 167 (Worldwatch Inst. 1992).

Pradhan, Rajendra, Franz von Benda-Beckmann, Keebat von-Benda-Beckmann, H. L. J. Spiertz, Shantam S. Khadga & K. Azharul Haq, *Water Rights, Conflict and Policy* (Intl. Irr. Mgmt. Inst. 1997).

Rees, Judith, *Regulation and Private Participation in the Water and Sanitation Sector* Global Water Partnership, Technical Advisory Committee, TAC Background Papers, No. 1 (GWP/Swedish Intl. Dev. Coop. Agency 1998).

Reichert, Götz, *The European Community's Water Framework Directive: A Regional Approach to the Protection and Management of Transboundary Freshwater Resources?* in *Water Resources and International Law* (Laurence Boisson de Chazournes & Salman M. A. Salman, eds., Martinus Nijhoff Publishers 2005).

Rivera, Daniel, *Private Sector Participation in the Water Supply and Wastewater Sector—Lessons from Six Developing Countries,* Directions in Development (World Bank 1996).

Rogers, Peter, *Comprehensive Water Resources Management—A Concept Paper,* World Bank Policy Research Working Papers: WPS 879 (World Bank 1992).

Rogers, Peter, & Alan W. Hall, *Effective Water Governance,* Global Water Partnership, Technical Committee Background Papers, No. 7 (GWP 2003).

Rogers, Peter, Ramesh Bhatia & Annette Huber, *Water as a Social and Economic Good: How to Put the Principle into Practice,* Global Water Partnership (GWP), Technical Advisory Committee (TAC) Background Papers, No. 2 (GWP/Swedish Intl. Dev. Coop. Agency 1998).

Salazar, Carlos, *Water Resources Management in Chile,* in *Water Policies and Institutions in Latin America,* Water Resources Management Series (Cecilia Tortajada, Benedito P. F. Braga, Asit K. Biswas & Luis E. Garcia, eds., Oxford Univ. Press 2003).

Saleth, R. Maria, & Ariel Dinar, *Water Challenge and institutional Response—A Cross Country Perspective,* World Bank Policy Research Working Paper 2045, 13 (World Bank 1999).

Saleth, R. Maria, *Water Institutions in India—Economics, Law, and Policy* (Inst. of Econ. Growth, 1996).

Salman, Salman M. A., *United Nations General Assembly Resolution: International Decade for Action, Water for Life, 2005–2015,* 30 Water Intl. 415 (2005).

———, *From Marrakech Through The Hague to Kyoto—Has the Global Debate on Water Reached a Dead End?* Part One, 28 Water Intl. 491 (2003); Part Two, 29 Water Intl. 11 (2004).

———, *Inter-States Water Disputes in India: An Analysis of the Settlement Process,* 4 Water Policy 223 (2002).

———, *Groundwater: Legal and Policy Perspectives,* World Bank Technical Paper No. 456 (World Bank 1999).

———, *The Legal Framework for Water Users' Associations—A Comparative Study,* World Bank Technical Paper No. 360 (World Bank 1997).

Salman, Salman M. A., & Siobhán McInerney Lankford, *The Human Right to Water—Legal and Policy Dimensions* (World Bank 2004).

Salman, Salman M. A., & Laurence Boisson de Chazournes, *International Watercourses—Enhancing Cooperation and Managing Conflict,* World Bank Technical Paper No. 414 (World Bank 1998).

Sands, Philippe, *Principles of International Environmental Law,* vol. 1, 9 (Manchester University Press 1994).

Savenije, Hubert H. G. & Pieter van der Zaag, *Water as an Economic Good and Demand Management—Paradigms and Pitfalls,* 27 Water Intl. 98 (2002).

Schwarzenberger, George, *A Manual of International Law* 36 (Professional Books 1976).

Sharma, Sudhindra, *Foreign Aid and Institutional Plurality: The Domestic Water Sector in Nepal,* 16 Intl. J. Water Resources Dev. 119 (2000).

Shen, Dajun, *Water-Related Risk Management in China: A Legal, Institutional, and Regulatory View,* 30 Water Intl. 329 (2005).

———, *The 2002 Water Law: Its Impacts on River Basin Management in China,* 6 Water Policy 345 (2004).

Sherk, George William, *Dividing the Waters—The Resolution of Interstate Water Conflicts in the United States* (Kluwer Law Intl. 2000).

Simas, José, *Issues Affecting the Irrigation and Drainage Sectors in Latin America: Lessons from Mexico, Argentina, and Brazil,* in *Institutional Reform for Irrigation and Drainage,* World Bank Technical Paper No. 524 (Fernando J. Gonzalez & Salman M. A. Salman, eds., World Bank 2002).

Simonovic, Slobodan P., *Tools for Water Management—One View of the Future* 25 Water Intl. 76 (2000).

Singh, Chhatrapati, *Water Rights in India,* in *Water Law in India* 8 (Chhatrapati Singh, ed., Indian Law Inst. & Sweet & Maxwell, Ltd. 1992).

Sitarz, Daniel, ed., *Agenda 21, The Earth Summit Strategy to Save Our Planet,* (Earthpress 1994).

Solanes, Miguel, & Fernando Gonzalez-Villarreal, *The Dublin Principles for Water as Reflected in a Comparative Assessment of Institutional and Legal Arrangements for Integrated Water Resources Management,* Global Water Partnership (GWP), TAC Background Papers No. 3 (GWP/Swedish Intl. Dev. Coop. Agency 1999).

South Africa, Department of Water Affairs and Forestry of, *White Paper on a National Water Policy in South Africa* (1997).

Stein, Robyn, *South Africa's Water and Dam Safety Legislation: A Commentary and Analysis on the Impact of the World Commission on Dams' Report, 'Dams and Development'* 16(6) Am. U. Intl. L. Rev. 1573 (2001).

————, *South Africa's New Democratic Water Legislation: National Government's Role as a Public Trustee in Dam Building and Management Activities,* 18 J. Energy & Nat. Res. Law 284 (2000).

Stephenson, David, & Bruce Randell, *Water Demand Theory and Projections in South Africa,* 28 Water Intl. 512 (2003).

Stevens, Jan, *Current Developments in the Public Trust Doctrine and Other Instream Protection Measures,* in *Water Law, Trends, Policies and Practice* (Kathleen Marion Carr & James D. Crammond, eds., American Bar Association 1995).

Subramanian, Ashok, N. Vijay Jagannathan & Ruth Meinzen-Dick, eds., *User Organizations for Sustainable Development,* World Bank Technical Paper No. 354 (World Bank 1997).

Teclaff, Ludwick, *Water Law in Historical Perspective* 6 (William S. Hein & Co. 1985).

————, *What You Always Wanted to Know About Riparian Rights but Were Afraid to Ask,* 12 Nat. Res. J. 30 (1972).

Tortajada, Cecilia, Benedito P. F. Braga, Asit K. Biswas & Luis E. Garcia, eds., *Water and Environment Policies and Institutions in Mexico,* in *Water Policies and Institutions in Latin America,* Water Resources Management Series (Oxford Univ. Press 2003).

Tortajada, Cecilia, *Environmental Impact Assessment of Water Projects in Mexico,* 16 Intl. J. Water Resources Dev. 73 (2000).

————, *Legal and Regulatory Regime for Water Management in Mexico and its Possible Use in Other Latin American Countries,* 24 Water Intl. 316 (1999).

Tsur, Yacov, Terry Roe, Rachid Doukkali & Ariel Dinar, *Pricing Irrigation Water—Principles and Cases from Developing Countries* (Resources for the Future 2004).

United Nations, Earth Summit, Agenda 21, The United Nations Programme of Action from Rio, U.N. ISBN 92;92-1100509-4; Sales No. E.93.1.11.166 (U.N. Publications 1993).

United Nations, Report of the United Nations Water Conference, Mar del Plata, March 14–25, 1977, U.N. Publications, Sales No. E 77.II.A.12 (1977).

Voivontas, Dimosthenis *et al., Public-Private Partnership in the Water Sector—A Case Study in the Cyclades Islands, Greece,* 27 Water Intl. 330 (2002).

Ward, Christopher, *The Political Economy of Irrigation Water Pricing in Yemen,* in *The Political Economy of Water Pricing Reforms* (Ariel Dinar, ed., Oxford Univ. Press 2000).

Water Environment Federation, *The Clean Water Act, A Desk Reference* (WEF 1997).

Welch, Anna R., *Obligations of State and Non-State Actors Regarding the Human Right to Water under the South African Constitution,* 5 Sust. Dev. L. & Policy 58 (2004).

World Bank Operations Evaluation Department, *Bridging Troubled Waters— Assessing the World Bank Water Resources Strategy* (World Bank 2002).

World Bank, Asian Development Bank, FAO, UNDP, and the NGO Water Resources Group, in cooperation with the Institute of Water Resources Planning, *Vietnam— Water Resources Sector Review, Main Report,* A Joint Report, Vietnam (World Bank et al. 1996).

World Bank, *The Water Resources Sector Strategy—Strategic Directions for World Bank Engagement* (World Bank 2004).

———, *Armenia: Towards Integrated Water Resources Management,* ECSSD Working Paper No. 35 (World Bank 2002).

———, *China: Agenda for Water Sector Strategy for North China,* World Bank Report 22040-CHA (May 9, 2002).

———, *China—Air, Land, and Water: Environmental Priorities for a New Millennium* (World Bank 2001).

———, *Yemen Water Strategy Report,* World Bank Report No. 15718-YEM (World Bank 1997).

———, *Toolkits for Private Sector Participation in Water and Sanitation* (World Bank 1997).

———, *Water Resources Management—A World Bank Policy Paper* (World Bank 1993).

———, *World Development Report 1992, Development and the Environment* (World Bank 1992).

World Commission on Dams, *Dams and Development—A New Framework for Decision-making (the Report of the World Commission on Dams)* (Earthscan Publications Ltd. 2000).

World Water Assessment Programme, *Water for People, Water for Life,* United Nations World Water Development Report (UNESCO Publishing 2003).

World Water Council, *Report of the Panel on Financing Water Infrastructure, Financing Water for All* (World Water Council 2003).

World Water Council, World Water Vision (Commission Report) *A Water Secure World: Vision for Water, Life and the Environment* (2000).

Index

Notes are indicated by n.